HOLY ROCK & ROLLERS

THE STORY OF

Kings of Leon

JOEL McIVER

OMNIBUS PRESS

LONDON / NEW YORK / PARIS / SYDNEY / COPENHAGEN / BERLIN / MADRID / TOKYO

Cover designed by Fresh Lemon
Picture research by Jacqui Black

ISBN: 9781780381473
Order No: OP54197

Exclusive Distributors
Music Sales Limited,
14/15 Berners Street,
London, W1T 3LJ.

Music Sales Corporation,
257 Park Avenue South,
New York, NY 10010, USA.

Macmillan Distribution Services,
56 Parkwest Drive
Derrimut, Vic 3030,
Australia.

HOLY ROCK & ROLLERS
THE STORY OF
Kings of Leon

Contents

Introduction

Rock music is a fickle thing. Bands come and bands go, usually sooner rather than later. Only the best stick around for long, and it's always because they have something unique – a key factor that is theirs and theirs alone. Whatever it was about the Kings Of Leon, four unkempt preacher's boys from the American sticks, that made them so beloved to the public – and more weirdly still, the British public – it has turned them into superstars. The band's metamorphosis from mumbling, naïve hairballs into model-squiring darlings of the fashion press has been nothing less than miraculous, and it's this transformation that lies at the core of this book, the very first Kings biography.

You may be looking for lurid stories about drugs, booze and overflowing condoms. Well, they're all in here – but I've focused more deeply than that. Bands like this mean much more than all that stuff, especially in this particular case: the four Followills have had the tricky (some would say impossible) task of balancing their religious roots with the opportunities for debauchery that immense fame and fortune presented. How they did this is the real story, and it goes above and beyond the fights and the hangovers to anchor an overall picture that I couldn't have imagined when I started writing this book. You will be amazed.

Joel McIver, 2010
www.joelmciver.co.uk

Acknowledgements

Emma, Alice, Tom, Robin and Kate, Dad, John and Jen plus Chris Akin, Naomi Alderman, Chris Amott, Mike Amott, Carlos Anaia, John Araya, Tom Araya, Steve Asheim, Adrian Ashton, Tony Bacon, Fraser Baillie, Dan Balaam, Max Baroni, Scott Bartlett, Geoff Barton, Duff Battye, Chris Barnes, Jeff Beçerra, Nick Beggs, Glen Benton, Jeff Berlin, Terry Bezer, Jakub Blackman, Diego Bortolaso, Mark Brend, Alex Burrows, Chris Catalyst, Chas Chandler, Darren Charles, Chris Charlesworth, Stevie Chick, Ian Christe, Ben Christo, Carol Clerk, Ben Cooper, Neil Daniels, Rob Dimery, Malcolm Dome, Helen Donlon, John Doran, Jason Draper, John Dryland, Eddie Duffy, Jeff Dunn, Daryl Easlea, Mark Eglinton, David Ellefson, Jerry Ewing, Tom Gabriel Fischer, Ian Fortnam, Caren Gibson, James Gill, Ian Glasper, Spencer Grady, David Gray, Ross Halfin, Hannah Hamilton, Matthew Hamilton, Sara Harding, Vanessa Hards, Alex Herron, James Hoare, Glenn Hughes, Ken Hunt, Roland Hyams, Ihsahn, Bill Irwin, James Isaacs, Talita Jenman, Patrik Jensen, John Jolliffe, Tim Jolliffe, Tim Jones, Jonathon Kardasz, Jake Kennedy, Michelle Kerr, Jacquire King, Molly Knight, Chris Korff, Dom Lawson, Stephen Lawson, Sarah Lees, Brian Lew, Alan Lewis, Dave Ling, Frank Livadaros, Sian Llewellyn, Dave Lockwood, Corinne Lynn, Gavin Martin, Joe Matera, Patrizia Mazzuocolo, Jason Mendonça, Bruno McDonald, James McNair, David McNamee, Alex Milas, Jon Mills, Greg Moffitt, Eugenio Monti, Anthony Morgan, Emma Morgan, Albert

Mudrian, Bob Nalbandian, Joachim Noske, Alex Ogg, Harald Oimoen, Will Palmer, Ravi Parsan, Scott Patrick, Martin Popoff, Valerie Potter, Dave Pybus, Raz Rauf, Steven Rosen, Scott Rowley, Nick Ruskell, Darren Sadler, Adam Sagir, Ian Salsbury, Rudy Sarzo, Jonathan Selzer, Ian Shirley, Joe Shooman, Kirsten Sprinks, Scott Steele, Zoe Street Howe, Louise Sugrue, Carl Swann, Darren Toms, Dan Travis, Jerry Trimble, Jr, Katherine Tsang-Orr, Andy Turner, Luke Turner, Tommy Udo, John Varvatos, David Vincent, Sarah Vincent, Jeremy Wagner, Mick Wall, Jeff Waters, Alex Webster, Dora Wednesday, Clint Weiler, Nick Wells, Elton Wheeler, Ian Whent, Jonathan Wingate, Jamie Woolgar, Henry Yates and the families Barnes, Bhardwaj, Bowles, Cadette, Carr, Clark, Cooper, Edwards, Ellis, Eschapasse-Carr, Foster, Freed, Gunn, Harrington, Hoare, Hogben, Houston-Miller, Knight, Lamond, Lamont, Legerton, Leim, Maynard, Miles, Parr, Sendall, Tominey, Tozer, Webb and Woollard plus the many visitors to www.joelmciver.co.uk and www.facebook.com/joelmciver.

CHAPTER 1

Before 2000

Rock'n'roll rumours are always a hoot. Here's a good one.

One day a singer called Caleb Followill goes into a pub in London. A man is standing at the bar nursing a pint of beer and looks over at the newcomer, noting his generous beard and shoulder-length hair. He chuckles to himself and resumes drinking. Followill sees this and indignantly asks why the guy is laughing. "You look like a Kings Of Leon wannabe," comes the answer.

That very afternoon, Caleb shaves off his beard.

It's a good story. But not actually true, as the other members of the Kings Of Leon confirmed. It was just another of the many rumours that have swarmed over the band, from the moment when they entered the UK in 2003 to the current point in time seven years later, when they can justifiably call themselves the fastest-rising rock band of the last decade.

The problem is that the Kings Of Leon arrived on British shores with such a conveniently unusual back story to present to the press that people tended to dismiss them as the creation of some management team or record company. It's a fact universally acknowledged that we Brits (excuse me if you're reading this book overseas; we'll come to you shortly) are suckers for a bit of Americana, and we have a history of welcoming with open arms American acts who weren't initially popular in their home country, Nirvana being a prominent example from the Nineties and Seasick Steve another in more recent times. Marketing people at record companies are fully aware of our appetite for all things Stateside-oriented, and exploit it whenever possible.

The bare facts about the Kings Of Leon seemed so tailor-made for marketing purposes, because they added up to a picture of life in backwoods America that no-one believed still existed. The claim was that a huge family, the Followills, exist in different parts of the South, coming together once a year for a family jamboree in Talihina, Oklahoma. Three members of the band were brothers, ran the spiel, with drummer Nathan the eldest. He was born in Oklahoma in 1979, while Tennessee-born guitarist and singer Caleb was born in '82. Nathan and Caleb were more like-minded than their guitarist cousin Matthew (Oklahoma, '84) and their bass-playing brother Jared (Tennessee, '86), effectively splitting the band into senior and junior camps. Note that each member adopted his middle name for professional use – as in Ivan 'Nathan' Followill, Anthony 'Caleb' Followill, Cameron 'Matthew' Followill and Michael 'Jared' Followill.

The Followill family is large enough to call itself a dynasty. The three brothers' parents are an ex-Pentacostalist minister called Nathan Leon Followill and his ex-wife Betty Ann Followill: details of their 1997 divorce have largely been kept private. Most information about the senior Followills' family history has remained behind closed doors – quite an achievement for a band of this magnitude – while the only skeleton in the closet that has been openly discussed is the exit of Leon Followill from the church, allegedly the result of a drink problem. As he put it in a 2007 interview, "I was not defrocked, I was forced to resign."

The life of the children of a United Pentacostal preacher was, to say the least, an eccentric one. Leon's job took him around the country from church to church in an itinerant lifestyle that provided much excitement, if little stability. Although the family finally settled near Memphis, Tennessee after Jared's birth in 1986, before that point (and to an extent, afterwards) Leon took his kids with him on the road – to much acclaim, Caleb later recalled. "He was a big deal," said the middle son when asked about his father. "He was in the upper echelon. When we walked into a church, everyone knew it. We sort of had this rock lifestyle before we became a band. It was good for meeting girls: we had our pick of the litter. The only thing is we couldn't do too much. Mostly kissing. But it taught us how to kiss, man. To this day, girls think I'm a great kisser..."

The youngest brother, Jared Followill, later identified the period in which the family did most travelling as approximately 1991 to '95. As he put it, "It was a good four-year span... we would rent a house for three months at the most during those four years. My dad would travel and preach in a different church in a different town almost every night. We'd stay in motels and churches, and just weird places like that – maybe relatives' houses. My dad would preach every night. They would have real Bibles and my dad would revive the church, then we'd leave. It was pretty weird, you know?"

Much later, Nathan – who often played drums while his father whipped up the congregations – compared the life of a travelling preacher and his family with that of a rock band, saying: "Growing up, me, Caleb and Jared, our life was eerily similar to the life we lead now. We'd pull into a town on the Monday, set up shop, have three, maybe four services, then we'd break everything down, stick everything into the trunk of the car and drive on to the next town. I did that for 15 years of my life, so now we come and do this and it's pull the bus into the town, play a show, maybe get a hotel, if not hop on the bus, drive to the next town. That way though, we'd get to stay somewhere for two or three days. Now people say we're so lucky to see so much of the world, but in reality, you pull into the place sound asleep, soundcheck, play a show, party 'til you pass out and wake up in the next town, so we don't get to see anything at all."

One popular destination for the Followill boys was a preachers' conference in Alexandria, Louisiana, called Because Of The Times. This event, which lasts three days and is designed as a meeting-place for clergymen and their families, is the American Christian equivalent of the Glastonbury festival, according to Nathan: "You'd pick your favourite preachers like you'd pick your favourite bands."

"It's a festival, but instead of bands, it's with preachers," said Caleb of the event. "That was really one of the funnest [sic] times of our lives as kids, because it was the one week we got to hang out with all the other preachers' kids and meet up with your little make-out partner from the year before. It was for preachers and their families only, and you felt a little special because everyone was pretty much on the same level. It's still held each year."

Although 'home' was a nebulous concept – "We were pretty young and travelled around all the time. We never stayed in one place longer than five years, so we never got to go to high school and make proper friends," said Caleb – this brought the family members closer together. Certainly the four young Followills would be the first of their family to spend much time overseas: the rest stayed pretty much where they were, at home in Oklahoma, year in, year out. The clan didn't live in luxury, either: there was, Caleb later explained, more than a dash of hillbilly in the Followill gene pool.

"The people there, they don't leave," he said. "We've been year after year, and you see the same process. Different high-school kids [getting] pregnant. Here comes the new kid, and the same thing happens. Drugs or whatever. Everybody goes through the same shit and no-one ever sees it coming… Dad's side of the family are real mountain people. They drink creek water and only eat stuff they've shot. A cousin built a house in the forest, but the last time we went back it was nothing but a concrete slab. Their methamphetamine lab had blown up."

The Followill kids had ambitions, but not ones that were radically different from those of their classmates at the schools they sporadically attended. Caleb and Nathan both assumed that they would become preachers like their father, with the latter even graduating from a private school called the Christian Life Academy in Tennessee. "All our friends would go to Bible college after high school," said Caleb. "Two years learning how to preach. That was just what everybody did. And we pretty much knew that was what we were going to do, too."

Other aspects of the kids' lives were more orthodox. Like so many other teenagers, Caleb worried about his looks, revealing later that he used to overexercise to try and lose weight. "I always thought I wasn't good enough," he explained, adding that he drank large amounts of coffee ("Anything to keep my hands and mouth busy without eating"), and that even as an adult, he wants to be in better shape. He remarked:

"I want to look like I can defend myself. I want a guy to look at me in a bar and know that he can't talk shit to me or run me over, even though he probably could."

The lack of a permanent base was the first unusual aspect of the Followills' childhood; another – a direct result of the Christian fundament in the family – was the boys' near-complete ignorance of non-religious culture. The boys' parents played the occasional album by Al Green, Gladys Knight and Creedence Clearwater Revival, but barely anything else. Leon and Betty Ann didn't allow them to listen to rock music or watch films, forbidding them to visit cinemas: "I thought they were smoking and drinking and having orgies in there," said Caleb later. However, they found ways to get around these restrictions, with Nathan listening to Bob Dylan and Neil Young when his parents weren't around, and Caleb taking solace in a portable radio.

"I was really lonely because we were always in a different place, usually sleeping in a back room at a church," he said. "It was always really scary in there, so I would put my little radio under the pillow and just listen to the oldies station, listen to doo-wop and 'Stand By Me', and that finally got me to where I'd fall asleep." When he finally got to hear more secular music, it was a relief, he added: "It just lifted the blanket of fear. I heard stuff that made me forget about all the things I would hear in church every day, things that made me feel as if everything was wrong. Music gave me my own little world."

Music was the answer, it seemed. What's more, it already existed in the Followills' lives, and in a big way. The sermons that Leon Followill gave were more like rock concerts than traditional services, with the music loud, rhythmic and passionate. At least that was how Nathan recalled it: "I don't think people realise when they hear that when I played the drums and we grew up and sang in church, it was black gospel. Most people think [it would have been] Protestant, very chilled out, maybe an organ up there, *a capella* singing, very reverent… no, the churches we went to and the music we played, it was like a juke joint: people dancin' and sweatin' and screamin' and hollerin' and runnin' around. It was more like going to an underground club, back in the day when that music was frowned upon."

For Nathan, this music lay at the core of his future band's sound, coming as it did at such a crucial juncture in the Followill brothers' lives. He reasoned: "Aretha Franklin caught a lot of flak early on – she was a preacher's daughter and she grew up singing in church. Even Ray Charles had a couple of songs where he changed the lyrics around and took 'em from a song being about God, to a song being about a girl. That was so taboo back then. It was sacrilegious and they wanted to burn him at the stake. [Those artists] were bold enough to step out on a limb and take a lot of flak in the beginning, but they were paving the way for every band after that – from the Stones to Led Zeppelin to The White Stripes to us – who were influenced in some fashion by Motown or by that sound that originated in church music. There are thousands of standard gospel songs that come from blues riffs and vice versa. It played a much bigger role in shaping music than most people think."

Gospel and devotional music shaped the music to come just as much as religion itself, which had once inspired the 10-year-old Caleb to write a sermon with the ponderous title of 'Why Beg For Bread When You're Living In A Wheat Field?'. It's quite a back story for a young band arriving in overseas territory. If all this was invented by some marketing goon in North London with a portable scooter and a hair-fin, it was a remarkably durable scheme: the band have insisted that it's all true for the seven years since their arrival, and by now it seems only reasonable to believe them.

Nathan, when he looked back later at his band's sudden explosion to prominence, knew perfectly well that the Followills' archaic back story had been a crucial part of it. As he said: "We made a little five-song EP in Memphis, and I guess a publication over there [in the UK] picked it up, but honestly, at the beginning it was all about the story... Three sons of a travellin' preacher, you know, lived in this world of good and didn't listen to rock'n'roll or watch TV or live the normal life, and we're plucked from that world and stuck in the world of debauchery that is rock'n'roll. They had a field day with the whole good-versus-evil thing, and I think it was just kind of a novelty to them."

"I think at first people liked our story, our looks... pretty much all the wrong reasons for liking a band," observed Caleb. "They saw what we looked like and where we were from, and wanted to jump all over it. But then they found out that we were actually a pretty good band... We came out at a time when it was this 'New Rock Revolution', whatever the hell that is. Everyone was pretty much trying to be louder than each other and party harder than each other. We knew from the beginning that people weren't going to take us that seriously because we were younger, and we were family. So we had to make sure that our songwriting was something that people couldn't talk about in a negative way."

Not that the band looked particularly as if they were gospel-trained and church-raised when they arrived in London. Sporting manes of shaggy hair and, in the two older boys' case, mountain-man beards, the Kings Of Leon seemed a touch more contemporary than their unsophisticated backwoods story would suggest, from the super-tight cut of their jeans to their fashionably insolent gazes into the camera. Guitar music had transformed them, it seemed, elevating the brothers from their purely religious roots to a more rounded world view.

Caleb Followill had started to play the guitar when he turned 11 in 1993 – for the usual reason, not one that reflected Christian values in any way. "As a boy, I just wanted to play guitar because it looked cool," he said. "I feel like music comes very naturally... It's definitely fun to play music. I think it comes natural to all the guys really – we're in a band, and it's kind of our job. Maybe it's in our blood?"

Hooking up with Nathan, who could already play the drums, Caleb began writing songs. With little experience of popular music to draw on, the songs he and his brother wrote were raw and basic. As Nathan later explained: "When the band started we had never made music together, so that was what came out of our instruments. It wasn't like we set out to become the modern-day Allman Brothers or Lynyrd Skynyrd or Creedence Clearwater Revival... we'd never even listened to any of these bands before, so we had no idea what people were talking about."

The music bug bit Caleb instantly, and while Nathan was still at Christian college and his younger brother, Jared, was still at school, he dropped out in the middle of his high-school senior year to concentrate on writing and playing songs. In 1996, the pair moved to Nashville, where country music – the scene that most fascinated them at the time – was focused, now and always.

In reality, the move meant taking on various temporary jobs while they worked on their music. Caleb worked in construction and both brothers did stints as house painters, which (by their own admission) they executed badly. This was a stressful existence, exacerbated by the first in a long series of sibling disagreements, which – as is the case with so many bands formed by brothers – often got significantly physical. Nathan said later, "Being family is a double-edged sword, because when you fight you know exactly what to say to get them wherever you want them to go. If you want it to be a fist fight, you know that one thing to say. On the other side it's great, because if we do have a blow-out, it's Nathan and Caleb – brothers fighting – not the lead singer and drummer of Kings Of Leon. When we get on that stage… we're a band. We've had times when we've hated each other before we walked onto that stage, then we'll get up there and smile and rock out and have a blast, then get off stage and it's right back to, 'You shithead motherfucker! I'm gonna beat your ass!' And it has to be that way. You have to draw that line, because once your personal life starts spilling into your professional life, you're screwed."

Caleb added: "We've always been competitive because we're family. Growing up, anything we did, no matter if it was sports or anything, we always wanted to be the best. And that would sometimes lead to a few problems… I think it makes you more proud, doing this with family. Having your brothers and your cousin there, it's so fulfilling. I can't imagine being a solo artist, or being up there with people who don't have the same blood running through their veins. It makes it a more beautiful thing to me… I don't know how other musicians have done it. It's weird and it sounds kind of cheesy, but it's really like, 'We're family, and we know what's going to happen because we're psychic'. It does feel natural when we're in the studio: I look at Nathan, and we'll know where every part fits. There's definitely a comfort level to know that nobody's feelings are really getting hurt. They can tell me whatever they want to."

The appeal of painting houses by day soon wore off, and the idea of making a living out of music grew not just more attractive but urgent, and Caleb and Nathan realised the need to step up and be more professional. This came when they renamed themselves The Followill Brothers and began playing gigs in Nashville bars such as the Bluebird Café. By now the duo's exposure to rock music had expanded, as Nathan recalled: "We discovered rock'n'roll in the way most people did – break out a joint and listen to a Led Zeppelin record. We decided we wanted to do this when we got tired of painting houses in the summertime and working our asses off, so Caleb started writing songs with me and we thought, 'Let's give this a try'. We thought if we could sell 10,000 records we'd be happy…"

Initally Caleb and Nathan shared the lead vocals, as both brothers are accomplished singers. After a while, Caleb took over, saying: "In the beginning, we wrote songs together, and if he was writing a song, he'd sing, and vice versa. It came to a point where I knew I wanted it and, as opposed to us literally fighting for it, I just went to him and said, 'Look, man, if we're going to do this, we need a clear vision, and I think you should play drums and I'll sing'. There were some tough times between us, but I pretty much said, 'I'll do it. I'll be the singer. I'll take all the girls and all the drugs. I don't want to, but I will'."

Nathan, despite having been a possible candidate for lead singer, knew that Caleb was the right man for the job. As he said: "He's got the right amount of cockiness, the right amount of friendliness. He's not a big talker, likes to let you do the talking. It's kind of weird to talk about him as a lead singer 'cause he's my brother. All those things I hate about him as a brother might be the things I like about him as a singer… He's great. He's cool. He's open to pretty much anything. He has a lot of responsibility. I couldn't keep it up all day, every day like he does."

The brothers were now spending most of their free time writing songs, usually devoted to the subjects you'd expect from teenage brothers whose family leash had recently been untied for the first time. Caleb remembered: "We'd devote hours a day making songs, we'd get three or four a day… [about] alcohol and women and love."

Not that the brothers' Christian beliefs deserted them, by any means – Caleb's relatively sudden immersion into independence left him slightly shellshocked, he said: "I can recall every night trying to go to bed and something was saying, 'If you leave, you can never come back [to the church]'. It was like being a kid again – sleepless nights, over and over – and I would have to turn on the TV to drown it out. And then one day I looked at myself and said, 'You know, this is what you wanna do', and it was like a weight was lifted. It was almost as if God was smiling down on me, saying, 'Finally, you made a decision, you quit struggling with yourself.' And the voices went away. For a little while..."

Fortune smiled on the Followills in the year 2000 when a prominent music publisher and manager, Ken Levitan, caught one of their performances at the Bluebird Café. Spotting something in the band that he thought made them unusual, he approached the brothers, arranged to manage them via his Vector Management company and asked a Nashville-based songwriter and producer called Angelo Petraglia to work with them on their sound.

Nathan recalled his first meeting with Petraglia: "We wanted to do some songwriting for pot money and called this number. They thought Angelo would work well with us, so we went and met with him." Caleb added: "Before we ever wrote with Angelo, we hung out with him and got to know him some. From the very beginning, he got it. He used to be religious, just like us. He was a Holy Ghost guy. Instead of trying to chug out some bullshit song for some bullshit country artist, we sat there and listened to records and hit it off so well. Angelo is a big part of what we do. He's a sweetheart, just a helluva guy."

This was a key moment in the evolution of the band. With Levitan's business connections and Petraglia's musical talents on their side, the Followills were in a much better position to make serious inroads into a career as musicians – one that actually paid the bills and didn't require them to paint any houses. While their new manager arranged auditions with record companies, Petraglia organised songwriting sessions, co-writing new material for possible release.

In his mid-40s at the time, the New York-born musician had moved to Nashville after achieving some success in Boston with his band, The Immortals. After signing to MCA, Petraglia became known as a co-writer with a golden touch, working with a range of artists including Emmylou Harris, Martina McBride, Tim McGraw, Trisha Yearwood and Sara Evans. His speciality lay in identifying songs' unique vibe, he once explained: "The kind of record I always wanted to make [is] where you just kind of camp out and experiment. Anybody can jump on anything. It's not always being totally proficient at your instrument that leads to a beautiful sound."

In the case of the Followill brothers, Petraglia sensed that a refinement of name and style was necessary, after jamming on co-written original songs that owed more to the new (to Nathan and Caleb at least) sounds of The Clash and The Rolling Stones. When Levitan came back with the news that he had set up an audition with BMG subsidiary RCA in New York City, the brothers agreed on a new band name – one that honoured both their father and grandfather.

When the Kings Of Leon – all two of them – played for the RCA execs in NYC, they made a decent fist of it, leading the label to make them an offer. One stipulation was that the Kings would have to add other musicians to form a full band – musicians whom the label would suggest. This made no sense to Nathan and Caleb, who decided to sign with RCA on condition that the new musicians would be their younger brother, Jared, on bass and their cousin Matthew on guitar. Although the latter was already a competent guitarist, Jared had literally never picked up a bass before, but this didn't seem to deter the older brothers, and nor did the fact that he was a mere 15 years old at the time.

As Levitan recalled, Nathan and Caleb "came into my office and sang *a cappella* in the corner". He added that when they told him about Matthew and Jared's recruitment to the band, "there were some raised eyebrows. But when we heard the music and saw the determination and that they had a vision, it was like, 'Let's put this together and roll with it'." While the band's new record company wasn't sure of this move, Nathan shrugged. "OK, we'll just buy our brother a bass and our cousin a guitar… [they] haven't questioned anything since." Caleb was more forthright, declaring: "They were like, 'This is fucking suicide'. I told them to fuck off and give us six weeks – we'd show 'em."

As Nathan put it much, much later, "We kidnapped our cousin from Mississippi, told his mom he was coming for the week and just never let him go home. We locked ourselves in the basement with an ounce of marijuana and literally spent a month down there. My mom would bring us food down. And at the end of that month the label people came and we had 'Molly's Chambers', 'California Waiting', 'Wicker Chair' and 'Holy Roller Novocaine'."

Jared, it emerged, was the clued-up one when it came to popular music, despite his tender years. As he explained: "I pretty much got in the band based on my music credibility – I introduced them to all kinds of cool bands. I would always tell them, 'Man, you guys need some rock.

Fucking-A. That's where it's at'... Caleb introduced me to The Rolling Stones and Johnny Cash and that sort of thing, and I introduced them to The Pixies and The Cure and Talking Heads and Joy Division... I was totally into my music. It's because I really wanted to make soundtracks for movies. That was like my big-time goal in life."

A little later, when Jared had acquired some bass skills, he explained that he had a clear image in mind of who he wanted to look like. "Paul Simonon from The Clash [is] somebody I think of... he's the kind of person I want to look like on stage. As far as writing [bass-lines] and stuff like that, there are a lot; guys like Peter Hook, who was in Joy Division and New Order."

One major influence brought by Jared into the band was The Velvet Underground, whose urban art-rock ethos might have been worlds away from the country-rock the Kings were playing at the time, but whose punk approach to musicianship resonated perfectly. Asked why the Followills liked the Velvets so much, Jared mused: "Maybe it's because they were really bad at their instruments... You just hear it and you're like, 'Fuck, I could do that!'... it's so different. It's really dumbed down. [They] was the first songs that I heard where [the musicians] embraced their fuck-ups. Somebody would mess up on the guitar or the bass and it would be a really stand-out mess-up, and that would make it even cooler. They would even mess up on violins and stuff like that... it makes people believe in themselves, that it's not necessarily about playing and talent and stuff like that, as much as it is being original and having your own style and being different."

"My little brother, Jared, and cousin Matt always hung out with the indie girls who would turn them on to cool music that we'd never really heard of, then they'd turn us onto it," Nathan said of his introduction to new music via the younger Followills. "We kinda learned this music and discovered it along with other young kids who were discovering it for the first time... It's like 40 years of rock history has happened, now we get to sit back and sift through the greatest hits."

The educational process went both ways, said Jared: "They taught me about the older stuff, and I teach them about the newer stuff. They love Otis Redding, Sam Cooke, The Ronettes, Tommy James & The Shondells – music that basically influenced what I was listening to, bands like The Velvet Underground. Lou Reed once said that the first song that made him want to be in a band was 'Be My Baby' by The Ronettes. I can see that. It's an incredible song."

"The way that we were raised, we were kind of musically neglected," Caleb explained. "We didn't get to experience a lot of music because of our religious beliefs and things like that. But these past few years we've kind of been lapping it up, and anything that we hear we feel like we can at least try to give our take on it. Obviously there are bands and musicians that are much more talented than us. But we feel like if we listen to something and we get inspired by it, we can try to give our interpretation and be a million miles away, but it still might sound like something fresh."

Nathan added: "We weren't raised listening to the music that everybody else was raised listening to. So, when we hear something that we've never really heard before, it hits us in a totally different way. Most bands hear a record and can name you five bands that it sounds just like. We don't have that luxury, or maybe that curse. If something moves us, then shit, it's hitting a spot that's never been hit before. We can't compare it to another feeling we've had, or another record we've heard or another song or another band. We respond to the way it makes us feel right then. It's very natural."

The month spent in the basement mentioned by Nathan was a turning point for the band. Having rechristened themselves, the three brothers and cousin were attempting to write music that would resonate with rock audiences, as well as mesh together as musicians – no small undertaking when the intra-band relationships were so volatile. Matthew Followill, only 17 at the time of his recruitment into the band and still at high school, was evidently conflicted about his new role, recalling later: "It's kind of weird. Sometimes it's great because you can talk to your family about stuff and have someone to hang with at three in the morning when you can't sleep, because your brother or cousin is also still awake. But then, there is the other side to that too. Like when you're with your brother or cousin you tend to say whatever you want, so there is no common courtesy – like you have when you're with someone other than your family member. You don't hold back saying stuff like, 'Your hair looks stupid, go fix your hair!' where it can piss off the other, and it can be tough at times."

Jared summed up his older brothers' formative years in Nashville in an interview with journalist Molly Knight, saying: "Nathan and Caleb started writing some country tunes, because they lived in Nashville and that's what you do – write some fucking shitty songs and make a little money. That's kind of what they did, and then they met this guy named Angelo and he was a really cool songwriter. They started writing songs with him that were fucking shitty, and so they started kind of, like, singing them themselves, and Angelo would play the guitar. From there they started realising they had some pretty fucking cool songs and it wasn't just a little side job to get weed money any more. So after they figured that out, they went and started a band because... after writing all that shit they became pretty good songwriters. They had had a year of practice or two years of practice, and so they wanted to put a band together. And we knew that our cousin Matthew played guitar."

Matthew had endured a similar background to those of his three cousins, he revealed: "I moved around a lot, moved to seven or eight different houses growing in different towns. We had the same religion. It was exactly the same for me – not being able to listen too much to secular music. We pretty much grew up together. I'd go to their house for three weeks in the summer. There'd be family reunions out in the hills of Oklahoma where we'd hang out for a week. Me and Jared were always close because we were close in age. I knew they had songs and stuff: they'd play them for me when we got together. They were great, great songs."

Recalling his younger years, Matthew revealed: "It was pretty cool I guess. I went to mostly private schools, really tiny. Sometimes I would have, like, two people in my grade. [The educational system] was called 'Paces'. You do your own work and read and answer questions and stuff. It's all I knew. I had some friends that were in public schools and stuff like that, and what I was doing was a lot easier. And at the time I thought 'This is great', but then later I realised it was a bad thing because I wasn't learning everything I needed to be learning."

Matthew had dabbled in the guitar in a small way before joining his brothers, as he explained: "I had a teacher that played guitar and he started to give lessons. I was 12 and there were like, five guys in the class, and we all started to play... I don't know if I have [any influences]. Maybe a couple of guitar players. Chuck Berry is great, some guitar players that played [in] Thin Lizzy were great. I hear guitar players all the time that I think are great, I just never know who the guitar player is… it all goes back to that teacher. He'd play, and my uncle had given me this classical guitar, and I always had it in my room. I could take lessons and play this guitar, and my mom was like, 'Yeah, go for it'. She paid for it, so I did it."

Asked how it felt to play in a band with his kinfolk, Matthew replied: "It seems like there's a chemistry there. You always feel comfortable playing with your family. Sometimes it's weird, maybe not on stage or whatever, but like hanging out. Sometimes we'll argue and stuff, but it's cool. We take our own space."

He added: "One day I heard they were looking for a record deal and before you know it, they got signed to RCA. They called me and said they wanted me to join the band. I finally thought I'd never get an opportunity like it — so I dropped out [of school] in the 11th grade. It made me nervous. I was like, 'But I gotta go to high school'… I thank God it worked out – because I'd probably be painting houses now."

Joining the band was no small step for Matthew, who was a top student at high school, as he explained: "I had no idea what I wanted to be, but I knew that I kinda wanted to be rich. That was my main goal, really. So I came up with all these different things. When I was really young I wanted to be an anaesthesiologist… I was kind of a dork. I was a really smart kid, and was on Honour Roll and made straight As, and was in all the honour classes, and stuff like that. And I had glasses and wanted to be an anaesthesiologist because I got my appendix taken out when I was nine. The guys who gave me the medicine – I remember as I was passing out – they were talking about the Sooners, because we were in Oklahoma; they were talking about the college football team that we support. I remember trying to talk to them and I just passed out. I remember thinking, 'Man, this guy has the easiest job'. And so I asked one of the nurses, 'Do those guys get paid a lot?' And she was like, 'Yeah, definitely'. So I was like, 'Awesome, man. I want to do that'. Just like put a mask on my face – not to mention how much they huff themselves… And then I kind of wanted to be a photographer, and then the whole soundtrack thing came along and then my asshole cousins made me get into this fucking stupid band."

He looked back in amusement at the hurdles he'd had to jump in order to join the band: "Well, I was in 11th grade, and the guys were like, 'Look, we just got signed to a record label, and we need a guitar player. Jared's gonna play the bass and if you're gonna do this, you need to do this right now'. I told my mom I was going to Oklahoma City to visit my dad and I went to Nashville instead. And I didn't come back. My mom could have never imagined then that it would be what it is now. I wanted to tell her that I could see it, and I just did it. That was a hard phone call, I just had to call my mom and tell her, and she was like, 'I know'… Jared did the same thing. He was about 15, and he dropped out of school too. And there for a couple of years he didn't go to school or anything."

Matthew recalled that his first job with the band was to find some decent gear. "The week that I moved in with the rest of the boys, they had said, 'When you get here we have to buy equipment and stuff and good guitars'. So I went to Gruhn's in Nashville, and they had this [Gibson Les Paul] that looked incredible and sounded great, and I've had it ever since. I love it."

"When I got up there [to join the band], I immediately started writing guitar parts," he added. "I went for the Les Paul and Marshall [combination]. I jumped right in: 'Can I play solos?' 'Sure, you can play solos.' It was my favourite thing to do. I was into that dirty old Rolling Stones, Led Zeppelin sound. As I progressed, I listened to a lot of different music. I got a different guitar and amp. I bought a pedal with a bunch of effects on it and realised I could apply new sounds to [both] the new songs and the old songs."

Between writing new songs and rehearsing them into shape – a time-consuming process when Jared was learning the play the bass, while Caleb and Matthew also had some way to go before mastering the guitar – the band also played the occasional gig. Their newfound freedom led to some wild times in those early days, even if the two junior Followills were too young to drink legally. This didn't prevent Caleb and Nathan from indulging, with the former acquiring the nickname 'The Rooster' because of the aggressive attitude he displayed when he drank whisky. A popular rumour that circulated later on was that three of the band members didn't lose their virginity until after the first Kings album was released in 2003, but that was later dismissed by Matthew as one of Nathan's jokes – and anyway, given the lifestyle the Followills were leading while the band were getting their act together, it's unlikely that any of them waited that long to do the deed...

Bizarrely to most of us, but reasonably enough given the circumstances, the Followills got into the habit in their early years of bonding before each show by singing a gospel song together. "It's a gospel song called 'Just A Little Talk With Jesus'," explained Caleb to one interviewer, singing, "Now let us have a little talk with Jesus / Let us tell him all about our troubles / He will hear our faintest cry / He will answer by and by / Now when you feel a little prayer wheel turning / And you know a little fire is burning / You will find a little talk with Jesus makes it right."

Band life suited the brothers and cousin from day one, for various reasons. The constant movement of the musician's life paralleled the travelling-preacher existence they'd experienced for so many years (Caleb: "We were always on the move, but that wasn't always a bad thing. It meant that every week you could become a different person a little bit – you could have a different reputation every week"), and it gave them an outlet for their creative urges. The four young men had seen some sights on the road with their father – sights that weren't always pretty or innocent. Caleb explained: "I don't want people to get tired of us and tired of our story, but we're naturally drawn to storytelling. Most people assume that, because we're preacher's boys, everything was regular and good – but what it really means is that we were living behind the scenes and got to see the really bad parts of life, too. We knew which members of the congregation used to be prostitutes, which were alcoholics or whatever."

"We have family members that are on both ends of the spectrum," explained Nathan. "I think that has definitely added to our imagination, because we definitely see the good side, the good way to live, and then we see the bad. I think that totally broadened our imagination. I mean we, *per se*, haven't been fucked up, but we've seen that world first-hand."

Nathan added that the similarities between the rock'n'roll life and the missionary counterpart were greater than they might at first seem: "In a sense, it's kind of the same thing. We're not preaching, but we're trying to get a message across [through] all of our hard work. It's hard not to view our audience as a congregation. We learned from our father how to put on a show." Given the ecstatic nature of Leon Followill's preaching, and the beatific effect that it had on all those Southern congregations, this isn't too far-fetched a claim.

Still, the Kings Of Leon had their problems – inevitably, given that the intra-band power structure was still in the process of being established. Caleb, as the most creative and the most naturally driven, took some time to learn the fine art of diplomacy. In later years, he looked back at this early period (when he was, let us not forget, only 18 years old or thereabouts) with obvious embarrassment at the way he had behaved: "We're all a lot closer [now], especially compared with the beginning. I used to have an idea of how things should go and didn't let other people's opinions matter to me. All that did was hurt our relationship and it took a little while to gain the band's trust... Now we're a lot stronger. Obviously the work can get to me and I lash out at the people I love, but we're accomplishing so much more than we ever thought we would."

Jared, still in his older brothers' creative shadow at this early stage, commented: "I remember taking a class at high school called inter-personal communications. I learned about this wheel of abuse that involved couples arguing and then making up with champagne, flowers or candy," leading Nathan to quip: "For us it's fight, flowers, chocolate, champagne, drunk, fight. On second thoughts, fuck the flowers and chocolate – it's fight, champagne, drunk, fight, champagne, drunk."

Meanwhile, the Followills were continuing their secular music education. The gaps in the brothers' collective knowledge might never be filled, but perhaps that gave them a certain advantage. Jared even reasoned that his lack of exposure to commercial pop and R&B was a benefit to him as a rock musician: "MTV never shows a good band, and magazines in America never feature decent bands. I mean, The Raconteurs are pretty big in America but they're not as big as they should be. Over here, cool bands that people would actually listen to are on the cover of the *NME*... The kids in Britain are more open-minded because they're fed a bigger variety of stuff. They're not just force-fed Beyoncé."

He added: "The fact that we didn't listen to that corporate sort of stuff definitely helped. The first band that really changed my perspective on music was The Pixies. Once I heard The Pixies, a flood of what I now consider the greatest bands in the world followed. Joy Division, Television, The Clash, The Cure... And that led me to cool American things we hadn't been listening to before – like Johnny Cash, and Townes Van Zandt, and all the great songwriters like Bob Dylan and Led Zeppelin [*sic*]. And then The Strokes emerged and we thought, 'Wow, those guys are like us'. And Black Rebel Motorcycle Club and The White Stripes. We suddenly felt, like, 'We can do this!'"

It's interesting to note that Jared, from his position in the shadow of his older brothers, was able to sum up the Kings' early progress with great precision. As he explained, "[Nathan and Caleb] wanted to get into music, but there was no rock'n'roll scene [in Nashville], so people were like, 'Yeah, come on over to our house, write a song with us and we'll see what we can do'. They both had really good voices, and so they'd go over there and write songs, and the songs would be country. I think all along they knew that they didn't really like it, but they got paid for it. And they didn't have to work a real job, so it was cool for them, you know, they'd just go over there, get drunk and write a country song, then bring it home and put it on a CD."

He went on: "I'll tell you how I got into the band... Once I started to delve into more diverse music, I began to make mix-tapes for them. I remember one that had The Pixies' 'Where Is My Mind?', The Cure's 'Boys Don't Cry', Billy Bragg's 'New England' and a song by Clinic called 'Return Of Evil Bill'. I could see it kinda opened their minds, and they'd ask me to make more mix-tapes for them. So I made more mix-tapes, and by the time they decided they'd stop writing crappy country songs and start a band, they asked me to be in it. This was based on no talent at all. I had *no talent* for playing anything. I was just thrown into it, but they just thought that maybe my musical tastes could further the band along. And it worked out really good. I'm still not a good bass player, but I still know what sounds good."

In fact, Jared became a fairly accomplished bass player in a remarkably short time, with the funky, unusual bass parts – usually produced on a Gibson Thunderbird, with mid-tones that suited the band's sound perfectly – soon becoming a prominent part of the Kings' songwriting. Caleb confided: "He's a fucking madman. You better not print this shit 'cause he's already cocky as hell… He doesn't love being on the road. He doesn't love what he does. He loves having a vehicle, a house and a pretty girlfriend. But that little motherfucker, man, if he keeps at it – if we don't drive him crazy or if he doesn't get too big for his britches – he'll end up going down as one of the great ones."

"It does get to a point," Jared reflected, "where you play normal bass-lines for so long [that] you almost try to do the weirdest thing that you can do, as long as it sounds good. Mine is definitely not normal bass-playing. I just keep trying to play the weirdest things I can and make it sound cool, because I wanna be different."

While the mood was optimistic – Jared remembered that as far back as high school, "We used to tell people we were going to be famous and nobody believed us" – it emerged in later years that there was something of a dark heart in the Kings Of Leon. While the musicians' upbringing had been beneficial in many ways, lending them an appetite for travel and fuel for creativity, their father's fall from grace when he left the church and his subsequent divorce from their mother made a lasting impact. This was most evident in Caleb, who said some years later: "I'd put my faith in my dad and I wanted to follow in his footsteps. I'd always looked up to ministers, but at about 15 I started to see that they were just normal men and it broke my heart. I closed myself off to pretty much everyone and dropped out of school. I thought I was smarter than everyone else, but I was wrong. Now I'm trying to go back and figure some things out, and writing songs is a good way to do that."

According to Caleb, Leon and Betty Ann "took [the idea of the boys being in a band] pretty well. They supported us pretty good. We had to lie our way through it a little bit. Matthew's family didn't know he was actually going to be in the band. We told them he was going to spend the summer with us…" He also explained how the band's early songwriting sessions went, joking: "We were two Budweisers away from being the next Oak Ridge Boys… We never wrote country songs. We had a friend that would sell songs. He would sell these cheesy country songs to this publishing company and they'd pay him $500 a song, $1,000 a song, which, now that I know the whole game of publishing, he was totally getting ripped off. But, [with] the shit that he was writing, he was ripping them off. We were like, 'Fuck it, we can write shitty songs just as easily as he can,' and we started writing songs and then eventually got fed up with it. We're like, 'Why would we write these things that we would never even sing? Yet we're putting our name on 'em'. So we sat down one night and tried to write a song that we would actually be proud of."

Those songs slowly took shape, pushed forward by Nathan and Jared's evolving rhythm section and laced with riffs laid down by Caleb and Matthew. In later life Nathan was asked who his drumming heroes were, to which he replied: "It's hundreds of nameless, faceless drummers, in churches everywhere from Mississippi to Alabama. I never knew these people. Every night it was a different style of drummer… the best way to describe it is Al Green, Aretha Franklin, Otis Redding: music with soul! Like, making the ugliest faces in the world and you don't care because you're so into the music, feeling it."

One thing was for sure – the Kings were interested in playing 'real' music with traditional instruments: no electronic beats for them. As Caleb told Paul Elliott: "I never understood how someone could like electronic music. Back in the day I would go to a club to try to hook up with girls, and the music the whole time was so bad, I would sit at the bar going, 'What the fuck is this?' There were girls up there dancing, and every other guy would go home with a girl because I couldn't stomach the scene."

And so the sessions continued. Thousands, maybe tens of thousands of bands have been in the same position: struggling to find an identifiable selling point, something that would make them stand out from the rest. The Kings Of Leon had their unlikely back story to sell, of course – but would it be more of a hindrance than a benefit?

CHAPTER 2

2001–2003

Jump forward two and a half years.

On the afternoon of February 8, 2003, the Kings Of Leon were no longer in Nashville. They were in a pub in the unlikely environs of High Wycombe, in the English county of Buckinghamshire, about to play their first British show. The venue, a slightly run-down place on the west side of the town called The White Horse, hosts bands by night and strippers by day – which came as something of a shock for the still-teenage Matthew Followill, who explained: "When we got there, there was a bunch of naked women in our dressing room, changing clothes. We thought this is definitely the life! I was 17. I was just thinking about boobs."

The band had recently acquired two press officers, Jamie Woolgar and Jakub Blackman, who worked at the time at one of the UK's better-known agencies, Coalition. Woolgar recalls: "The band came over to play in High Wycombe, which was the first gig they played in the UK. Apparently they came on and everyone was like, 'Who the fuck are these hairy bastards? Get your hair cut!' But despite the boos and the catcalls they proceeded to play an absolutely monstrous gig – people were going mental at the front."

Caleb added, "We were sweating bullets, but every show was sold out. At that first one we couldn't get onstage because all the kids were on there!"

The previous two years had passed quickly. Having rehearsed a set of original songs, the four Followills had improved their musicianship – although Caleb and Matthew still felt obliged to strap their guitars high on the chests ("to see our hands better" as the former put it). Manager Ken Levitan and RCA's US office had put their heads together and decided that a pre-emptive strike on the UK, then in thrall to hip new American bands such as The Strokes, would be a more sensible move than an attempt to convert the immense American market. Levitan recalled later, "We tried to break it out of Europe first. We thought they really might get the music and the story quicker there than they did here. So basically we hopped on a plane, got the guys over, hired a publicist, got the label fired up and away it went."

So it was that the Followills ended up flying to Blighty to try their luck. Levitan prepared the ground for the Kings Of Leon's arrival by setting up a meeting with Woolgar and his colleague Jakub Blackman at Coalition, where he played them a short EPK (electronic press kit), comprising some footage of the band. As Woolgar recalls: "Myself and Jakub started doing their publicity in 2003. Their manager, who looks like Elliott Gould, came in with a DVD of the band in 2002, and the three of us had a meeting. He showed us this little movie, about 15 minutes long – an EPK – and the opening scene is the lads sitting on a sofa outside an office in Nashville, and they introduce themselves one by one. This was interspersed with them playing in the studio and then driving around places where they were brought up with their mum and dad. They looked incredible – they were in their Creedence phase at the time – and we were in the middle of doing The Strokes at the time. They wanted to go with the company that had done The Strokes, because they'd seen what they had done and were a bit in awe of them."

Talking of The Strokes, Caleb explained that the kinship between the bands was both a blessing and a burden: "When The Strokes took us out on the road [in 2003] we were shocked. They were, and are, the coolest band in the world. Then for a long time people saw us as 'the Country Strokes', their little inbred brothers, let out of the cage in their basement. Over a lot of time, though, we've slowly but surely killed that stigma… We just came out of the gates, we never had the opportunity to have a bad show. We never had the opportunity to have shows where there isn't anybody in the crowd except seven drunk guys in Denver who couldn't give two shits. There was always someone gonna be there, someone important, someone famous, whatever."

The impact of the EPK was instant, Woolgar adds: "We saw this movie and we were blown away, because it's not often you know that a band is going to be big. But we knew then: we heard the songs, and we saw what they looked like, and the story – it was almost too good to be true."

Acquiring their first passports, recruiting their cousin Chris 'Nacho' Followill as guitar tech and flying out to the UK – a country that no Followill had even considered visiting before – the Kings Of Leon were stunned by the differences, even the minor ones, between their homeland and foreign turf. Woolgar remembers the band's first contact with the finest elements of British culture: "They came to London, and stayed at the Columbia Hotel, where we went to meet them. Jakub and I walked into their room and all four of them were sitting on this bed, with their cousin Nacho, who turned out to be the fifth King Of Leon, and they looked like the Beverly Hillbillies! They looked like they'd all been sleeping in that bed for years, top to toe, sharing one room. They were all quite shy initially, so we decided to take them out, because they'd never been to a pub. We ended up taking them for a drink at the Uxbridge Arms in Notting Hill, and they looked like they'd just walked out of Hicksville and into the big city – gobsmacked. Then they were hungry, so we took them for some fish and chips at a place called Carlito's just up from the pub. They were all like, 'This is amazing, I ain't never eaten nothin' like this before!' and calling everybody 'sir'. We decided to go for another drink, and as we were walking down the road they stopped when a red bus went past and said, 'I ain't never seen no red bus before!' It was unbelievable."

A show on April 10 at the London Astoria in support of Liverpool indie darlings The Coral followed, where the Kings were noted for their tight, bluesy set by a small number of critics. The Followills' shyness and silent determination to perform at their best came across to some observers as arrogance, as Nathan told *Mojo* in later years: "We always wanted to be the best at anything, and we will settle for nothing other than the best. And when we first started out, a lot of people mistook that as being cocky. These people don't realise, we took our 14-year-old brother and our 16-year-old cousin out of high school. Caleb was 18, I was 20, we'd grown up in this little bubble, and all of a sudden, 'Here's your passport, we're taking you overseas where you're gonna be adored and playing sold-out shows to 500 people'. To us, that was huge. Holy shit, 500 people! So compared to the way that we could've turned out and the direction our band could've taken, we did pretty good."

The band's unusual appearance was construed by many as a kind of effortless panache, perhaps because the young musicians knew no other way to dress and thus carried their look off with confidence. Nathan and Caleb sported mountain-man beards and long, unkempt hair, while Matthew and Jared's asymmetrical haircuts suited the emo-loving crowds of the early decade just fine. All four were skinny guys in even skinnier jeans, a look sported by indie bands since the rise of the wholly regrettable 'heroin chic' a decade and more before. "We were definitely a different-looking bunch!" laughed Matthew. "I had long curly big hair, I wore pants that were way too tight, shirts that were too small, cowboy boots. I don't know what we were thinking. We didn't think, 'Let's look like we're from the Seventies', but we did." Jared added: "We didn't really expect anything, we just threw a band together really quickly. Everything happened so quickly – much quicker than with most bands. We came [to the UK] and things got big on the radio and in magazines. It took a year to even process what was going on. It was all so exciting and depressing and every mix in between."

The sound and the look were just right for the UK at the time, it emerged, and within a matter of months a small but vocal cult following had grown around The Kings Of Leon. This must have been gratifying for the band, their press people and their label, but the early success had its downside. Caleb recalled that it took serious courage to step up to the plate: "We got thrown right in – thrown to the wolves. All these bands we toured with, some of them were 30 years old, and here's my little brother, aged 15, on the bass. We would pump ourselves up every night. Like, 'These guys are fucking gonna blow us off the stage unless we go out there and fucking do something!' And so, night by night, we would do something a little closer to being, you know, a confident band. I remember we played with The Datsuns, and they got up there and were going crazy, and then we got up there, just kinda doing our thing. Now, when I look back on it, we were pretty fucking cool! We wore our guitars really high because we didn't know how to play our instruments good enough, so we had to watch our hands. It looked like a schtick but it wasn't. It was four guys that were really uncomfortable, trying to make people think that they were comfortable."

2003 was the key year for The Kings Of Leon, with RCA releasing two singles and their debut album, all containing songs written by the band and Angelo Petraglia. On arrival in the UK, the press interviews drummed up by Coalition all focused at least in part on the young men's religious background and how it affected their playing and songwriting. For example, Nathan was noted for his immobility while playing – an inherited tendency from church: "You know, there's times when Caleb's like, 'Dude, you need to show some more emotions. It's like you're about to fall asleep!' It's not that I'm bored – it's just the way I learned to play in church. I don't thrash about. It's all business."

Still, when asked about his memories of playing drums in church, Nathan insisted "Most people hear, 'Oh, you played in church,' and they picture an organ, and just very quiet. It was very lively and wild... it was like the blues. With a little Jesus," while Caleb added: "The thing that inspired me about the music we grew up on is that it was human music. The people that got up to play, they basically just got up there and told the story of what happened to them that day... 'Today, I went to Walmart. Da da da da. I saw someone walking down the aisle, da da da da...' For me, it was inspiring. I thought, 'Man, I want to make up some songs'."

Caleb mused in one interview, "I grew up with my dad as a preacher, and so you hear Bible verses. I've always looked at the Bible as poetry, so I kind of learned to write in that style from time to time. And a lot of people misconstrued that as me trying to push something on someone. We're all sinners... I've always drawn from things around me, the guys in the band, the people I see on the streets. I try not to write too much about myself, other than stuff that's risqué and that turns people's heads... We got hold of something and the next thing you know, we've got an entertainment attorney and a lawyer and a manager and a publisher, and meetings with labels in New York. It literally happened that fast. It was silly." Nathan added that the band's attraction came from their down-home image just as much as the songs: "At first it was the story. They thought it was our publicist's fabrication. Half the people didn't even believe it, so we had to convince people it was true."

"They thought some publicist spawned this whole story, they stuck us in with Angelo, he wrote all our songs for us," he laughed later. "We actually had a publication in Europe that brought swabs to an interview – they wanted DNA, they didn't believe we were all related. My idea was to take the swabs and get samples from a black fan, a little person, a Japanese fan and a woman and send them back. They'd get the results and say, 'See, they're not related'."

The story of the band's past rears its ugly head again. As we saw earlier, the Kings Of Leon emerged from Tennessee – which might as well be Mars, from a British perspective – with what appeared to be such a full-formed history that few took it seriously. "As we went along," remembers Woolgar, "people started questioning whether the story was true, and to a certain extent I did too, because I was thinking that some of it was just too good to be true – this couldn't be the case!"

Not that any of this deterred the Followills, who recounted endless tales of their family background for the benefit of the disbelieving limey journalists. "A few [of the extended family in Tennessee] are house painters but a lot are unemployed – folks who don't own a pair of shoes, and you've never seen them wear a shirt," said Caleb. "But all the time there's a pig cooking and no-one's any better than anyone else. They can all sing good, but we just got lucky… I guess we lived a sheltered life. I never thought I'd go to places such as Paris, London or Sydney. And, to tell you the truth, as a kid, I didn't know much about those places, either."

The unmistakably Southern look of the first Kings Of Leon release, an EP called *Holy Roller Novocaine*, immediately caught the eye when it was released on February 18, 2003. From its artwork to Caleb's laconic drawl on the lead track, 'Molly's Chambers' – its title taken from a line in the traditional song 'Whiskey In The Jar', made famous by Thin Lizzy – the EP was a deliberate or otherwise nod to traditional American country-rock. The sound wasn't lo-fi – the producer, Ethan Johns, had given the songs a widescreen sound, if not quite a digitally crisp one – and the mix was perfect, placing Caleb's understated, almost *sotto voce* lyrics at the top.

'Molly's Chambers' was, like the first work of many groundbreaking bands, an early triumph. The song is tight, mid-paced and compelling, brimming with barely contained energy within a simple, two-chord riff that expands outwards in the chorus. Matthew's guitar solo is raw and unsophisticated, but not (you can't help but sense) deliberately so: the 17-year-old guitarist is playing to the best of his ability.

Asked by interviewer Molly Knight where the song title came from, Jared laughed: "Actually we've been following you for the last three years, and we're just totally intrigued by you and so that's where it came from… No, we used to just mumble that part because we didn't have a line, and we were listening to this Thin Lizzy song called 'Whiskey In The Jar' and he sings this one part and he's like, 'I went to Molly's chambers and blah blah blah'. So we got it from that. We totally ripped it off, and nobody's said anything about it, so… We were kind of nervous that maybe it would be a copyright thing, but I guess because it's just a small line from the song that it wasn't that big of a deal. But yeah, that's where we got it. That and you!"

There's more subtlety, but not much, in 'Wasted Time', a more upbeat song based on a slick, almost punkish set of chords and a thumping, insistent bass-line, and 'California Waiting', a slice of naïve, Eagles-indebted rock with thick layers of guitar. The pace slows for 'Wicker Chair', the Kings' homage to vintage American blues, where Caleb's voice gets its first real workout and reveals itself as classic blues-wailer's pipes, all bourbon-soaked warmth. The four minutes of the sublime 'Holly Roller Novocaine' end the EP, book-ending the release with two excellent songs.

The press being what it is, much speculation followed about the role of Angelo Petraglia on the *Holy Roller Novocaine* EP. Had he written all the songs? Worse, were the Followills just a front for his work? Petraglia himself was quick to put all this nonsense to one side, saying: "There was a misconception from the beginning, where some people thought this band was put together, which is so untrue. I mean these guys have so much talent, whether it was in the beginning very raw – talent is talent. To me, it was just guys that I hit it off with and dug making music with, and the writing was really cool… I've known Nathan and Caleb before the band even started. To me Kings Of Leon are like family. I feel like their older brother. The main thing that the Followills bring to the table is family. It runs through the way they play, write, sing, perform and party. The thing I dislike about them most is that they always seem to be right!"

The …*Novocaine* EP went some way to convincing many listeners of the Kings Of Leon's credentials: it was just too authentic-sounding to be fake, even if – like most British rock fans – you had no real idea what the current sound of Nashville was. 'Molly's Chambers' might have been used in a Volkswagen Jetta advert further down the line, but despite this tacit admission that the Kings were working for The Man just like the rest of us, there was something real at the heart of the music, even if it was merely youthful enthusiasm. As Petraglia put it, "At first, when I met Nathan and Caleb, it was pretty obvious that they had a thing – they had a sibling thing that was pretty powerful, and when they sang they had the sibling harmony that's hard to get anywhere else. That was pretty special, there, right off. They just had a lot of soul… They grew up in this whole Pentecostal background, and that was their experience in the world. People have heard [this story] a million times, cruising around with their father as he was preachin' and stuff, travelling the South, going to all these church meetings. But initially, to me, it was like they had a pretty old soul when it came to music."

Caleb and Nathan, then as now the prime movers behind the band, knew right from the off that their roots made them a draw in merrie England – always an Americana-loving nation. "When the dust cleared and the smoke cleared, we had a good first record," reminisced Caleb. "The UK has always had a fascination with the South. Where we came from had something to do with it."

Matthew looked back at these early days in amazement, marvelling: "We just went over to the UK, having never been there, so didn't know what to expect. We were selling out our EP and some radio stations and magazines were talking about us. So we went there and it was crazy – and at our shows people were freaking out. We had never seen anything like that before. We were used to playing bars to about 20 people back home, but over in the UK it was different."

Things moved rapidly for the band after the release of *Holy Roller Novocaine* and the EP that followed, *What I Saw*, issued on three formats (including blue 10" vinyl) on May 26. As press officer Woolgar remembers: "Everything started to take off: they put out the first couple of singles and the story just got bigger and bigger as we went along. I went along to their gig at the Zodiac in Oxford, and again the gig was just awesome because they were starting to build up a head of steam – and after the gig their mum was there, Betty Ann. She's like a proper Southern mama – saying, 'My boys, my boys!' – and once I'd met her and talked to her, you knew it was all real. None of it was nonsense. That was quite an eye-opener, because I was starting to doubt it, slightly."

Not that everyone agreed that the Kings were the next big thing. One major newspaper remained unconvinced, at least initially, says Woolgar: "One night they were playing at the Garage in Highbury, supporting My Morning Jacket, and a journalist came down to review it for the *Guardian*, and they came on and played. Remember, the thing about American bands is that they are incredibly tight live, whereas new British bands take so long to get good live. It had been the same with The Strokes – they were straight on it when they played at the Barfly. The Kings Of Leon were fantastic that night, I thought they were incredible and we were all blown away by it. Afterwards we hung out and had a few more drinks and they were getting a bit more friendly, because they didn't know anybody there and they wanted to see some familiar faces. The review of the gig ran the next day, and it got one out of five – and it was one of the only times that I've been actually angry about a review. I thought, 'I'm sorry, but I know what gig I saw, and that's not one out of five!' so I rang the journalist up and said, 'Look, come on! You know this band's going to be huge and you know that gig was good', but he said, 'No, I didn't like it'."

These dissenting views were few, however, and coverage in the press grew steadily as the year passed. An early milestone to which the band members still refer to this day was that summer's set at the Glastonbury festival, which the Kings delivered in the New Bands tent. This was the gig that really signalled the band's acceptance among the great and the good of British pop culture, thanks to the presence of Noel Gallagher and Kate Moss, whose attendance was a clear sign to the *Heat* and tabloid-reading demographic that the Kings Of Leon were worth their attention.

"I was at the Glastonbury gig," laughs Woolgar. "They were having a great time. They were coming out of themselves, without a doubt."

Appropriately, the band were beginning to shake off their early shyness and, their confidence boosted by the open-arms welcome that Britain had offered them, began to show what they could really do. On July 7 their debut album, aptly titled *Youth And Young Manhood* – its name culled from either a biblical verse or a line from a Hemingway novel, depending on where you read about it – was released. As Caleb put it: "We were going through a box of all kinds of stuff, and we found my dad's old preaching Bible... There was this cool-looking tree in the back of it called the 'Tree of Life', and on each branch it said something different. One of them was 'youth and young manhood'. The album title says a lot about us and our band, where we are and the things that we're going through." On the other hand, there's a line from Hemingway's *A Moveable Feast* that runs, "I had already seen the end of fall come through boyhood, youth and young manhood, and in one place you could write about it better than in another". Take your pick...

Most critics gave the album a cautious thumbs-up, aware that the storm of attention the Kings were receiving might obscure the quality of the music, but generally they were in agreement that the arrival of the band on these shores was a good thing. In an interesting twist, which became an ongoing feature of their career, rock buyers in the USA (where the album was released a month later than the UK) were almost completely indifferent to the Kings' charms – at least for now.

Youth And Young Manhood is the sound of four boy-men who have just found out what rock music is about. There's punk, country, blues and pop in there, with Caleb's deliberately impenetrable mutter the central feature of the sound. Producer Ethan Johns (son of the legendary Eagles fader-tweaker Glyn Johns) knew exactly where to place the band, keeping the guitars raw but clean and the rhythm section tight and swinging. Johns impressed the Kings instantly, recalled Nathan: "He was awesome. He let us keep it as raw as we wanted it, while still keeping it within the boundaries of a record that sounds great. He was very patient with us, very understanding. He just got the songs; he was in it from day one. The first demos we heard he was ready to go. He just basically let us be as natural as we could be making the record, and just played off that. We got awesome sounds. Awesome guitar sounds, awesome drum sounds… he was definitely the man for the job. Definitely couldn't have made a better first record!"

Sounding like a bluesman of twice his age, Caleb barks and mumbles into the mic on the opening track, 'Red Morning Light', a punkified country stomp, and into the slightly unhinged-sounding barnyard hoedown of 'Happy Alone'. Asked about this song, which mentions Montana in its lyrics, Nathan revealed the band's love of the American outdoors, saying: "We just fuckin' love Montana. I'm serious. We were thinking, it seems so beautiful to us because it's just wide open and it seems very chilled out. It definitely seems like the kids don't have a fuckin' thing to do on the weekends but get shit-faced, which sounds very much like Tennessee. I don't know, we just thought about how amazing it could be to have all that beauty around you, yet still think you don't really have anything because you're kind of in the middle of nowhere."

He added: "I'm serious, man. That's our dream. We wanna be *Legends Of The Fall* and *A River Runs Through It*… We wanna ranch and all share the same woman and fight over her. But we always fight over who gets to be Tristan. Every single time, and it's always Caleb who wants to be Tristan. I always get stuck with fucking Alfred. I'm the oldest and that's probably why, but oh well. I'm the mean one that gets the girl, yes-sir-ee… I would fuckin' love to play Montana. I would come out there just to hang."

There's plenty of light and shade in the band's sound, too, with the riffs decaying for subtle moments when the bass and drums keep the momentum going. 'Wasted Time', from the *Holy Roller Novocaine* EP, leads into 'Joe's Head', a more mellow country-pop composition with a sweet, melodic bass-line from Jared. Like the other songs, it has an upbeat chorus and a jangling guitar sound that is pure Nashville. Towards its end, Caleb's vocal descends into a harsh-edged rant: there was passion aplenty in the band, evidently.

One of the debut album's standout songs was 'Trani', for which none other than Bob Dylan expressed a liking a couple of years later –

unsurprisingly, as its understated, confessional edge is highly Dylanesque. It's one of the darker tracks on the album, and Caleb explained its subject as "a transvestite, like the kind we'd see in London, trying to survive in one of the places in the [American] South, where that doesn't really happen".

"I watch a lot of murder mystery shows on TV," added the singer of his darker songs, "and the whole thing about those shows is that you can see there's this brutal murder that goes on, but when they delve back into the life of the people, you see that the psycho really feels as if he loves the woman. So much so that if he can't have her, no-one can have her, and it ends up becoming some brutal story. I tried to pick the good parts out of that, but for a lot of my slow songs there's a woman in the trunk of the car!"

'Trani' builds into a droned, multilayered climax before leading into 'California Waiting' and then 'Spiral Staircase', a high-speed guitar workout with more than a nod to Bo Diddley and Sixties Rolling Stones, especially in Matthew's gritty solo, the handclaps and the bass-line.

The superb 'Molly's Chambers' follows before 'Genius', a quirky tune based on a nifty, questioning guitar riff, and 'Dusty', an acoustic blues wail straight from the Delta. 'Holy Roller Novocaine' winds up the album, before a hidden track dedicated to the Kings' annual family gathering, 'Talihina Sky'. Thanks to the band's immersion in Nashville, their careful handling by Levitan, Petraglia and Johns and their youthful energy, none of this sounded any less than completely authentic, even to those doubters who couldn't see beyond the haircuts and jeans. Few debut albums have set out a band's mission statement as clearly, although the Kings' later albums bore little resemblance to this early work.

Some of the album's rootsy sound can be attributed to the vintage gear provided to the band at the studios where they recorded, Sound City Studios, California (where Nirvana's *Nevermind* had been laid down) and Shangri-La Studio in Malibu. Among the instruments was the third Fender Telecaster ever made and some ancient Rolling Stones gear, as Caleb recalled, marvelling: "Every now and then we'd break out the Number Three Telecaster or Charlie Watts' drum kit... That stuff sounds so old."

The pressure was mounting on the Kings Of Leon as 2003, their Year Zero, passed by. Two singles, an album and several club and festival appearances since they stepped off the plane, their world had effectively expanded in ways they could never have predicted. Caleb remembered of their first few days in London: "We saw a lot of crazy things in the couple of weeks that we were there the first time... The first couple of nights [at the Columbia Hotel] we were sitting there just looking around laughing. It was like a movie, but worse. It was like, 'What the fuck?' People were snorting coke off the tables, pissing and puking out the windows, throwing champagne bottles at people's heads. It was absolutely, completely crazy. Like a damn circus."

It didn't take the band long to join in. Matthew Followill, whose tender years prevented him from overindulging at home in the States, remembered just how debauched those early times in the UK were, saying: "When we started out we had been so sheltered that we kind of went crazy for the first couple of years, and we kind of ripped our way through with a kind of rebellion so we could get that all out of our system."

"We're not naturally bad; we're fairly considerate people," added Caleb. "But occasionally you have to go a bit crazy, otherwise you're fucked from the pressure. Sometimes you just have to act like a kid." Luckily, the band's family background was a constant support, he explained: "Of course we have our disagreements. We're brothers, and you can take it too far sometimes. But because we're brothers, it is great at helping us stay grounded – no matter what you're reading about in the papers, whether it's good or bad."

He needn't have worried: at this stage in their career, pretty much everything that appeared in the media about the Kings Of Leon was good. A sold-out show at London's Electric Ballroom – attended by Sadie Frost, Stella McCartney and other A-list red-top regulars – only added to their allure, and it soon became clear that as well as enjoying the Kings' music, a significant proportion of the British population actually wanted to have sex with them.

"Basically everybody just wanted to shag them," recalls Woolgar. "That was the bottom line. It was chaos. I remember they wanted to go to the London nightclub, Trash, and me being slightly older than them and a bit tired, I didn't particularly want to go, but I took them there anyway. I remember going into the club and going downstairs, the doors flinging open and me at the front and the band behind me, leading into this club – and basically a sea of women coming towards us! They'd been given a spot in the VIP area and I pushed them in there, with all these women running towards me – and at that point I said, 'I'll see you all tomorrow!' and ran up the stairs and out of the club. I left them to their wicked ways."

From the start, however, the band – more savvy than they looked – knew that a reputation for endless hedonism could backfire after a while, and attempted to play it down a little. Nathan insisted, "It's not like we're trying to be these party animals or the most fucked-up band in town or whatever. It's just that, whether you're playing a show or not, you spend every night in a bar," while Matthew played up the contrast between the UK and US: "I didn't turn 21 till we'd been a band for a few years, so coming to England was awesome. We'd play the show and immediately start drinking beer. Then we'd get home in the US and try going to a bar and immediately get kicked out. That sucked so bad".

Asked why he thought the UK had welcomed his band so readily, Caleb mused: "When we started, we were from the South and we looked the part. Plus there was sex and violence on our first album. People immediately attached themselves to it, especially outside of America, because they see the South as a mythical place." He was also wise enough to know that in 2003, Britain's pop-consuming masses were in the grip of Americana fever, thanks to the success of The Strokes. Ethan Johns had also worked with that group, although there was almost nothing in common between the NYC band's sharp urban pop and the Kings' Nashville-flavoured wig-outs. In fact, both bands played together for a handful of US dates that year, creating an even greater connection between them in the eyes of the music-buying demographic. "When we first came out, we sounded like The Strokes," Caleb sighed. "They were popular, so if you were in a band you were either the 'Southern Strokes' or the 'English Strokes' and so on."

The constant references to The Strokes were clearly starting to get under the Followills' skin. Matthew protested, "The Strokes are good and everything, but you don't want to be compared to anybody. I don't think we sound anything like The Strokes, and we don't sound like Lynyrd Skynyrd. No offence, but we don't even listen to Lynyrd Skynyrd."

Nathan added: "Just because they're from the South [and] we're from the South, long hair, country boys. So obviously, it's either Lynyrd Skynyrd or The Allman Brothers. We'd rather be compared to The Band. That's our favourite band… After Nirvana came out, every band that came out after them were branded the next Nirvana so, y'know, [we're] just kinda taking it in [our] stride. Obviously The Strokes and The White Stripes have been huge recently. So all the new bands are gonna get tied in with them; obviously they make the comparisons, but we just do what we do. If it gets branded [or] labelled [as] that, then so be it – we just make music that we like and hope people dig it, I guess."

Jamie Woolgar reports that even at this early stage, hysteria was growing around the band – but still not in the USA. "I went over to Philadelphia to do a press trip," he explains. "I went from Philly to New York with them, and they were so unknown – most people thought they were from the UK. One of the journalists who interviewed them was [the late] Steven Wells, who was working for the *Philadelphia Weekly*. I thought he was going to hammer them, but he didn't – he actually quite liked them, and he loved the show and thought that they would go on to greater things. After one show at the Bowery Ballroom we all went out, and The Strokes were there. Then they came back over and the shows were getting bigger and bigger. The album went in the top five and it was just out of control."

Back in their hometown of Nashville for a few weeks towards the end of the year, the Kings reconnected with their families for a welcome dose of normality. "I went to Nashville with them, which was quite interesting," recalls Woolgar. "Jared and Matthew couldn't come out in the evenings because they couldn't get served booze, and also their mum was cutting their hair that night! Really, she was cutting their hair… so we went to a party with Nathan and Caleb and just hung out, and Angelo Petraglia came."

Leon and Betty Ann Followill (who were now living in Oklahoma City and Lebanon, Tennessee respectively) were, reported the band members, happy with their boys' progress – although it's not known quite how much they knew of the endless partying in which the Kings were indulging in their absence. "They're super proud," said Nathan. "We come from a great family… anything we did together, they were proud of. So, yeah, they're very supportive, very loving. They're getting a little too comfortable now, like having a box of the CDs sent to their house that they promised everybody they've met in the last six months they would have their boys sign for them."

"I love living in Nashville," he went on. "We all love it. It's great. It's a good place to come off the road to. All of our friends, they live in LA and New York and stuff. And the last thing I want to do when I come off the road from three years is to go to a party every single night, or you just get caught up in the whole scene, and you never really take a break... either you've got to slow down, or your body is going to slow down whether you want it to or not. So we like living in Nashville. LA and New York are a plane ride away."

It must have been a relief to be on home turf once again. Although the band had enjoyed the delights of the UK rock scene to the fullest, they had also seen its downside – the sarcasm and spite for which certain sections of the press in this country are infamous. Certain other bands had been less than welcoming to the Kings Of Leon, perceiving them as outsiders. Nathan commented, "They wanted nothing to do with us until we got famous, but now we're like, 'Fuck you, you had your chance'... An eye for an eye, brother." Caleb also revealed an inner insecurity when he said, "I hated talking to anyone at the start: I thought they'd think I wasn't intelligent because I came from Tennessee", and, "I always used to feel intimidated and tried to hide what I was saying in case people didn't like my opinions." Nathan backed this up, adding that Caleb deliberately sang in a raw manner "so people couldn't understand a word" as the polar opposite of his "all good and clean" church singing.

The negativity of it all, as well as the shock of their sudden success (Nathan again: "When we first started out, we said we wanted to have one record that sold 10,000 copies, and then to play one show a year and know that at least 10,000 people would come"), must have been unsettling. Not to mention the fact that the senior Followills were avidly following their young relations' progress in the print media and TV from home. Asked what they thought of it all, Jared explained: "My mom can never really understand the lyrics, so when I tell her about them she gets so sad she almost starts to cry. So I tell her to think of it as like a little movie or something," while Caleb added: "Our family have learned to listen to our music selectively. Someone asked our grandpa – Grandpa Leon himself – what he thought of us cussin' in the music, and he said, 'Well, I can't understand a word they say, but I know that you've got to do stuff like that these days to make it in the business'."

It had been a pivotal few months. Over the course of 2003, the Kings Of Leon had played endless support acts, opening for Adam Green in the States, The Warlocks in Europe and Travis in the UK; playing festivals such as the relaunched Lollapalooza, Austin City Limits and T In The Park as well as Glastonbury; headlining a few of their own dates at mid-sized provincial clubs in the UK and select venues such as the Viper Club in West Hollywood, and completing the year with a New Year's Eve show supporting The Strokes in Sydney, Australia. The band had taken a professional step upwards, too, improving their stagecraft significantly while remaining focused on their goals. As Caleb remembered, "When I found music I thought, 'That's what I want to do', but the idea of it being a job never crossed my mind. I just wanted to be good enough to pick up a guitar at a party, or if I saw a girl I liked, to work up the courage to play a song," while Nathan said, "When we're on stage, we're not thinking about anything but trying to play the most kick-ass show we've ever played, and those kids leaving thinking that's one of the best shows they've ever seen."

Still, their fondness for a party would be the reputation that clung most tightly to the Kings of Leon by the end of this year – a whiff of debauchery that was difficult to dismiss, even years later. By their own admission, the band didn't help matters by inserting provocative statements into their interviews, such as when Nathan smugly remarked, "The thing is, we're really horny bastards and we get a lot of sex on the road." Jared protested, saying, "See, that's what fucks up every interview when you talk like that...," to which his brother retorted, "We're supposed to be in a fucking band, and you're telling me I can't talk about sex?"

Like true homebodies, the band couldn't wait to get home to Betty Ann's home cooking and a Christmas vacation. Caleb chuckled, "I don't think we'd be very welcome in our church this year. We'd go in there with our long hair and tight pants and crotches bulging with the mistletoe in our belt buckle. It'd be a little weird," but the others' minds were on baser subjects. Nathan gloated, "We're just going to lie around on the couch and let our mom get us fat. I can't wait to get so fat that I can balance a coffee cup on my belly. Then there's always *It's A Wonderful Life* on TV. That's the fuckin' raddest. We just play cards, play dominoes, watch the football. Every now and then, like once every five or six years, it snows on Christmas Day."

Bands come and bands go. What was to stop the Kings Of Leon disappearing back where they came from, as so many others have done over the years? Caleb Followill knew that this was a very real possibility. Although he confidently declared: "We already have six songs written for the second album. We want to keep on making music and having a really good time while we have the opportunity," he added, "because pretty soon there's a good chance that fashion will turn against us again, and no-one will care any more…"

CHAPTER 3

2004

In early 2004, no-one seemed to think that the Kings Of Leon had anything other than a glittering future ahead of them. They had Australian dates with The Strokes to finish and a raft of summer festival dates booked several months in advance, including the Big Day Out back in Oz, the Bonnaroo event in their home state of Tennessee, a second slot at Glastonbury and then Roskilde, Oxegen, T In The Park, Benicassim, V Festival and other European festival slots. After that, there would be a series of headlining club and university dates in London and the British provinces – still a heartland for Kings Of Leon-related appreciation.

Then, of course, there was the small matter of the next album, which the Kings knew full well would be their make-or-break release. *Youth And Young Manhood* had been a hit, but not a huge one, and if the follow-up flopped then their career was likely to follow. A release date was scheduled by RCA for October 2004, and the musicians spent a solid four-month period in the spring and summer working on new material. The new songs, their engineer (and later co-producer) Jacquire King told me, embodied the band's attempt to deliver their own material – in other words, without the co-writing skills of their longtime mentor Angelo Petraglia – for the first time.

King – a multiple Grammy-award-winning producer, engineer, mixer, manager and artist – has worked with a range of musicians as diverse as Buddy Guy and Tom Waits, so he knows what he's talking about when he says: "The Followills have this musical background which brings them together, and even if their talent was a little bit rough back then, you could tell straight away that they had that sort of intangible quality. I've been longtime friends with Angelo Petraglia, so I've known about the guys since the beginning. They were very young back then and they had a lot of raw talent. They were definitely very driven. Their voices always blended really well together, and the feel of the way they connected in their music always felt special, even when they were young and Jared was just learning to play the bass. All those things were apparent."

He goes on: "They're family, so they love and fight like family. Sometimes it gets kinda heated in a brotherly sort of way, and tempers can be pretty quick to ignite, as well as heal. I've seen situations where one or two of them will be at each other's throats and then, if an outsider gets involved and takes a side or has an opinion, the argument is dropped between the brothers and the other party becomes the enemy! Because of their upbringing, and being on the road with their dad, they're used to being in close quarters and travelling and being sort of insular. They changed schools a lot when they were young, they never had friends for very long periods of time, so all these things kinda make sense."

The early sessions developed, slowly but smoothly, into productive songwriting. As Jared – still relatively new to his instrument – explained: "Sometimes Caleb will have a guitar part and a vocal idea ready; sometimes he'll just have a guitar part or I'll have a bass part. Each and every song always starts from one musical part. We all just get the music together first, and I'll play my bass part and Caleb will play his guitar part and Nathan will come in with a drumbeat. Then, we just write around that musical idea during soundchecks until we get the musical idea first. Then, once we have the basic musical arrangement done, Caleb starts to think up a vocal melody. Sometimes that comes naturally and quickly while we're writing the music, and sometimes it takes a little bit longer. When it comes down to it, the steps of our creative process are music, vocal melody and then lyrics."

Having witnessed the Followills' modus operandi at first hand, King was impressed by the band's work ethic and their drive to succeed on their own terms. As he explains: "Angelo had helped them prepare their material for their first record, and they really wanted to have more of their own input and ownership of the second one. They'd spent four solid months working on the material that they'd written themselves, and they were very, very intense about it."

Not that much of this intensity was revealed outside the pre-production and the recording sessions. The band were still fond of a drink and a joke, revealing to one interviewer that their famous beards might have a lifespan. Caleb declared, "I put a little dab of wax on there and just slick it back when I'm about to eat... Seriously, though, if people start coming to our shows in moustaches, we'll shave and cut our hair," while Nathan asserted: "Yeah. For the second record, we'll come out clean, crisp handsome devils. The ladies just won't know what to do."

Meanwhile, the partying went on, with Jared – who was starting to emerge from his youthful shyness – admitting wearily: "I swear to God, I don't think I've ever gone to bed in London before the sun comes up. It's terrible..." He added, to much amusement: "I overheard some girl talking about which guys in bands she wanted to get with, and she said, 'Matthew Followill, but not Jared, that'd be too weird'. I don't understand. Why? Why is that too weird?"

The songs were going to tackle more serious subjects this time, it emerged. "All that most music really is right now is crappy fairy-tale songs about boy-girl or love or whatever," sneered Nathan. "We'd rather put ourselves in the shoes of some of the people we've encountered... We don't necessarily feel the same way as some of the people in the songs, but I guess that you just have to try and take yourself to that place." This inevitably led to some rather grim subject matter, Caleb added: "Every one of our songs has something about it that's a bit dark. It can be the best melody, but will have lyrics about a transvestite or a murderer."

Of course, a year and more spent enjoying the fleshpots of London would have an effect on the creative output of anyone, especially so in the case of four young men from the sticks. This also manifested itself in the subject matter of the new songs, explained Nathan: "Our first album, I'd say about 30 per cent of what we were writing about was autobiographical and 70 per cent was wishful thinking. We were writing about things we hadn't seen yet. On this album, at least 90 per cent of what we're writing about is things we've experienced, nights we've had. There's still that other 10 per cent, though…"

The band were also growing up, to an extent. While Nathan quipped, "We're a whole lot richer, dude. Like, literally hundreds of dollars richer. Hundreds and hundreds," it was evident that the perspectives on the new album would be rather more sophisticated than on the debut. Caleb observed, "We're definitely not the same people we were 18 months ago. We've just all grown so, so much. Seen so many things… For this record, I pretty much wrote a song about everyone in the band. There's a song about Jared, a song about Nathan, a song about Matthew… I wrote a bunch of songs that were about me as well, because I'm a fuck-up and the only method I have of changing my ways is to write."

Part of the role of a 'fuck-up' apparently continued to include fighting within the band, sighed Matthew, who – like Jared – was beginning to establish himself more. "The press always says 'three brothers and a cousin, Matthew'," he mused, "but it's not that way. There might be more fighting between the brothers, but that's it… we're all together. I call them my brothers. I grew up with them. There's no common courtesy between us. Everybody says what they want to each other. That's why we've brawled so many times… We've been pretty good lately. Egos fly. I swung at Caleb one time. But that was a long time ago and he was drunk and being an ass."

The specifics about the extent of the Kings' partying didn't become public until July 15, 2009, when *The Sun* ran a tell-all feature about what went on behind closed doors. Nathan was quoted in the tabloid as saying, "Oh my God, it was just sex, drugs and rock'n'roll… Jared and Matt were only 15 and 17 – it was just crazy! I'm looking at my 15-year-old brother and he's got a 21-year-old girl travelling around with him. One of the perks of being in this band is that 80 per cent of our crowd is girls. We're super-competitive so, after a show, if your girl's prettier than my girl, I'm gonna try to take your girl from you."

Matthew was reported as saying: "In the end I was sick of feeling hungover. When I went home for Christmas one year I was 10½ stone. I'm over 14 stone now. I just didn't eat, ever… That's cocaine. I'm so glad it's over. I just feel better. We never touched it again. I try to not even drink that much now."

As well as using cocaine, *The Sun* alleged, Caleb had explored the joys of ecstasy. He was said to have revealed: "Oh God, ecstasy, man! One night the guys were looking for me – I later found out someone had slipped me some really strong ecstasy. Finally they found me behind a huge speaker. It was the loudest music ever and I had a huge smile and tears pouring out of my eyes. I was crying and enjoying it at the same time… When you do drugs you're thinking, 'I'm doing this to keep me going, otherwise I'm just gonna fall asleep and I ain't gonna wake up'. When, really, doing drugs is probably gonna be the way you fall asleep and don't wake up."

The band's press officer, Jamie Woolgar, noticed that the band's lifestyle was having an effect on them, and says: "You could tell that the partying and the never being at home was starting to get to them quite a lot. Inevitably, if you're on the road that much, cracks are going to start to show."

Caleb looked back on this tumultuous period later, remarking: "When we first brought drugs into the band, they messed everything up. It took a long time before we could trust each other again." Nathan clarified this, saying, "Any time you're a band and you're known for something other than music it becomes a novelty. I mean, sure it was fun for us to make out with supermodels and get shit-faced every night, and it kept us in the papers for a little bit of time. But a lot of bands think that they have to be out there being stupid, and it's a form of insecurity because their music isn't good enough to hold people's attention. So they have to smoke crack, play with baby mice and put it on YouTube. Not naming any names, of course."

Not only were the Kings Of Leon getting tired of the endless debauchery, it seemed, but they were also becoming fed up with people writing on the subject. "Eventually we got tired of reading about it," said Caleb. "You'd read an interview you supposedly gave where all you did was talk about celebs. Except you never actually gave the interview! It's weird, walking offstage and looking in the mirror and knowing you look like shit, but also knowing that someone pretty and famous is coming back to meet you. But that only happens in Europe. We've always had the chance to come back to America where not even our next-door neighbour knows who the fuck we are..."

However, Nathan faced up to the rumours with good humour, saying: "It's only the magazines who write about the partying. We don't brag about it or anything, but you can read magazines where every single paragraph is all about rootin', tootin', drinkin' and snortin' with Kings Of Leon. They're always going to write horrible stuff about you. Like how I fucked two girls with the same condom or something. Everyone loves 'rock'n'roll', you know? And everyone loves to put people with greasy hair and beards on the cover, but it's about the band, really, and how good you are. By the way, I didn't fuck two girls with the same condom, please don't print that. It's a myth."

Although the band were some way from cleaning up at this stage in 2004, it's apparent from what they said later that a general detox needed to take place for the band to function efficiently and, indeed, to survive. Booze, of course, is the lubricant that makes long tours bearable, and it had rapidly become an essential component of the Kings' daily routine, explained Caleb: "I'd wake up at four o'clock on the bus, just sweating, and we'd get up, go to soundcheck, go straight from there to dinner – because you have to eat a couple of hours before the show or you'll hurl – and me and Nathan would drink at least a bottle of wine at dinner, if not more. Then we'd go back to the venue, start shaving and stuff for the show, drink a bottle of wine while we're waiting, drink a bottle of wine onstage and, as soon as we get offstage, start doing cocaine and tequila shots. And this was all night long. You wake up the next day and it's four o'clock and you think, 'Man, I'm not going to do anything today', but then you find a little bit of cocaine in your pocket..."

This wasn't good for any of the band but especially not for the singer, who added that the end came after a visionary experience. "I'm a sleepwalker, especially back when I was really belligerently drunk," he said. "I just came to, standing there, and I was like, 'What the hell?' I was walking down the hall thinking, 'I hope no-one's here'. I stumbled to the end of the hallway and there was a closet. I opened it and one robe was hanging there, illuminated in a spotlight. It was honestly like a miracle, a gift from God. I used to drink so much that I forgot everything that happened. That was someone's way of saying, 'This time you're not gonna forget'… If we had kept going the way we were, the lifespan of this band would have been cut short. We went from being best friends to enemies. Touring became no fun… you throw cocaine and every other drug into the mix and things can't last long. You have really bad nights, waking up thinking, 'Who puked in my bed?' Then later on, you have a flashback and go, 'Oh, it was me'."

Jared didn't escape the consequences of too much of a good thing, either, suggesting: "It would've been the same if we hadn't been in the band. It's definitely something in our family. We just have communication problems, so with us, the only way to understand and fix things is by getting into an argument… It's hard to have somebody tell you something bad about yourself when you know you're a rock god… it's like, 'Who did I have a fight with? My rib's hurting'. It's a never-ending cycle. You're like, 'Well, I'm so hungover I might as well have a beer at lunch to make myself feel better' and that turns into an all-day thing…"

All this was fuelled by the changing times in which the band were operating. No sooner had the Kings Of Leon established a toehold than the media were focusing on another band of the moment, in this case Arctic Monkeys – whose indie credibility was perceived as a bonus, on top of their own fully-formed back story (ie that they were a Myspace phenomenon). "The Arctic Monkeys were everywhere," recalled Caleb glumly. "We used to read magazines and people would always refer to us. When it stops you get jealous. We're so competitive that when we hear a good record by someone, we think: 'All right, if that's what we gotta beat, we're gonna do our best'."

The other band of the day, at least in what remained of the indie press, was Babyshambles, the briefly fêted band featuring ex-Libertine, tabloid regular and drug hoover Pete Doherty. The Followills were aware of Doherty as a fellow nightlife traveller: as Jared commented, "That's a fucked-up situation. I wish the press would stop fuelling it… now he's joined another band that are totally cool with his fucking habits, and they're playing the venues that we're playing, and we've been touring for two and a half years, trying to get up to this point. And because he's got such crack credibility he gets to do his thing now. And now nobody cares. He's just gonna end up dying… The sad thing is he's great. His new thing, Babyshambles, is fucking amazing. It sounds like Built To Spill or something like that."

Doherty's predicament made Jared consider his own situation within the band, frequently rocked as it was by internal strife: "It just gets to the point where we're kind of different people. And now when we go home we don't really see each other, and it's great. I fucking love it. I don't know. I'll just hang out with all my old friends and my girlfriend, and stuff like that, and stay away from the whole band thing. It makes things a lot better. It makes people appreciate having each other around a lot more if you're not around each other all the time… you start to just see their habits and the deterioration, and all kinds of crazy shit. We're all in that age group and we have to watch each other change, so you try to get involved and it just kind of fucks up the process. You see people and they're like, 'Yeah, he's different', and it's because you just get older, you get smarter. Sure you don't want to get fucked up every night, and that should be like a normal thing, but I don't know."

Other new bands were inspiring the Kings too, it emerged. Nathan raved about The Kills ("That stayed in the CD player the longest time") and My Morning Jacket, observing: "See, we name bands more than CDs because we're discovering bands every day that we've never heard before. We're not well-informed enough to go, 'Oh well, the record they made back in '79 was much better than the one made… whenever…'"

The pressure was mounting, but the band were becoming more rounded in response. Jared was coming out of his shell a little, claiming: "If people liked the first album, they'll like this more. They have to, because we're better at everything," adding with a chuckle, "If anything we've gone from bad to pretty good…" Having reached the ripe old age of 18, he and his brothers could look back on the past couple of years and gain some perspective on their progress. He explained: "Every new band that comes out, they label the new Killers or Strokes. But it's really hard – styles can pigeonhole you and we're constantly changing… Just by being able to take what little we'd known, and come up with our own style and sound, is one thing I'm proud of in our past. It's helped us a lot because we are still being inspired every day by music, old and new." Caleb added: "It's never been important to try and name what it is we do. I don't know what we do, [but] you can expect a lot of growth in our sound, a lot more confidence in the things we want to do and accomplish. Not in a cocky way. But we're pretty young, and musically on the first album we were scared of what we were doing."

Scared? For many fans, this admission of insecurity didn't square with the perfectly formed vision of the Kings that had emerged with *Youth And Young Manhood*. Caleb had admitted that his raw, mumbled vocals were deliberately low-key as both a reaction to his clean-singing church background and a defence mechanism against the crowd, but for all that the Kings Of Leon had still come across to the public as a sturdy group full of cocksure confidence.

It only emerged much later that Caleb's muttered vocal delivery was a deliberate front. "Early on I wasn't confident with what journalists or people all over the world would think about what I had to say, and my phrasing," he explained. "So I tried to kind of hide it all. I was also really scared of the record company trying to push us out there as some good-looking brother band. So I wanted to make it a little difficult for people. I wanted people to have to go on this journey with us. I never felt like we were good enough early on to have a huge, smash record, because I find that all too often when a band comes out of the gates and has a big hit, there's really nowhere for them to go."

The group's fans could see how quickly their idols were growing up. Caleb's songwriting was more real this time, an unmistakable mark of maturity – as he put it, "Every emotion you can feel in the course of two years of being in each other's hair is there. There are lots of stories about a lot of things we don't really remember… This album is just us being ourselves. It's not about record sales or if we reach one or 10 in the charts – it's none of that. What we were making was a record that we were happy with. This album – we're thrilled with it. It doesn't really matter what people say or think."

Again, not a statement that seemed entirely believable at first. No-one goes from being insecure to confident in a matter of months. Still, soundbites like this gave the anticipation that was building towards the release of the Kings' second album an extra boost, helped along when the band debuted a couple of new songs on the 2004 summer festival circuit, including the V Festival and Benicassim in Spain. "We played in front of really big crowds," remembered Caleb. "They were sobering moments

– we were playing in front of bands who inspire us, like The Pixies and The Cure." This was a clever move: of one new song, Matthew said: "No-one's ever heard it before, but the crowd react like they've seen us play it 50 times before and they just can't wait to hear it again."

At these shows Matthew – the other junior King – was also beginning to stamp his presence on the band, stepping up his guitar solos. "They stick out in the live show more so than on the records," he told writer Molly Knight. "They let me off the leash. I've been working atmospheric stuff into the music, but the next album could be more rockin'. We've been listening to punk and grunge, and the next album could be quite a bit different." Asked about the new album, he said: "If you listen to all the records, you'll hear songs that some people would say sound Southern rockish, or punk, and there's some country influence. And you have atmospheric and poppy. That's the main thing I love about the band – that we don't have to play one style of music. We do whatever we want to do, whatever we love. It's worked out for us. We can do anything we want."

A mass of evidence was building up on the subject of the new album, thanks to these and hundreds of other interviews the band gave in summer and autumn 2004. The second Kings record would genuinely reveal a different side to the band, it seemed. Caleb summed it up when he said: "We had more of an open mind and learned not to second-guess what we like… we don't pay attention to anything but what we like. We like what we like and that's the only satisfaction we get. We love going out and meeting people and playing our music for them, and what we do is only about our band… the only tip, really, is to always think you are never as good as you could be and to always think what you've done is shit."

From the interviewing journalists' point of view, the Kings' advancing progress was obvious. Press officer Jamie Woolgar observes, "On the first album they had a single minibus that would pick them up, and on the second they had a limo each and their own bouncers. That shows you how far they came in that time," while the interviews themselves often took place in London's most prestigious venues. One notable occasion saw the Followills rising from their hotel bedrooms to meet the press after yet another mis-spent night, this time in the company of musicians from Whitesnake and The Quireboys: "We came to the bar at 20 minutes to closing time, took two shots and four or five beers, just downed 'em... It was miserable," complained a hungover Matthew. Clearly not everything had changed, then.

Nathan was eager to discuss the new album – and confirmed that Matthew had found his true position within the band at last. "This is the first record that all four of us were part of, we all wrote it together," he said. "Matt played really well on this record, it's the first one that he's been a part of 100 per cent. We did it really quick. We didn't give ourselves time to get sucked into the sophomore jinx that so many bands worry about. We had toured for 18 months straight, so we were given a month off to be normal guys, but within one week we were already recording the new album. We called the label before the month was up and told them we were ready to go. The label didn't even get to hear it until it was done. That's kinda ballsy."

As ever, the Followills' family background both sustained and plagued them. Their father, Leon, had, they reported, embraced his sons' (and nephew's) transformation from country boys into fully-fledged rock stars. "He loves it," declared Caleb. "He gets busted stealing magazine articles now, though, like he'll go to the store and instead of buying the whole magazine, he would walk out with pullouts from ten British magazines. They've got him flagged, you know, they keep an eye on him. He has to buy the magazine."

Meanwhile, some of the instrumental parts on the new album had come about simply because the band members had annoyed each other into using them, chuckled Matthew: "Jared will be walking around just playing the same stupid bass-line, and we'll tell him to shut the hell up... we tell him, 'We'll write a song with it, so quit playing it!' Or maybe Caleb will be playing the same thing on his guitar for about a week, and we'll eventually all join in, one by one."

In between writing, rehearsing and recording the album, the Kings played a second set at Glastonbury alongside the cream of the year's rock talent – including Goldfrapp, Nelly Furtado, Keane and many other acts, some of whom have faded from view in the past half-decade. For the Followills, the experience was more terrifying than it had been the previous year, because they were no longer confined to the new bands tent. "It was the biggest crowd we'd ever played for," said Caleb. "As far as you could see, there were people. We were like, 'Fuck it, boys, don't look, just play'… I want it to be a party, though it sure as hell won't be a party to us: our assholes will be fucking clenched, we'll be scared shitless."

In late summer 2004 the title of the Kings Of Leon's second album was revealed as *Aha Shake Heartbreak*, with two tasteful sleeve variations of an unmistakably vaginal orchid design, rather resembling a sexualised version of *A Night At The Opera* by Queen. The album had been recorded once more with Ethan Johns at the helm and had been cobbled together in a hurry: Nathan revealed that he had a "favourite pair of jeans, that I wore every day during the recording of the record. Me and Caleb wore the same outfit, didn't change once! We didn't smell too great afterwards, but I'll be damned if we didn't make the best record we could."

Comparing *Aha…* with their first album, Nathan recalled: "The first record, we were scared shitless. We didn't know how to make a record. With the second one, we kind of had an idea what we wanted to do but we still relied on the producer quite a bit." Caleb added: "With *Aha Shake Heartbreak*, it was all live, so pretty much the only thing the producer can do is tell you to relax and do what you do. So, we'd go in there and do it, but the whole time we'd be bitin' our fingernails wondering what the fuck it sounded like… We heard other bands layer all these sounds on their records, and we thought that it really sucked. They were just putting shit on top of shit. We realised that you don't have to do that."

Nathan clarified: "There's nothing worse in the world than going to watch a band play live whose record you love, and you hear them play, only to realise that they overdub 20 instruments on every song. It just sounds so naked up there. So, that was the first thing for us. We wanted big sounds and effects, but we didn't want to put anything on this record that we can't pull off live. Luckily for us, we had our sound man in there during the recording of the album so he could write down every pedal we used, every effect, every amp, anything and everything we put on the record, so that we could play it during a live show. We wanted our live shows with these songs to be as close to the record as you can possibly get."

Audio engineer Jacquire King was brought in again to lend his skills to *Aha Shake Heartbreak* and recalls: "We did it all in the same room together, right there: there wasn't a control room. It was an intimate and intense affair, and it went pretty quick. These guys work pretty intensely and there's a lot of horsing around and a lot of good times, but it all balances out because when they sit down to work, things get done very quickly."

King reported that his talents came in most useful when it came to getting the musicians in the right frame of mind to deliver their best performances – and then capturing those sounds. "My skills are record-making in a live setting," he explains, "and being able to create a comfortable environment that is technically up to great record-making. I make it a transparent experience, and I remain very keenly aware of what things about a performance are magical and make for good record-making, and when it happens, I'm able to identify it and discuss it and shape it."

At this stage in their careers the Kings themselves were still finding their way around the studio ("They were starting to get the hang of things, but we provided a lot of assistance in that way"), but everyone had a good time nonetheless. "The sessions were fun, and there was an intensity," King recalls. "They're singing about their experiences of the first album, and so *Aha Shake Heartbreak* is a little bit of a hangover record."

"When we made the first record, we were these guys living in the middle of nowhere," Caleb said. "We hadn't seen everything that we've seen now. So we wrote a lot of songs about wishful thinking, things that we were longing for. With this album, we didn't have to turn to anyone outside of ourselves. There are songs about each and every one of us. When you live in each other's hair for two years, it's easy to know everyone's ups and downs."

Nathan said of King, "He's a really cool guy. He's laid-back and lives in Tennessee, which made us like him right off the bat. I still remember those sessions for *Aha Shake*... so clearly. We were in the studio early on and Jacquire got a Fed-Ex package. Now anytime somebody gets a package, your natural curious instinct wants to know what it is. We were like, 'Let's see what it is'. Instead of opening it, he put it up on the shelf behind him and left it sitting there all day long. By the end of the day we were all dying with suspense, like, 'Fuck it already, open the stupid package'. He knew the whole time what was in there, he was just letting it eat away at us… Turns out it was a Grammy that he won after working on a Buddy Guy recording!"

As someone who has witnessed the internal relationships of the Kings Of Leon at their most creative – and therefore most stressed – King is in a unique position to comment on the dynamics of the band. "I would say in the end that the balance of things is fairly equal," he remarks. "The four of them come together as a group and they have their different strengths: certain guys are relied on for certain opinions. Sometimes we'd get into very heated discussions about things and sometimes, depending on the way it was going and who was forming what opinions, if you weren't in agreement with someone, you just had to look at their contributions and their skills and say, 'OK, we'll go with that opinion, because they've proved themselves to be reliable in that way'."

It seems that this trust repaid itself in spades, because when *Aha Shake Heartbreak* was released by RCA on November 4 in the UK and three months later in the USA, it was another immediate hit. Fans loved its expansion on the basic country-rock formula established on *Youth And Young Manhood*, beginning with its opening track, 'Slow Night, So Long'. Dominated by an upper-register bass-line from Jared, which gives the song a Joy Division and New Order flavour, 'Slow Night…' alternates between a fast-strummed country-funk workout in its chorus to more atmospheric sections in between – for a far more eclectic sound than anything the Kings had recorded before. Its second section features Latin percussion, a sweetly tinkling piano and jazz guitar chords. Only two and a half minutes in length, this outro comes and goes before you know it, a vignette that buffers the bigger sounds of the songs before and after it.

'King Of The Rodeo' amps up the pace and the tone immediately and became a set-list staple. Although its guitar parts owe a certain debt to The Strokes, whose influence is all over the early Kings records, it's a Followill song through and through. Beginning with a drum pattern that fans of The Stone Roses' 'I Am The Resurrection' and Iron Maiden's 'Run To The Hills' will recognise, 'Taper Jean Girl' is a slow-burning classic, even if it caused some upset among the Followills' relatives for its line, "Cunts watch their bodies, no room for make-up". Caleb mutters rather than sings the offending word, but it appeared in black and white on the CD lyric sheet, causing Betty Ann Followill some distress. As Jared reported with slight embarrassment: "My mom cried. She hates the C-word really bad. And that's a really big one to fucking put on your record. So, um, I think we're going to maybe put characters in place of that – a little exclamation point and money sign and all that bullshit – to cover that [word] up for the American version. But I don't know. For the rest of the family: those were the people that were telling us that we shouldn't play music, that it wasn't going to go anywhere; that we were going to go to hell… all kinds of crazy stuff, so we don't really give a shit about them." As a result of this song, *Aha Shake Heartbreak* is the first (and only) Kings Of Leon album to carry a Parental Advisory sticker.

It's back to boy's-own territory with 'Pistol Of Fire', a modern equivalent to Kiss's 'Lick My Love Pump' in a freaked-out country-stomp style. There's a speeded-up midsection that almost approaches AC/DC or ZZ Top territory, too: the band were clearly throwing all they had at the album this time, an approach that was paying off hugely. This album isn't all riffage, though: 'Milk' is a heartfelt acoustic ballad, focusing on Caleb's racked, reverbed vocal and plaintive lyrics. Precision-engineered by Jacquire King, the song rises and falls with great subtlety, avoiding the power-ballad trap with ease.

'Milk', it emerged, was inspired by one of Caleb's female acquaintances. As he told MTV, "There were some girls. Like a song on the new album, 'Milk', that's about an, um, experience that happened while we were making the record. Um, I love her. It was a good experience, you know, got a good song out of it. Hope she's doing all right… Everyone over there had such a long time to examine us, and want to make us look like rock stars and making a bunch of stuff up. The new album comes from having a little bit of celebrity on the other side of the world, and dealing with it and reading what everyone thinks they know about you. We got a chance to come back home where no-one knew who we were, and write a record that's completely honest and completely pure about everything we've experienced."

'The Bucket' became one of *Aha Shake Heartbreak*'s best-known songs, thanks to its anthemic nature. Released in the UK as a single, it became an early radio and TV hit in this country and for the summer of 2004 it was difficult to avoid, giving the band another major boost. As for its subject, this song was another autobiographical look at what had happened to the Kings since 2002, with its line, "Everyone's gathered to idolise me" explained by Nathan with the words: "'The Bucket' is about the person you turn into when you're on the road. It gets to where you can't even stand yourself, you know? And when you get off the road, you realise how much of a dick you really are. It's just about killing that guy off and trying to get back to normal." Not that he would take back the on-the-road experience, even if he could: as he added, "When we first started, we weren't that good of a band. But when you're playing, like, 180 shows a year, you can't help but get more confident in what you're doing… the highlight – maybe kind of a lowlight, actually – was coming home after seeing so much of the world."

"I'll come into your party but I'm soft!" yells Caleb in the next song, 'Soft', one of only two songs co-written with Angelo Petraglia on this album. Too much booze makes him an inadequate lover in this song, may or may not be based on the band's real-life adventures and which ends with a reference to his desired lover's "perfect nipple". Note Caleb's downhome pronunciation of "soft", which comes out as "sowft".

There's more Nashville blues-wailing on 'Razz', written about and for Jared, whose funky octave bass-line towards the end of the song is its highlight. "I wrote the song about him because it had the coolest bass-line on the album," said Caleb. "He loves playing it. It's his favourite song on the whole record… Jared is the Razzle Kid. I dunno what it was he did that day to piss me off so much that I had to go write a song about it, because he pretty much pisses me off all the time. Everyone in this band is always pissing each other off!"

'Day Old Blues' is a melancholy song, in which Caleb refers to becoming ill, girls loving him and boys hating him – a perfect post-tour song in other words, even if his bizarre cuckoo impression in the word 'blues' (rendered as a falsetto "blue-hoos") caused more than a few fans to reach for the skip button. Caleb later said of this song, "The rest of the guys had decided to go shopping, and I was sitting on the hotel balcony with my guitar. I was thinking about my mom a lot, and I just started playing and singing. When they got back I was crying. I've never cried while writing a song, and I've never written a song that quickly."

'Four Kicks' is a stomping rock workout that is a close cousin to 'Molly's Chambers' from the band's first album. Although Matthew had referred to keeping his solos under wraps on record, he's on fire on this song, which ends suddenly and is replaced by the two minutes of 'Velvet Snow'. A fast song on which Caleb spits out the lyrics – again, seemingly inspired by the debauchery of the road – '…Snow' comes and goes in a flash, followed by the much more thoughtful 'Rememo', which begins like an old country-and-western ballad from the Fifties. "The motherfucker's gonna go to jail," intones Caleb in a doom-laden sonic environment, all throbbing bass and ancient-sounding, echoed guitars and creepy fairground sounds.

It's a gloomy way to end an album, although a hidden track – 'Where Nobody Knows', available on the black-sleeved version of *Aha Shake Heartbreak* only – supplies a more upbeat touch. A droned ballad of sorts, the song mentions an unknown female – 'Jessica' – before its end, causing a froth of excitement among Caleb's fans. Still, it's a downbeat song topping off a largely introspective album, which – despite a handful of uptempo tracks – has a much more sombre atmosphere than *Youth And Young Manhood*. Little wonder that Caleb was quoted as saying, "If *Youth…* was the party, then *Aha Shake Heartbreak* is the hangover."

The differences between *Youth And Young Manhood* and *Aha Shake Heartbreak* were subtle, but easily spotted once you knew what you were looking for. They could mostly be attributed to the experience the Kings had gained in between the two albums, as Jared told writer Molly Knight: "I think that's all the difference, just because since we recorded that's all we've done – play live for a year straight, basically. There was really nothing else in it. We wrote most of the core of the songs during soundchecks and stuff like that, and we got a lot better on our instruments having played all those shows. We have a lot more stories to tell now."

Sombre or otherwise, the Kings' growing legions of followers loved the album and bought it in huge numbers. Jamie Woolgar remembers the impact that *Aha…* had on the band's profile, saying: "When the second album came out, you could sense that things were getting bigger: what was quite strange was that they never had friends or women or anybody by the side of the stage at their shows, because they didn't actually know all that many people. I remember standing at the side of the stage at one of their shows at Brixton Academy – and this was when I knew that they'd really made it, because a door opened and security were saying, 'Bring him through, bring him through' and we heard this guy saying, 'Aren't they great?' and it was Mick Jagger. He was there with his daughter."

He goes on: "We also bought a footballer called Gareth Ainsworth down to see them at Hammersmith, because Nathan had adopted Queen's Park Rangers as his British football team. Gareth loved the show, and I got him to meet the band afterwards – and Nathan's a massive sports fan, so we got him a QPR shirt with 'Kings Of Leon' on the back. So after the show me, Jakub, Gareth and Mick Jagger got put in this kind of holding room to meet them. Jagger was raving about it."

Despite all this fame and fortune – not to mention rubbing shoulders with rock legends - the Kings Of Leon were still yet to fully emerge from the cultural vacuum that had enveloped them as preacher's boys. Woolgar shakes his head in amusement as he recounts this particular gem, which occurred as Christmas 2004 approached and the usual raft of seasonal movies were released: "They went out to the cinema in London one day when they had a day off, and afterwards they said, 'Oh Jamie, we went to the cinema today and we saw one of the greatest movies of all time!' So I said, 'Oh really? What movie did you go and see?' And it was *Elf*, with Will Ferrell. Apparently they all sat in the front row, because it was an afternoon viewing and the schools weren't on holiday yet – it was literally just those four sitting in the front row watching *Elf*! I was like, 'Er… have you never seen *The Godfather Part II*?'"

CHAPTER 4

2005

L et's put the frankly improbable career of the Kings Of Leon thus far into perspective. In 2005 Nathan Followill turned 26, Caleb 23, Matthew 21 and Jared a mere 19. They had released two albums, played innumerable gigs and festival dates and become darlings of the fashion press as well as of the music trade, thanks to their still-outlandish image, debauched lifestyle and knack for a soundbite. Could things get any better for them?

Well, yes. Things got much better when the Kings were invited to open for the biggest touring band on the planet.

Say what you like about U2. You may think that their singer, Paul 'Bono' Hewson, is irritating for his messianic tendencies, and that guitarist Dave 'The Edge' Evans is wholly reliant on his rack of effects. Possibly you find the band's lantern-jawed seriousness and endless political flag-waving a little grating, too. However, any band that can sustain a career over almost three decades (much of it at the very highest level of commercial success), without playing disposable pop music, deserves a modicum of respect. U2's brand of confessional rock speaks to a hell of a lot of people, many thousands of whom are willing to shell out a large sum of money to see their heroes play in gargantuan sports arenas, over and over again. When a band such as this asks you to go on tour with them, you tend to say yes.

The genesis of the U2 tour remained in Caleb's memory for a long time afterwards. Months later, he explained: "We did some TV show or something like that with them in the UK. We finished our set and someone came over and said the band would like to meet you. We walked in the back, and there was a line of people on both sides of the room and we're like, 'Fuck this shit'. But the folks who brought us told us to come on, and they walked us through everyone to this little room. We were sitting there by ourselves looking at the door but didn't realise there was a door behind us, too. The door behind us opened and all four band members and a woman with drinks walk in. They sat there with us for a few minutes and talked about our music. They knew a shitload about our music. To be honest, they knew a lot more about us than we knew about them at that point. We were just floored. I'll never forget Bono saying, 'Man, with the records you guys are making, we'd love to open for you guys one day'. We all laughed our asses off and then three weeks later we got the call that they wanted us to open for them."

Twenty-eight American dates with the Kings Of Leon in support of U2 were announced at the beginning of 2005. Stretching from late March to the end of May, the shows took place both on individual dates and in clusters at the same venue, with the latter the most logistically efficient method of bringing the music to the masses because of U2's vast stage set. With the Irish band's backdrop, which included enormous 'LED curtains' (the last true extravagance that U2 toured with before their later, greener tours) behind them, the Kings Of Leon were literally and metaphorically dwarfed.

Asked if he was excited by the prospect of touring with U2, Matthew revealed some pre-departure nerves: "It's kind of weird. Travelling in a band isn't really travelling. You're in a bus and a backstage area and a hotel. You don't see that much. On the last tour we did a few things, like we went to the Eiffel Tower and Stonehenge, but for the most part it was depressing... I don't act too excited. It makes me so nervous thinking about playing Madison Square Garden and Staples Center. We could play terribly. I'm super-excited about seeing U2. I'm just not so excited about us playing. If people are booing us, it could be the worst."

Now, in case you're thinking that this was just another support slot and just another crowd for the Kings to conquer, think again. Close proximity to the behind-the-scenes organisation of the U2 dates made the Followills sit up, shape up and consider where they were going with this whole rock'n'roll career thing. Did they want to sit around snarfing drugs and making downhome country ditties, or did they feel that an update to the game plan was in order?

Let's be perfectly clear – the impact on the band of the U2 tour was huge. Not only did it encourage the Kings to rethink their musical approach, it also forced them to examine the way they led their lives. After the two-month tour, Caleb marvelled: "It was just like, fuck! The scale of it! That was back when we were doing drugs, but the U2 tour in particular was so good that I can remember every minute. Just seeing how professional everyone is in their team, it made us think that if we worked hard we could get to that level."

"U2 would get up there every night in these huge places that weren't made for music," echoed Nathan in equal astonishment, "and just make the place sound so amazing. And that kind of intrigued us a little to try to make music that was big-sounding."

Matthew, too, was left awestruck by the Bono experience, saying: "I only knew a couple of U2 songs prior to going on tour with them, so I wasn't a fan. But by the end of the tour, man, I had become a huge fan. Their live shows were amazing and they're definitely a really good band to look up to, and the sort of band you want to strive to be one day."

Looking back on the U2 tour, Nathan mused: "I don't know if we were scared. I think it was just more of a confidence thing, you know? It's just playing, just touring our way from San Diego across America. I mean, it's a huge deal, getting offered to open for the biggest band in the world, especially since we didn't even know that they knew us, much less knew our music. We get to play a lot of big places in front of a lot of Americans, which is unusual for us, so it should be fun."

Caleb added: "I may or may not have seen some sunglasses in a dressing room that said 'Bono' on them. That's all I'm going to say. I mean, maybe they were his, but I doubt it. Maybe someone put them in there. I tried them on, but they were too big."

Recalling the first U2 date in San Diego, Nathan said: "Oh my God, we were scared to death! We had never played in a place that big and we were flying by the seat of our pants. That was the first time I played in a place so big that the snare drum [echo] slapped me in the face, a second after I hit it... We didn't know what to expect, and I'm sure our whole sound crew was in the same position. I think we were more excited about seeing U2's show than playing our own. I'm sure we used a whopping 31 minutes of our 40-minute set time, just because we played the songs four times faster than usual. We were really in awe. It didn't sink in how big a deal it was until the fourth show, when we were getting 50 calls a day from everyone from our 10-year-old cousins to our 65-year-old great-aunts."

"They're fucking awesome, they're one of the best bands ever. Absolutely," said Jared of U2, although he damned them with faint praise when he added, "They definitely made their way into, at least, my top seven favourite bands, maybe top eight." He recalled of the tour: "Nobody pressured us except for ourselves. Just getting up there in front of 10,000 or 12,000 people and it only being half-full, but it was still a shitload of people. And we just had to learn how to not give them one second to be able to say something. We'd play a song and then immediately start another one, then immediately start another one. It was like 45 minutes of music, so we barely had a chance to listen to them cheer because we'd just keep playing. Because we didn't want fucking hecklers or anything like that. When we first started, people would be like, 'Yeah, whatever' and by the next one they'd be like, 'All right' and you'd just keep on and keep on. And somebody would hear a song that they really liked, and by the end I think we won over a lot of the crowds."

The Kings managed to keep their feet on the ground, it seems. They still wanted to have fun with their fans, explained Caleb: "We've always been a fly-by-the-seat-of-your-pants sort of band and whatever happens, happens,' he explains. 'When we toured with U2, we saw that no matter how big the show was you could still have fun, even if there were 15,000 people out there, you can still make it intimate and be personal with the audience because you're still playing music for your fans." As Nathan mused later: "I think the U2 tour really planted a lot of seeds in our head, as far as the direction we wanted to go on [the next] record, as far as big-sounding songs, and songs that would sound good in Madison Square Garden."

"U2 are great guys," he added. "They're so sweet, you wouldn't know that they're the biggest band in the world – apart from their setup: they have 57 tractor trailers on tour… Luckily for us, our first show after *Aha Shake Heartbreak* was playing Glastonbury right before Oasis for 110,000 people. So once you play for that many people, even a big crowd is gonna seem kinda small to you!" He snickered: "By the end of the tour, we all had our own U2 nicknames. Matt's nickname is now 'The Curve'. Nathan had a beard so we called him 'Hairy Mullen, Jr'… Jared was 'Jaydam Clayton'. And I was 'Wino'."

It didn't take long for the Kings to realise just how different U2's approach to pretty much everything was from their own. Returning from that tour to their own live schedule for 2005, the Followills assimilated what they'd learned and began to apply it, in as much as they could between shows. The year was shaping up to be a busy one: the band were set to play the Bonnaroo festival again, headline gigs at large UK venues such as the Cardiff International Arena, the Hammersmith and Manchester Apollos and the Birmingham 02 Academy, and play sets at the Reading and Leeds festivals before winding up in October with South American festivals alongside their old roadmates The Strokes.

The band spent as much time as possible in Nashville, although life there wasn't always tranquil. Despite the good vibes of the place, Nathan explained that there was a certain degree of antipathy towards the Kings in their home town: "All the bands in Nashville seemed to hate us. They kind of feel like we've hijacked Nashville as our town, that we haven't paid our dues by playing in some shitty bars and clubs for 10 years. It's a little better now: there's definitely more of an alternative scene other than strictly country music. There are some great bands in Nashville, and Jack White lives there now. But when we started out, the only good band in town was The Features. The only time you could hear good music in Nashville was when they played, once every six weeks."

Jared explained: "We don't really feel at home anywhere; Nashville never really accepted us, which is totally fine because we never really accepted them. As far as the Nashville music scene goes, they hate us, so we don't feel connected to Nashville at all, which is totally cool with us. Well, the thing is, our fans in Nashville are great and they treat us as though we're from Nashville, but the whole music scene there is really fickle. If you don't play certain bars for five nights a week, you're not a Nashville band. We literally formed in Nashville and started playing in a garage there. We don't really feel like we're connected to any particular spot and we don't really have a home base. No matter where we are, we never really feel like we're playing at home."

Matthew added: "Around 2002, Nashville was all country music all the time. There were guys we knew outside of town who played punk music, and we'd hang out with them. But there was nothing going on. Now I hear about bands all the time… there's another band called Bang Bang Bang, and in 'The Bucket', Caleb sings, 'Three in the morning, bang bang bang'. I don't know for sure if these bands are influenced by us, but I figure they are."

Meanwhile, the band's lifestyle – alternating between relatively peaceful co-existence in Nashville in the bosom of the family and tours – continued much as normal, although the Followills were gradually becoming aware that something wasn't quite right. "We looked in the mirror and we didn't like who we'd become," recalled Nathan a couple of years later. "It would be like, 'Shit! I did it again. I pissed everybody off'. You'd resolve not to drink or do any drugs that day, but that would only last until wine with dinner, and before you knew it, you'd be at a club with whoever doing whatever… It's amazing how blind you are when you're doing it. Now we'll be at a club and we'll see nine people going off to the bathroom together, and it's like, 'Don't you realise how blatantly obvious that is?' But we were just the same."

And who could blame them? The Kings Of Leon were now bona fide celebrities, with the opportunities to indulge in anything they wanted and an ever-attentive press (at least in Britain) that was eager to write about those indulgences. Nashville was just about the only American city that gave them special treatment, as its adopted sons: as Nathan explained, "Nashville's good in the sense that there's something if you want it. Sometimes, when you're home, you just want to sit on the couch, open a bag of potato chips, sit and watch TV and do nothing. We all live separately but within a three-block radius. We have a movie theatre, our favourite bars and restaurants. It's cool... It's not like New York or Los Angeles where things are shoved at you, and there's something every night."

He added that when the Kings did go out in Nashville, they were used to celebrity treatment: "For some reason they treat us like we're really famous. They'll put us in our big booth, and then Kid Rock and Pamela Anderson will come in and they'll put them in some shitty booth – you see Pamela Anderson saying, 'Who the fuck are those guys?' and they're like, 'They're the Kings'..."

Even cousin Chris Followill had become famous, it emerged, with crowds – in the UK at least – shouting his name when he appeared on stage. "Nacho is the best case scenario," said Nathan. "He's our first tech and I think he's done every show with us. He's also the athlete in the family, a great baseball player. But the band made it big first, so we brought him along with us. Nacho's been there since day one, man. He's a lifer!"

Caleb went on: "When you go to LA you feel like you're working every minute of the day. You have to get up early, get a bus and travel to the studio. You do your songs, but you can't get too drunk because you have to drive back to your hotel. Then you come back late at night and go to a club where the entrance is cordoned off with red braid and wait to be let in. It has nothing to do with making music. In Nashville we amble over to the studio around noon and talk about our woman trouble. Then we record a song and dive into a bar. That's what it must feel like to have your own studio."

Despite their increased profile, the band were growing wise to the ways of the music industry, retaining their faith in those close to them and investing in the inner dynamic of the band. Caleb and Nathan were still in control, in effect: as Jamie Woolgar explains, "It's definitely the older two who run the show, without a doubt. Nathan's a bright bloke – I think it's his band. You just subtly know that if there was ever an argument between them, he would be the one who mediates. Also, they're like no other band that I've ever worked with in that they all think the same thing without saying a word, because they have that family connection. Caleb drives the band: he's meticulous, and so professional about everything he does. You can see it in soundcheck and when they're gigging."

The internal structure of the Kings had crystallised by now, he adds: "Caleb has a very dry sense of humour. When he laughs, he really laughs – he looks quite scary! Nathan is very laid-back, and controls the band in his own subtle way. I like him a lot. The kids are brilliant. Matthew, because he's the cousin, is a little more the outsider, although he's not picked on or anything. He can be a bit of a whipping-boy sometimes. He is a sweetheart and very shy, but when you get to know him he's really fun. Jared is the nipper of the bunch."

Matthew remained just slightly to one side of the other three for a long time, simply because he was a cousin rather than a brother. Caleb described him as "the outsider – we're three brothers, he's the cousin. He's quiet and stays in the background, but when he goes up there and plays he takes it to another level.

Matthew has always had great opinions. We'll end up leaving a song off the record that later on we looked back and regretted, and Matthew was the one pulling for it. He's got a great sense of style as far as music goes."

"He's pretty shy," added the singer. "He's not as confident as he should be. He's one of the better musicians in the band. He can fucking rip on the guitar. The thing is, he'll play something really cool but think it's stupid. So, he'll come up with something else and something else again. He just doesn't have the confidence. But man, when he gets onstage, wow. Have you ever seen his legs? When both his knees bend, he's fixin' to wail, man. He's fixin' to get into it."

The older and younger Followills had assumed opposing responsibilities on certain issues, said Nathan. When Ken Levitan and the other staff at Vector Management called meetings on business matters, he explained, "Me and Caleb will weed through the shit and then take it to Jared and Matt. They could give two shits less about some of this stuff. The same way there's stuff me and Caleb could care less about, but Jared and Matt are really into, like who styles us on our photo shoot. As far as publishing or something like that, me and Caleb are like, 'That's the money side of it. We need to really pay attention to it'."

However, the divide between the older Followills and the juniors became less pronounced as time passed, explained the drummer: "It's a lot better now. At first it was kind of funny, my little brother coming and telling me that he's going home with some girl or something, and getting the brotherly approval... That was funny at first. But I guess as the oldest I'm always going to be kind of looking around the bar – I like to know where everybody is at. Yeah, it's pretty much democratic. Everyone has their say-so, and we go with, not necessarily majority rules, but intelligence rules, I guess."

The Followills still fought between themselves, though. "Girls and jeans" were, according to Caleb, the usual causes of disagreement. "We'd fight over who was supposed to wear the skinny blue ones – and the skinny black ones. We'd have the biggest knockdown drag-outs, but every night we'd tell each other 'I love you' then go and do the show. As the band, we've never lost sight of wanting to conquer the world."

Despite three years as virtual exiles from their home country (Nathan recalled that he and Caleb had spent only 48 nights at the house they once shared), the Kings' bonds with their other family members had only strengthened. Regular listening parties were organised and hosted by the Followills' grandparents when any new Kings Of Leon music was released, with the matriarch ruling the proceedings with an iron grip; as Matthew reported, "The last two years [our family] were first to hear our new records. We sneaked off and got hammered and could just about hear the applause after each track. Everyone had to listen good, or our grandma would take off her shoe and hit them."

Perhaps most noticeably of all, the band had found their position, gaining an understanding of where they stood in the pantheon of rock as it was in 2005. Of their transformation from geeky kids to a more self-confident plane, Caleb mused, "I was talking to Angus Young about this a while ago... he showed me pictures from the time AC/DC had their breakthrough in the USA. They were walking around New York in bare feet because they were so used to doing that in Australia. In the end no-one cared how they presented themselves; it became their strength. Maybe we've got a bit of the same thing going on?"

Perhaps, although AC/DC never made the fashion sections of the glossy magazines. The Kings Of Leon's unfocused country-rock chic had evolved into a more polished look: the jeans remained tighter than skin-tight and the facial hair was more groomed than before, but the haircuts – which remained long and luxurious until 2007 – were the asymmetrical stuff of art directors' wet dreams. Fortunately, the band could get away with their popinjay look because their songs were so gripping. The Followills had established themselves as songwriters with *Aha Shake Heartbreak*, but they retained a profitable working relationship with Angelo Petraglia. Nathan explained of their long-term writing partner, "He's a good guy, he's got a good soul. He brings good vibes, for sure… he's still the man. He kind of tutored me and Caleb in songwriting. He was the first person that taught us how to write a song that we'd actually be proud to play on stage… And luckily, as our songwriting skills have progressed, he might not necessarily have the same role as far as songwriting [goes], but we definitely wanted to keep him in the team, whether it be helping produce, or just being there and helping us find great sounds and try shit that we would never in a million years think of trying."

A dash of maturity was evident in the Kings' survival methods on the road. Faced with months on tour but unable and unwilling to satiate themselves with distractions in quite the way they'd done in 2003 and '04, the band retreated to their core values – the things that made them feel good. "I'm a country freak," admitted Nathan. "I probably listen to that more than anything. The band will kill me for saying that, [but] I listen to country more than any other, especially on the road. That's another comfort thing. And to hear country music while you're in Germany, oh, my Lord, amazing… When I'm home, I'm happier on the road. When I'm on the road, I'm happier home. There's no happy medium. That's a double-edged sword right there. We love to play shows, we love to tour. And luckily for us, we've kind of figured out a way to keep our sanity on the road… Stay at a decent hotel, and treat yourself to a decent meal every night. I've played golf on the most beautiful courses all over the world on off-days. You got to keep your sanity on the road. You got to do whatever you got to do to keep it fun and interesting."

"Caleb, Jared and our cousin Nacho, our little guitar tech, are all golfers," Nathan observed. "We have beautiful courses around here, and they don't give us any shit, since we went out on tour with U2. All the country clubs around here love us, and all the old members hate us because these long-haired tattooed boys are running around the golf course, taking up their space."

Golf, it emerged, had become a major part of the Kings Of Leon's on-tour schedule. A welcome blast of fresh air after the stuffy confines of the tour bus and hotel room, a round of 18 holes was now the Followills' way of avoiding cabin fever while touring. It also represented an escape route from the Kings-related rumours that were continuing to fill the gossip columns – as Nathan groaned, "I heard this story the other week that one of us was supposed to have tested positive for chlamydia. Dude, it wasn't even chlamydia. It was crabs! I mean, they're totally different, right? One just itches…"

The younger Followills had grown wiser, too. For example, despite his youth Jared was aware that there might be a life after the band, saying: "I wouldn't mind being a college student right now. I think I'd be pretty content with whatever I was doing. I think eventually I will go to college and do that whole kind of thing," and demonstrating that his church upbringing was still with him when – having been asked what his favourite hymn was – he exclaimed: "I wish I had thought about this, because that's the best question anybody's ever asked us. We're totally into those things. God, there are so many great ones that my mom would sing and my dad would sing. There was this one song called 'Only The Sound Of The Trumpet', and that was pretty fucking great… We're never really home. We're in Europe a good 70 per cent of the time, so [regular churchgoing] would be kind of impossible. My mom maybe will drag me out of the bed every once in a while when I'm home, and we'll go for like a special occasion. But, I don't know. It's kind of awkward when I walk in. I feel like everybody knows who I am, even though they don't. They're really just looking at me because I have long hair."

The band's upbringing had finally begun to reassert itself, too, in the wake of the endless debauchery. As Caleb put it, "You know, our dad was a preacher, we went to church on Sundays… Everybody remembers the way they were brought up, and you take from it the good and do away with the bad. But yeah, I still think about it. I'm sure my dad does too! I try not to think about it these days but sure, in the past I've felt guilt over the things I've done… I've been scared before." Nathan clarified: "We still have uncles that are preachers. Our grandma is a Sunday school teacher. We're not the same people we were, but we say our prayers every night and are thankful for the opportunities we've been given. If our grandma's cool with it, we're OK with it."

Movies, like music, were one of the missing ingredients of a secular upbringing that the Followills were now catching up on. Jared exclaimed, "I saw *Win A Date With Tad Hamilton* on the airplane ride over. It was surprisingly good! I swear to God. I mean, it's not good. I watched it as a joke because I thought it would be really cheesy, and it wasn't that horrible. But I did watch *Apocalypse Now* last night and that's a crazy fucking movie… It's like three hours. I started at like two in the morning, had no idea how late I would be up because I didn't know it was three hours and 15 minutes. It's one of the craziest movies I've ever seen… I was in my bunk, like, hearing machine-gun fire and explosions. I was peeking my head out of the bunk looking around; looking for Charlie."

It wasn't all maturity and movies, though. Jared, the youngest and least experienced when it came to drinking, found the constant on-the-road intake pretty depressing after a while. As he later reported, "We all partied together and did it for a year straight. After one tour, I got home and I was so fucking depressed. I could just barely stand it and I was like, 'Jesus, I've never felt this before'. And then I was like, 'Holy shit. I've been drunk for a year. Every single night'. And I just started to realise I needed to fucking quit doing that shit. So when we did the next record I completely quit drinking. I quit doing a lot of things I used to do. And once that happened it kind of – I don't know – it just shows strength. I think that kind of pisses everyone else off."

This led to tension, he added. "So it became a thing, like, during the record me and Caleb argued a lot. Then Matt kind of quit drinking too, so now it's like different personalities. Like, I'll be on the bus playing X-Box, or calling home, or fucking listening to music and the other guys come stumbling in. I don't know. It's just a weird thing. It's either

Kings of Leon photographed in Memphis in March 2003. Their deliberately out-of-step image caught the attention of the press when they arrived in the UK the same year. *(Pat Pope/Retna UK)*

Nathan Followill, the elder statesman of the Kings. *(Jamie Beeden/IPC Images)*

The Kings' early shows were frenzied but tight: they were professionals from the very beginning. *(Jo McCaughey/IPC Images)*

Just the good ol' boys, never meanin' no harm: Caleb Followill, Nathan Followill, Jared Followill and Matthew Followill pose at a 2003 location session in Sunnyvale, California. *(Maurits Sillem/Getty Images)*

At the Reading Festival in 2003: the Brits' attention had been well and truly piqued by this point.
(Jo McCaughey/IPC Images)

The glitterati begin to gather: the Kings backstage with Kate Moss, Stella McCartney, Sadie Frost and Pearl Lowe. *(Jo McCaughey/IPC Images)*

The Kings were still learning their craft at this 2003 performance for *Rolling Stone* in New York. *(Statia Molewski / Retna Ltd USA)*

Skinny, sweaty and strutting their stuff: the band at Glastonbury. *(Hayley Madden/Redferns)*

Matthew Followill, deep in the moment at Northumbria University in 2004. *(Andy Willsher/IPC Images)*

Caleb's beard was gone but that weird asymmetrical haircut was still firmly in place at the Forum in London in 2004. *(Stephanie Paschal/Rex Features)*

Caleb and Nathan with Julian Casablancas of The Strokes, who in some ways were the Kings' early mentors. *(Stephen Lovekin/FilmMagic)*

Caleb reluctantly takes one on the cheek in Philadelphia in February 2005. *(David Corio/GettyImages)*

Somebody call a stylist! The *NME* awards, 2004. *(Brian Rasic/Rex Features)*

By 2005, the Kings Of Leon were starting to find their feet as a band – although Jared would have difficulty explaining his choice of fingerless gloves. *(David Corio/Getty Images)*

like, you can kind of fuck your life up and do what everybody else does, and I just don't really feel deserving of that yet. I feel like I need to accomplish a lot more in my life before I can just become a big fuck-up... and if you have the ability to change, all it does is make those other people that much more pissed off, and that much more depressed. And then they start hating themselves so much that they take it out on everyone else."

As 2005 rolled past, the band's thoughts turned to their third album – which, judging by the success of the first two Kings releases, was set to be something of a milestone. A renewed confidence seemed to fill the band, fortunately. As Matthew explained, "This was the first record where, going into it, we knew what we wanted out of it. We knew we wanted to go for insane guitar sounds, insane pedals that sound like a keyboard, but it's really a pedal. Like we wanted to challenge ourselves and we wanted to fuck with people's heads in the sense of, you're not gonna get a record full of two-and-a-half minute barn-burners that are undeniably Kings Of Leon. We wanted to not only challenge ourselves, but challenge our fans. Obviously you wanna grow with each record and you wanna make it a little better than the ones before."

One of the songs, Nathan revealed, was a mighty seven minutes long: "As soon as we recorded it, we were like, that's either gonna be the first song on the record or the last song on the record... either the starter or the closer. As the record progressed and we were finishing it up and it came time to sequence the record, we were like, you know what? Fuck it. Let's start out the record with that and let people know that it's Kings Of Leon, but it might not be the Kings Of Leon that you're expecting. Not to throw our fans for a loop or anything like that, but more of a ... we wanted to show that we were multi-dimensional on this record. That we were more than three-and-a-half-minute songs about sticking your dick in any hole you can find, which all of the band members still do on a regular basis."

He clarified: "This was the first record that we knew the sounds we were going for and wanted to experiment with guitar and drum sounds. People expected two-minute barn-burners. We started with the seven-minute song, so that everyone would know we grew. We never got caught up in the hoopla of what number record we were making. We saw this as an opportunity to show fans how much we've grown musically and as people. We've tapped into a different audience with this record."

Momentum had been achieved, albeit at the cost of some disruption to the Followills' personal lives: the question now was whether or not the band could keep it going before the pressure tore them apart. Caleb gave a major interview to *Shockhound* later in the band's career in which he revealed just how far down the left-hand path the Kings Of Leon had progressed before they chose to clean up their act. He said: "There's just a lot that was goin' on in our lives early on that was a… it was a downward spiral. To the point where our career was gonna be much shorter than we'd hoped. We went pretty hard for a while, until we were like, 'Look, man – if we wanna continue with this dream, this other stuff is just getting in the way. And we'll end up looking back and thinking that not only is it over, we don't even remember what happened!'"

Some of this, he thought, was down to the suddenness of the band's rise to prominence: "I think [that] a lot of pressure was put on us immediately with the first album. Not necessarily here in America, but definitely overseas. We were a young band, and we weren't prepared for the pressure. I mean, I know that my little brother was 15 years old at the time. And so with all that pressure, that's what we did – we were working hard and we were playing hard. And at first, we just dabbled in stuff. But by the end of it, it was something that was a necessity – we had to have things to keep us going because we were working so hard. And I know that's a cliché excuse, but that's how it was. And so, yeah, man – we were in it. And for a while, we were enjoying it. But one at a time, ya know… One day, somebody's not doing it. Then we all started to realise how much better they looked and how much better they acted. And one by one, we all just kinda gave it up. And we knew we were all on the verge of giving it up, because there wasn't anywhere else we could go with it. We got back to Tennessee and we had a couple of months off, and Tennessee's not exactly known for its cocaine. So there wasn't really anything around, and after a couple of weeks we just felt better. But we never counted out the drinking – that was always like child's play for us."

Nowadays Caleb knows that he can't simply dabble, like most of us. "I still have a lotta friends that can do the odd line here or there," he observed. "But for me, I'm obsessive-compulsive, so when I do it, I do it big and I do it all the way. I'm a pretty full-on guy. And some of the most depressing times of my life have been when the stuff runs out and everyone's wanting to go home. I'd be like, 'Whaddaya wanna go home for?' But you just grow up. Or I won't say 'grow up', but you grow out of it." The Followills took the cold-turkey route. "We all just kicked it ourselves," he said. "And it took us a little while to get the attitude down, because you can kinda take it out on each other whenever you're feeling down and out and you don't have your best friends around. And for us, it was drugs. But it got to a point where I would see pictures of us, and I never even realised it at the time. But now when I look back, I had on white makeup and red lipstick and was all bloated and just outta my mind. I was just crazy. Me and my brother Nathan would drink… well, we'd wake up about three o'clock, wherever we were in the world, on the road. We'd go to soundcheck at four, and at five we'd go have dinner and drink a bottle of wine, come back to the venue, and while we were getting ready for the show we'd drink another bottle of wine. We'd go onstage, drink a bottle of wine. And before we'd go onstage, we'd take a huge amount of Adderall [a presciption stimulant] to kinda tide us over, you might say. And then as soon as the show was over, we'd break out a bag of coke and start doing tequila shots and coke all night. And when we ran out of coke, if somebody had ecstasy or acid, pills or mushrooms – I mean anything – we'd do whatever kept the party going… I'm lucky I'm still alive."

Perhaps inevitably, he ascribed at least some of the band's swing to righteousness to the good Lord above, saying: "God was definitely on our side. It was almost like he gave us a little bit of a lesson, like, 'All right – go out there and see what all the fuss is about'. And we knew when it was over. We saw a lot of our friends in other bands going down the same path, and it was breaking their bands up and they were kinda disappearing. And we were like, 'Man, we don't want that!' We wanna be doing this for a long, long time. Or at least keep doing this until we get good at it… it's kinda weird, because the whole rock'n'roll revolution, or whatever the hell they called it, when all the bands were coming out, they kinda returned to the ways of old, where people were like,

'Damn, music is back!' And you could go to concerts and you could experience the things that your parents were talking about. And with that, everything was kinda magnified. And even though musicians have been on drugs since the beginning of time, I think with this new music, that experiment kinda hit the ground running. Everyone was like, 'Wow! He does drugs! He has a drug problem!'"

The media played their part, Caleb thought: "And it got to the point in the UK where all it was in the *NME* was Amy Winehouse and Pete Doherty and what they've been doing and how many drugs they've been doing. And it was like, man! This is supposed to be a music magazine – where's the music? They don't even talk about music any more – it's more of a lifestyle thing. And we grew to hate that. We'd put out an album that we thought was good, then we'd get a blurb in the back of a magazine over there while on the cover there'd be some cracked-out picture of an artist on drugs."

Nathan summed it up perfectly when he said: "You take a group of guys between the ages of 17 and 22 and give 'em their passports and basically give 'em a get-out-of-jail-free card around the world, and they're gonna go crazy, and that's basically what we did at first."

In the end, home comforts proved to be stronger than the temptations of the road, Caleb concluded: "[Our] farm was where we went. And I think in the end it was just me and Nathan. I think the other guys had given up the drugs and stuff like that. But me and Nathan were drug buddies to the end – we were going hard every night. And yeah, we went out to the farm. And at the farm, it was like I started to remember all the things that I loved growing up – I always wanted to be a cowboy or something like that, I just wanted the open range. And when I got out there, I started to forget about the hustle and bustle of city life and the parties and all that stuff. It's in Lebanon, Tennessee, and it really opened my mind. And I credit that place so much for keeping us around as a band. So after we gave everything up, we stayed out there and we wrote the record out there, and every day the guys would come over and we'd just put amps out on the front porch. And I dunno – it was like we were playing music again. It was beautiful."

Where would the third album fit into the Kings' discography? Caleb had a firm idea, it emerged: "We'd written the second record that everyone was calling the honest record. But it got boring as everyone wanted to talk about supermodels all the time. So we were like, 'Fuck that, man'. I got obsessed with old westerns and I started thinking about things in a different way. I wanted to write a real love song. It wasn't gonna be about this fairy-tale love, it's the kind of love you see in the westerns and that my grandparents used to have. I never heard my grandparents say one nice thing to each other, but there's not a chance in hell they would've ever divorced. So I was trying to write these songs like in the old movies, where the woman would slap the man in the face and the man would slap her right back and they'd talk about getting pregnant and dealing with it – passionate love."

"We've always tried to show where we are," Caleb told writer Rob Townsend. "We didn't have a lot of time between the first record and the second record, so there wasn't as much growth as there is with this one, where we got the chance to take a break. We were no longer happy with having a direction. We want to experiment with music… it's exciting to me. I never realised we were changing direction. It was never a conscious decision, and it's not like we've got millions and millions of fans to piss off."

Asked by Artistdirect where the band's songwriting inspirations came from, Matthew was obviously at a loss to explain, saying: "We get asked these questions, and it's weird because there's not really a straight answer to them. You know? The songs just come. We'll start playing, and they'll come. We don't ever really have an idea of what we want to sound like. Sometimes we'll start a song, and we'll say, 'We want this track to sound dark.' But it'll typically be a situation where Jared starts with a bass-line and we all build around it. The next thing you know, we're in the studio and we have a full song. We simply get the sounds together like that. It really is what it is, man."

"I know some bands will try to play something like *Sgt. Pepper* or whatever," he continued. "We don't really do that. We seize whatever comes. It's hard to explain. We try to write good songs, and that's about all that goes into it… It's one of those things. What comes will come."

The forthcoming third album, Matthew felt, was very much a progression from the first two. "On the first record, we were trying to be punks and badasses," he explained. "We were nervous about being a band, and that shows. On each record, we became more comfortable. On the second record, we started looking more comfortable. Then… we really got comfortable. We knew we had some fans and we weren't worried about it, so we did what we wanted to do. It worked out… We have found our sound, but we'll still try to spice it up and make things different."

Part of the challenge, he knew, was creating a whole album of songs that flowed coherently: "When you listen to a record, you should be able to listen to the whole thing without getting bored. That's one of my favourite things to do. There aren't that many bands you can do that with any more. You're going to get bored and change the song. We're always nervous about that, and we hate that feeling. When we're putting a record together and trying to sequence the songs, we don't want people to get bored after the third song. We try to get good sequencing together. To make an album that you can listen to from start to finish is tough. There are very few bands that can do it. We really try hard, though."

By the end of 2006, the band's new lifestyle had taken firm hold. "We play golf every day now," said Caleb. "Especially if we can get a day off, just to remove ourselves from the machine that is touring. At first, when we had to share hotel rooms, things got a bit crazy and we wanted to kill each other, but now everyone does their own thing and we have girlfriends now. The paparazzi thing is kinda funny though… At first it's great, we were like, 'We've made it!' but that sort of stuff isn't cool if they catch you picking your nose, scratching your ass or coming out of a club drunk!"

After two albums, the Kings were also starting to make some headway in the USA. New York City and Los Angeles, always hipper than the vast American interior, had taken the band to their hearts to a reasonable degree – but anywhere else, they had to fight their way to be heard like any other indie band. As Jared put it, "Now, when we play in the States, it's like England used to feel. It is just the beginning for us over there, people are just starting to go crazy. That's been happening here for the last year but it's taken longer back home. It's great because now, all of a sudden, they love you and sound really excited. Over here more people know who we are."

Asked if it bothered him that the Kings were still relatively small fry in their home country, Nathan explained: "At first, it kinda bothered us a little bit. You go from such a huge high over there and not being able to go anywhere without a security guard, to coming here and the only person that recognises you in the airport is your mom. At first, we thought that was kinda shitty, but it's pretty good to get to take a break when you get home. It doesn't bother us that much. We really didn't set out to conquer the world. We're just trying to conquer one city at a time, and I think we've got about 13 cities now. We're on our way!"

Looking back at the new album, Caleb later explained that its sound was a combination of processed and live, which he liked: "Yeah, it definitely was bigger than anything we'd done in the past. But, you know, to us it still had [...] something that I really love if a band has the balls to do it. I love it when you can feel the live vibe on the song. You can tell that it's not people going in there one at a time and recording. And that's something that we didn't do on this record. We did it in the same way. I just feel like with each album we're getting better and better at performing live, and so this record, you know, it had that bigger feel. But, you know, it sounds like we were going in there, almost like going in there individually and recording our parts, but really it was the same way that we do it. I think we're just getting better at it."

Of the songs themselves, he said: "We do things differently. I mean, as far as the subject matter and things like that, and just kind of having the last say-so as far as what's being said, that's me. But, you know, a lot of these songs... I mean, my little brother on the bass guitar, he'll inspire a song and I'll write around that. Or I'll hear a drumbeat and write around that. You know, obviously there are times when I'm at home by myself and I kind of put it together and come in and hope the guys like it."

Asked if booze was an aid towards inspiration, he mused: "Well, I mean, you know, I'm always having glasses of wine. But for me it's like, you know, the musical inspiration is always there. And that's the good thing about having a band that, you know... I don't know if it's because we're family. Or maybe it's just because we were so musically deprived growing up. But at all times, you know, there's something being played to where we all kind of pick our heads up and go, 'Hey, that's good. Let's work on that'. And that, too, is the reason why I think we all need to live together, because we inspire each other."

"But as far as lyrics go, I never allow myself to write lyrics until it's time," he added. "On a few of these songs, literally everyone's sitting there looking at me like, 'Come on. Let's go record the song'. I'm like, 'OK. Give me one second', and I'll finish the lyric and run in there and sing it. And usually I don't have it memorised, so I end up singing it the wrong way and that's how it stays, you know. A lot of times, the lyrics, the way it comes out is the way that it ends up!"

Guitar-wise, the inspiration never dries up for Caleb, he explained: "I'm pretty much always writing riffs. It just sucks, because there are so many that I just don't remember. We're always playing. We don't even soundcheck our songs, we just go up. I don't know about the lyrics, but I'd say we could easily put out a double record at some point. Every time we go into the studio, songs come really natural to us. We're lucky. A lot of people get writer's block, and we're showing no signs of that."

Like the rest of the band, Caleb's stagecraft had improved in recent times, he enthused: "Oh God, it's really evolved a lot. We used to be so nervous, but now we're really comfortable on stage. We've got a light show. We're playing bigger places, and we have a lot more songs. We spread the set list out over the four records. You play so much you're going to get comfortable doing this stuff. Our live show is better than ever, and it's only going to get better. Our live show might be the thing that we're most proud of. People say we're great live, but it feels so good because they also say we have great records. They're supposed to go hand-in-hand. Some have even said our live show sounds better than the record, which is the best compliment ever."

Nathan was asked by writer Martin Halo how he viewed the first two Kings albums. "When we released our first record we were scared shitless," he mused. "It was just one of those things. We were in Los Angeles ready to record and there was no turning back. They miked us up and whatever came out, that was the record. We were four guys from Tennessee who never had a passport."

He continued, "*Aha Shake…* was without a doubt more of an urban vibe rather than a rural country record. We toured between releases, and

I think it would have been impossible to not be influenced by being in another country every other week. The influences of Tennessee couldn't have been farther away."

In retrospect, that's an interesting statement – the sound of the third Kings Of Leon album did indeed come from another direction entirely. And not one that pleased everyone…

CHAPTER 5

2006

When U2 invite your band to support them, you might take a moment to consider your options before saying yes. When Bob Dylan asks you to support him, you don't need to take a moment.

In 2006, the most important year yet for the Kings Of Leon, Dylan was riding on a wave of renewed popularity and had booked a huge, three-leg tour, one of which would feature the Kings as his opening act. After six months of writing, rehearsing, recording and mixing album number three, the band were committed to an apparently endless row of dates. The Dylan tour was scheduled to begin in Missouri and proceed through Illinois, Indiana, Ohio, Kentucky and Tennessee before playing several shows in Texas, Oklahoma, New Mexico, Arizona and Nevada. Canadian dates followed before the tour headed to Washington, Oregon, California (where there were multiple dates), Colorado, Nebraska and Illinois, to finish at the end of October. After a break of all of two weeks, Australian shows were then set to follow in support of grunge legends turned stadium-fillers Pearl Jam in Brisbane, Melbourne and Adelaide. Finally, the tour was to head over to Philadelphia, before winding up in early December in Hawaii. And all this *after* recording an album...

It's interesting to note that these two tours, with a brace of the most popular rock acts ever, weren't even supposed to happen at this stage.

The Kings Of Leon had needed, and fully expected, a break from the road – but were unable to turn down the opportunity to go out with Bob Dylan and Pearl Jam. As Nathan admitted: "We were gonna slow the train down – and ended up going on tour with Bob Dylan and Pearl Jam... When you're on the road, you wanna be at home and when you're at home you wanna be on the road. It's a never-ending cycle... When we got home we were actually off the road maybe three weeks, and got right back into it and started pre-production on the record. Throw in doing the record for a month and a half and then festivals and two pretty big tours. What seems to us like we've had a shitload of time off, we maybe had three months, which is a lot for us, but to the normal person... After going hard at it for three-and-a-half years straight, three months doesn't seem like anything."

The Followills spent January and February of 2006 writing and demoing songs. Someone within their organisation – manager Ken Levitan, RCA, perhaps the band themselves – had decided that the third Kings Of Leon album would be recorded not in LA or New York City but at home in Nashville. Ethan Johns and Angelo Petraglia would share production credits. It was a welcome decision.

Caleb contemplated the differences between the production team, saying: "From a production standpoint, Ethan is like the stern father and Angelo's like the mother. You can always pull the wool over your mom's eyes. So, they complement each other well. Ethan's more behind the board and Angelo's out there with us, strapping on the guitars and saying, 'That doesn't work but maybe if you try this...' Or, he'll just sit there, watch you and say, 'You're on the right track. That's the way to go'. Angelo is the voice of reason and the shoulder to lean on for us. He's been there from the very beginning, man. We're like his kids. He believes in us and he fights for us. It was always kind of a stiff situation between them until now. Now they're buddy-buddy. They have turned into one of the great production duos. Whether or not they know it, they just complement each other so well."

"Ethan, man, he knows how to get it out of you – how to get you to perform at your highest level," Nathan added. "And Angelo wants you to perform at your highest level, but he wants you to have fun while you're doing it because that comes across in the recording. He's the one that gets us to step out on a limb and try something that we'd never think of trying in a million years. It's a great balance."

"This record," said Nathan later in the year, "we had so much fun doing this record. We were so chilled out, because we were doing the record at home here in Nashville. After being on the road for so long touring and stuff, the fact that we got to come home and not only get to sleep in our beds every night, and drink at our favourite watering hole, and all that shit, but got to make a record while we were getting to enjoy all the perks of being at home. So this record didn't seem like work at all. It was like playtime... Angelo is a cool cat, and just, man, makes us want to go in there and record every day, because he lets us do the front side of making music."

Matthew added: "It was cool, because you could drive to the studio in your own car and listen to the songs you just did, giving you the chance to figure out whether you wanted to add or change anything to the song. It was definitely a big thing to this record, of just feeling comfortable and being able to do whatever we wanted to do with the songs." He added that Petraglia was immensely valuable throughout the sessions: "Man, he is awesome. He is one of our best friends... he kind of co-wrote a lot of those songs with Caleb and Nathan on the first record. Then on the next record, he just helped arrange the songs and Caleb pretty much wrote the lyrics and we wrote the music, so Angelo didn't really write any songs but he was the producer. And on this record, he kind of did the same thing again. He was just in the studio producing the record, helping us get the songs together and getting them completed and done. He's great, and I don't know what we would do without him."

Album recording began in March, with sporadic progress reports from the band: "Man, we're sitting on a bunch of songs right now that we wish we could let the world hear!" Nathan told *NME*. The songs were committed to hard drive smoothly and quickly, thanks to the mellow vibes emanating from the studio: Caleb in particular appreciated the proximity to home and friends, saying, "When you travel a lot like we do, you forget what it's like to be home. But it was the writing of the songs for [the third album] that brought me closer to home. For us, it was absolutely clear that we couldn't record this album in LA but had to do it in Nashville. On the left of us in the studio, Hank Williams. Jr was recording, and on our right Keith Urban. We came in one day and heard our songs being played in a different version, and when we opened the door we saw Keith Urban playing our songs live. Isn't that beautiful? We're rock stars and they're country stars, but we can still appreciate each other's music and talent."

Caleb was, as ever, the main lyrical force in the band, although all the musicians contributed musical ideas. Nathan described his brother's lyric-writing technique, saying: "The way he writes, it's kind of weird. He just sits back and observes stuff. And he'll sing you a song that he wrote about something you did four nights ago that you don't even remember… whatever vibe he's feeling, he goes with the flow. He definitely hasn't pigeonholed himself into any one form of writing, by any means." However, the music came from many different sources, he explained: "Ah, man, this record we had songs that started from a bass-line, songs that started from a drumbeat, Caleb whistling a tune, or Matt playing a riff that was driving us crazy so we wrote a song around it. There's no formula for us, as far as songwriting goes."

The next album would sound rather different from the previous records, it seemed. Jared was quick to play down the country sounds on the first two Kings Of Leon albums, explaining: "It's just that our style has changed. We were just growing and I think Southern rock is a really easy type of music to play, truthfully… all [it is] is bringing country into rock'n'roll, and you listen to some of those bass-lines and it's really easy. We were really young musicians and the way Caleb sings has a lot to do with it. And I think on the next one we just kinda figured stuff out and got a little more technical… the next one will sound completely different from the other two. I think it'll always be that way."

Matthew explained: "I don't know whether we spent more time writing this album [than] the other two, but we definitely wrote the album differently compared to the others, where usually Caleb would come up with ideas and we would write around stuff that he had. But on this record, all of us came with ideas that sounded cool. Like if I came up with a guitar part, we'd all write a song around that guitar part. So that was different to how we did it before, though Caleb still writes all the lyrics and we all do the music. When it came to recording, we'd never start a song with, say, Nathan playing the drums and we'd try to get a drum track, then try and get a guitar track and so on. We would all go in live and then whatever we could get from that performance that was good, we'd keep."

Jared, whose contribution had become more notable recently because of the funkier riffs he'd been playing, explained: "Caleb will be playing on a guitar part, and we'll all chime in and figure out parts to it [and] if we can all get something that's cool, then that will become a song. It pretty much starts from a lot of different things, like Nathan will have a really cool drum part that we'll want to incorporate into the record, and then you'll match that up with a bass-line that I've been playing over the last few days. So the music just gets thrown together [and] we'll sit down and Caleb will come to us with the lyrics – not all of them – but he'll write some of the lyrics and figure it out and give a theme to the song, and we'll figure out the rest of it."

The new songs were road-tested in the toughest way Caleb knew, he explained – by exposing them to crowds in Nashville bars. "When I want to test new songs, I call a pub and go sit onstage with my guitar. There is no better test than that. Not only do the top musicians live in Nashville, but also the best songwriters. Hundreds of people live there who get up every day and write three songs. You can walk into a bar in the evening and see a guy sitting in a corner with a bottle of whisky in front of him. They are often the best songwriters."

"Nashville has so much to offer," he went on. "On Monday evening you can be in an old pub playing cowboy songs with George Jones' violinist or Merle Haggard's lap-steel guitarist. The only thing you can buy is a bucket of popcorn, a mediocre pizza and beer off tap – no hard liquor. And there we are with Jack White and LeeAnn Rimes, sitting between all these old people. But the players there blow you away, and those are the moments when we feel very small… My hero is Townes Van Zandt. He was the man sitting in the corner of the bar. The moment he got successful, he fled into drink and drugs, and once he was forgotten by the media, he would write songs better than anything he did before. Someone like Townes makes me realise every day that I haven't written a good composition. I am leagues below his level. Maybe I will never make it."

Caleb was clearly feeling the pressure to deliver in a way that the other Kings did not. Jared in particular was ebullient about the new songs, saying: "We feel like we did in high school when we used to tell people we were going to be famous and nobody believed us. We all feel like, 'Man, this record is going to be so big! So good!' Not big as in record sales, but just in the way it sounds and how much better... it's going to be a lot more anthemic than anything we've done."

Asked by one interviewer at MTV if the album sessions had been punctuated by bad behaviour (in his words, "There are a lot of stories in the British press about what transpired out there"), Caleb took it in his stride, answering smoothly: "Well, LA is just LA, which is LA. Whenever we're making a record, we're pretty focused on what we're doing. I mean, we still have drinks at night and stuff, but we know why we're there. We worked a lot, but luckily we finished a little earlier than we thought, so we had a couple of weeks of a little sun tanning. It was good... I think the fact that we played so many shows in between records, we just got comfortable with each other as a band, and as musicians. We weren't really scared to try stuff [on the new album], you know, whereas on the first record we were scared of trying some things."

Caleb knew exactly what this album represented for his band's career, saying: "Because of what we've done as a band, and because we haven't really blown up to a level where people hate us, I think a lot of people are trying to scare us into thinking this is our make-or-break record. But they say that with every record. The title sums up everything that could potentially happen."

Asked about the writing of the songs, he recalled: "I was on my front porch of the farmhouse where Nathan and I live, about 45 minutes out of Nashville. I was getting to enjoy the normal life and being at home. The last record was a lot about honesty and going for it, and pushing myself into having the confidence to let people know exactly what I think. I got a lot of stuff out of my system, so with this record I was able to sit down and write about the things I really wish I had that I don't have, things that fame and all this stuff don't really bring.

"We see things in kind of like an older sense. So many people, you can tell that they put too much thought into their records, and you can definitely put too much thought into a record and overproduce and put all this shit on there," Nathan added. "We just figure if you're a band, that's what you do – you record music, it means you make records as soon as possible. Soon as we write a song we want people to hear it."

The pressure on Caleb came from within, he revealed ("We're always going to try to beat anything that we've done – that's why it's kind of hard going out there and playing all the old songs"), but the influence of the U2 tour the year before could not be denied. Open-hearted, unashamedly emotional anthems such as those in which the Irish band specialise may have been the polar opposite of the Kings' songwriting approach before this point, but something of the Bono approach had definitely infiltrated Caleb's songwriting – tying in with a renewed confidence he was feeling in the wake of his band's success. "People might hate me for writing obvious songs, but I've started to on this record," he told writer Rob Townsend. "My songs are often puzzles. It's kind of a confidence thing, as I'm scared of people critiquing me too much, but I want to really intrigue people and tell good, old-fashioned stories. With this record I'm opening up a little more. It's the first time I've sung. I've been able to sing since I was a kid, but I would alter the way I sang so people wouldn't understand it. I even hear the guys in the band singing our songs and getting the lyrics wrong and it cracks me up."

Caleb observed: "We spent a big chunk as the opening band for U2 and Bob Dylan and Pearl Jam – and when we walked out into these venues, let's face it, there might have been 200 people in a 20,000-seat venue. And so we would start playing our songs, and when we'd play it, it would sound bigger than anything we'd ever heard, because it was bouncing off the walls. So then we'd start to soundcheck in all these big places, and the songs started to build. But you never know. The next one could be raw and dirty and gritty and really small. We like to keep people guessing."

The mood of the album, he explained, would oscillate from bittersweet to good-humoured and back again. The more introspective songs came, said Caleb, from their itinerant background: "We've always travelled our whole lives, and it creates a lonely feeling of knowing it's gonna end, and you're gonna have to say goodbye and go somewhere else. That was how it was when we were kids and that's how it is now. It kinda makes you a little bit hardened."

There was a positive side, of course. "I think it was awesome that we got to see the whole United States growing up," mused Nathan. "Of course we missed out on having the same friends for three years in school, or graduating with buddies who we've known for so long. But it was pretty much a week: meet them on Monday, best friends by Tuesday, and sad when you have to leave on Friday. But obviously, life on the road definitely prepared us for this."

Caleb also explained that one of his songs was designed specifically to attract *The OC* actress Rachel Bilson. "It's kinda funny," he confided. "I don't know her, but I'm hoping word will get out. I had a birthday bash, and they are always a big deal. Everyone was asking what I wanted to do. I said I didn't mind, but I requested Rachel Bilson was there. I was deadly serious, but no-one believed me. I told them: 'You can make this happen, I'm Caleb Followill'. Anyway, we had a party and just hung out with friends, but the next night we had another party and as soon as we walked through the door I saw her. I was like, 'Holy shit'. She looked up and the thing was, she recognised us. She was telling her boyfriend who we were. I didn't get to speak to her though…"

Together with Caleb's new-found willingness to write more personal, inclusive songs and sing his lyrics in a clearer, more confident style, he was also being more honest about his goals – at this stage, religion and sex. "I'm a sucker for beautiful women," he explained, "especially if it's someone you see on the TV or in magazines. When you see that person in real life, it's like 'Wow'… well, sometimes it's more like, 'Whoa! You look better on the billboards'." He added: "If I want to write a song and say 'Jesus' in it, then I'll say it, and if I want to open the album with a seven-minute track then I will… We wanted to take things to the next level. We're sick of being considered an indie band that opens for other bands. We feel we have got something to show and something to prove, and we just wanted to throw it all out there."

Of the record's new sound, Nathan mused, "A lot of those songs were written while we were on tour with U2… We wanted to make a record to sound as atmospheric in a small club as a big stadium. It opened our eyes that you're not limited to any room. You can make music that sounds great in any size room". Perhaps the dates with Bob Dylan, whose songs – even the most fragile ones – expand to fill the largest stadiums, and seasoned anthem-writers Pearl Jam, had alerted the Kings to the importance of full-bodied songwriting?

Matthew Followill, who so rarely stepped up to speak about the band and their music, told Australian writer Joe Matera: "We just evolved a little bit… it comes a lot from us playing in a bunch of big arenas, where we really liked the way that playing those arenas sounded. Because we toured with U2, Bob Dylan and Pearl Jam, there were a lot of big open rooms with a lot of reverb and we liked the way that it sounded. So we thought that the next record we made needed to sound like we're playing in a large arena with a huge sound. And that is how it all worked out!"

Matera, himself a guitarist, immediately spotted that Matthew's sound had become slightly reminiscent in parts of Dave 'The Edge' Evans, U2's guitar player. "Yeah," admitted Followill, "and I wanted to go through a reverb unit for every sound. But at the core of my approach, it was really because I wanted to do something different for this album rather than the same old sounds I had. So I went out and shopped for effect pedals and ended up getting pedals that gave me the type of reverb-y sound I was looking for. But the Edge influence wasn't a conscious thing. I was only thinking about it after the record was done… it just struck me how my guitar sounded like the Edge."

Nathan invoked the big picture when looking back on these sessions, explaining where the record sat in the Kings Of Leon's career timeline. "Since then, I look back on it… it was truly us just playing our instruments as good as we could. Y'know, like I tell a lot of people, if you do something for eight years in any walk of life, you're gonna change, I don't care if you're a car mechanic, an athlete, an actor, whatever, you're gonna figure out the right way and the wrong way to do things, and shortcuts to take to make it easier for you without losing the integrity of your art or your craft. The [sessions] were basically us getting comfortable and confident with ourselves and our instruments, playing together and being a little more bold. Trying stuff that we were either too scared or too ignorant to try on the first records. And what threw people off is you could actually understand what Caleb was saying."

You can also place the third album, to be released in 2007, as the first steps the Kings Of Leon took away from the drug-fuelled lifestyle that had made them so famous. "I think we caught up for all those lost years [as preacher's boys] in our first couple of years of the band," remembered Matthew. "Now we're pretty chilled, we don't really do anything but drink. I'm sure why we went crazy was because we were so sheltered. But we're way more low-key these days. And I don't want to sound like we're now pussies or anything, as we still party and stuff, but it's just not as bad as it used to be… or as good as it used to be!… [Our religion is] still important but it's not as extreme as it was at one point, like going to church all the time and stuff. But you know, I still believe and I keep what I believe in the back of my mind. I know what's right and wrong."

Like his brothers, Jared was thoughtful about the role that religion had played in his upbringing. "I think it provided me with an inside scoop on things that I would later have been asking myself. For instance, organised religion – now I question that kind of stuff and see the dark side of it, the brainwashing element. I think it's good that I got to see those mechanisms of it when I was young. But I do agree with the central message religion tries to push forward – that's to be a good person. What I disagree with is religions that think theirs is the only true way, that everyone else will go to hell. Or when they're trying to kill people who belong to other religions."

Knowing right from wrong is difficult enough at the best of times, let alone in the Kings Of Leon's situation. Still, it seemed that as 2006 wore on the band were starting to think in terms of stability: Jared and Nathan were both in relationships and the band were becoming a little more discreet about their partying. Caleb was still resisting the pull of monogamy at this stage, though – as he told one interviewer, "At times I want a real relationship and at times I don't. The grass is always greener. I see other people, both in my band and in other bands, and they have relationships, and most of the time I'm feeling sorry for them because for me the hardest thing is when the girl's not around, and on the phone she's telling you what she did that day, and it's so anti-climactic. Then you get to tell her what you did that day. After a while it just seems the whole relationship is you bragging about the things you're getting to do. That's the last thing I want to do. I wish it could work, but I don't know. It'll take a while before I turn into the relationship guy, unfortunately…

I get to have too much fun, I guess. But I've still got time to get serious. Well, I say I do, but I'm getting kind of old."

Note that Caleb was all of 24 when he made this statement. Then again, the band had spent a couple of years working their way through a series of female admirers, so monogamy was probably an interesting concept for them. Jared explained where the Kings' collective heads were at when he said: "We don't really take advantage, like, full advantage of all that stuff – but it is there. And there have been nights where, you know, ridiculous stories go down and ridiculous things happen. You play a show every night and there are pretty much groupies there every night [but] now a couple of us have girlfriends, so we're totally not into that. When you're writing songs you pretty much write about your surroundings. You're playing a show every night; you've got people around you having sex every night." He added, laughing: "You can't really write every song about playing shows because that's just kind of cheesy – but you can write about doing it doggy-style."

Jared clarified: "You just kind of lose interest in the whole thing after a while. In the beginning you think, 'Wow. These girls really like us. Awesome. They're, like, willing to do everything'. And after so much of that, you're just like, 'Ugh'. You start seeing through them, and it just starts to gross you out – the way the girls are. The things they'll do, the way that they beg to come backstage and stuff like that. We're just kind of like, 'Gross'. And then me and Matt got girlfriends, and we're pretty content with that."

This new, more common-sense approach seemed to be shared throughout the band. Nathan marvelled at the ride the band had been on for the past couple of years, saying: "No sleep. A lot of booze. A lot of drugs at first, not so much here lately. But, who knows, we're going back out again, we might start back up. I don't know, man. You don't realise how much shit you're getting to see, until it's all over and you're looking at pictures. You're like, 'Holy fuck. I was there and I was doing that'. It's a double-edged sword, 'cause you're proud of where you've been, but you're also ashamed that you didn't pay more attention to it." He described the band's newly rebalanced daily schedule: "When you're on tour, fuck, you wake up, soundcheck, eat dinner, play that venue, get shit-faced, pass out on the bus, wake up in a different town, soundcheck, eat dinner, play at the venue, get shit-faced, pass out. It's not really like you have that much time. Now we're all golfers, so we'll pick two nights out of the week to kind of take it easy so we can go play golf… we just take it one day at a time. It can all be gone tomorrow and if it did happen, we've far exceeded our expectations for our musical career. It's all good. Life goes on. We're happy."

Asked by Paul Elliott at *Mojo* if he seriously expected people to believe that the band had quit hard drugs, Jared explained: "I definitely got to a point where it was too much. It just got depressing and repetitive and monotonous. When I joined this band I wanted to get away from all the normal things that 15-year-olds do. I didn't wanna go to school. I wanted to be in a band and travel, but by doing those things and going to a bar every single night and having the same drinks and meeting the same girls, it just became as repetitive as if I'd stayed in school. We all kinda went crazy. We haven't really completely recovered yet, but slowing down on a lot of that stuff is definitely the right step forward."

"We were getting to the end of our rope," Caleb told another interviewer. "On tour we were going at it so much that we had to rely on, er, things just to keep going. So we got home last year all hot-headed, with each of us still thinking we were the cat's miaow and so we were always fighting. It took a while, but you slowly started to see people look better, and be nicer and you realised it was because they weren't doing any drugs. Then we knew what we had to do, y'know? Only then did we all become friends again – having dinner and doing fun stuff together, playing golf and shit and just enjoying each other's company – both as part of the band and outside of it. Now it feels like we're all brothers again."

Some of the impetus to clean up their act might have come from Betty Ann Followill, who had been profoundly shocked by her sons' appearance when they returned from touring on one occasion. "When our mom saw us, she busted out crying," recalled Nathan guiltily. "We were all 20 pounds underweight and couldn't breathe out of our noses and looked like we were two days from death. We looked in the mirror and said, 'Holy shit'. That was a reality check – we just made the decision that we're in a band to make music, not to party all the time."

This was a pivotal stage in the Kings Of Leon's career: the moment when the foursome stopped being all about their looks and their lifestyle and started to be something bigger. It emerged that some of the huge acts who were mentoring them in late 2006 had had a quiet word in their ears about some of their life choices, said Nathan: "A lot of these older bands that are so legendary that like us so much, I honestly think in some way, they see us as a younger version of them and it's kind of like, especially like a Bono or an Eddie [Vedder] or something like that, it's like they wanna shelter you and give you advice of pitfalls to avoid in your career… They're looking out for us, and they want us to succeed, and they want us to do it the right way, and that's cool that you've got so much time to actually wanna help us out. It still doesn't change the fact that we're gonna try to get 'em shit-faced and make them pee their pants every night after a show. Still, I think they kind of see themselves in us, and us in them. It's great. As a band, you've gotta accept the fact that you wanna sell millions of records and be that, or would you rather sell a handful of records and be respected by some of the greatest musicians of all time? For us, right now, being accepted by some of the greatest musicians of all time is working out just fine for us."

The experience of the Bob Dylan tour was clearly a crucial one for the Kings, even if actual interaction with the great man was something that needed to be approached with diplomacy. Nathan recalled: "The thing that helped us out with him, a couple of the guys in his band, they're from Nashville and they're friends with our producer Angelo. That was our way in. We just hung out with those guys and Bob would come up and talk to us and say 'Hey'. He's kind of a quiet, reserved guy… it was awesome to watch him get up there and play every night. He's changed. The sound has changed. Shit, it's gotta be worth something that he's still up there doing it. The first couple of times we saw him on tour, we kind of freaked out a little bit and then it was just, 'Shit, he's a man. He's a human. He's normal just like everybody else'. He's a cool dude, man. We really had a good time on tour with him. He's a sweetheart."

Caleb recalled in delight that Dylan had been highly complimentary about the Kings Of Leon. "There were three legs of the tour, and he said he'd let his people decide who the other two bands were, but that he wanted Kings Of Leon. Just to be acknowledged by him was a dream come true," he said. "On the last date he came into our dressing room and said: 'Man, I'm depressed'. We asked him why and he said: 'Well, I just want to call those other two bands and tell them to stay home'... We were inspired by him for years and years, and there he was giving us his stamp of approval. He asked us: 'What was that last song you played?' We told him it was 'Trani' [and] he said, 'That's one hell of a song'."

It can be assumed that Nathan was exaggerating when he added of Dylan, "He's got the softest hands I've ever felt in my life. I swear to God. Of a guy or a girl. That's not an insult... he literally has the softest hands of anything I've ever touched. Almost like the bottom of a baby's foot that has yet to take its first step," because the reverence of the Kings for him was evidently genuine. "It was great and an honour," said Matthew. "We were pumped each night going out with Bob, and did our best to put on a good show. We'd walk out there and you hear these golf claps, you know, barely audible as they didn't know who we were, but we came out and played our stuff. By the end of the tour, the claps were getting louder and more frequent as they became familiar with us."

Nathan recalled: "His people tell you not to even touch him, but when he walked into our trailer, I hugged him before I could even think about it. After that he had to hug us all... His security guys were furious." Matthew cringed in embarrassment as he revealed, "At the end of the tour he invited us backstage to say bye and stuff. So here we were shaking hands and doing the hug thing and when it came to my turn to shake his hand and hug him I knocked his hat off! I mean here is a real fragile old man surrounded by all these security guards and I knock his hat off. I felt very awkward, so I just put it back on and said bye..."

Caleb added: "I was and am a huge Dylan fan. For me, it used to be like, 'How do you try to learn to do what he does? How do you try to beat that?' Then, the other night, it really hit me. He was up there and every line was insane. He's a fucking poet, whether or not he can still hit those notes or sing it the same. He knows the words he writes down should be heard. It's an honour to play with him. I got to meet him a few nights ago. I was walking up to my bus and he was walking in front of me. I didn't think nothing about it. He went to his bus. A few minutes later, I came off our bus and I was singing, 'Christmas time is coming, Christmas time is coming'. I looked up and he was standing there with his bodyguard, looking at me. 'Hey', he said, so I said 'Hey' back. He was just like, 'Good to see you' and held out his hand to shake mine. Softest hands on any person I've ever met!"

Then, of course, came the Pearl Jam support dates in Australia – a huge boost to the Kings' profile. The Followills took advantage of the extended soundcheck time they were given to come up with some new riffs. "That was a pretty cool way to get to work out new material, playing with those guys," Nathan remembered. "It was a fun tour for sure. It really just made it easier in the sense we had nothing to lose. If you get up there and the place is only halfway full, you can look at it as that the people who are there at least want to see you, but if you suck the people don't care, as they came to see Pearl Jam. If you can kick their ass it's great, since they've got two good bands for the price of one."

As Nathan explained: "A lot of our records are worked up during soundcheck, because you get so bored, you know. No one wants to get into soundcheck and play a song that you've played 30 times in the past 30 days and you're gonna have to play two hours from then. You've gotta keep things fresh and keep things changing. At soundcheck we just play ideas. You know, eight soundchecks have passed and you've got a song pretty much there."

Sometimes, Caleb revealed, great songs were created almost in spite of the band's lack of musical expertise in some areas. "Matthew and Jared don't have great timing," he said bluntly. "Me and Nathan do. Of course, Nathan's a drummer and when my dad was a preacher, I was the backup drummer, so I'm a drummer too. Nathan and me keep the beats and the rhythms. Jared solos on the bass and Matthew, he solos and makes sounds. Because of that, Nathan and me get to have a ball with them. We get to play around. They'll start playing something, and me and Nathan will flip the beat. Jared and Matthew will get confused and we're just like, 'Trust us'. That's how a lot of the songs come together. We're playing beats against them."

Australia was a home from home for the Followills. Nathan gushed, "Oh God Almighty, the women! Australia has the best-looking women per capita anywhere… [Sydney] is like the New York of this half of the world!" while also observing that the week-long Big Day Out festival, the continent's biggest rock event, had certain advantages over its one-day European equivalents. "It's good in the sense that if there's something you like, you have five more chances to see it," he said. "If there's a band that you like, there's a good chance you'll get to know them. When you play festivals like Reading, it's great: you see good bands, but you might have an hour backstage to hang with them and then they're off to another festival and you're off to another festival, and that's it. But this is great – half the time you make friends with bands that you would never in a million years guess that you would hang out with."

After the U2 tour the previous year and two tours in '06 with similarly huge acts in giant venues, the band were becoming enamoured with the idea of writing bigger songs. Although the third album had already been recorded by the time the Kings hit the road with Bob Dylan, plenty of anthemic elements had crept into the sessions – to be crystallised by the end of the year. "We definitely wanted to go big on this record with these songs," said Nathan. "The fact that we worked a lot of these songs up during soundcheck on the U2 tour, in big arenas, meant that from day one these songs were born with a really big sound. I'd definitely say U2 was a big influence on this record. Man, watching them every night and hearing how great it sounded in these huge, cavernous rooms was amazing to us. The fact you could make music that sounded great on a CD but also in a 30,000-seat arena definitely planted a seed that you could make big-sounding music."

Once the third album was recorded and safely in storage, the Kings were happy to leave it alone for the rest of 2005 and early 2006. As Nathan said, with obvious satisfaction: "It's great. It's kind of like sitting on a secret. Most people would go crazy having to sit on a record for three months, six months: we sat on it for a year and we didn't listen to it. We haven't listened to it at all because we don't wanna get tired of it. We don't wanna get sick of it, and by the time we play these songs live for people, we've already heard 'em 300 times and we're sick of 'em and ready to move on to the next record. We tried to distance ourselves enough to where it still is refreshing to get up there and play these new songs every night and it still is fun."

One caveat, though – the band did debut some of the new songs on the Bob Dylan and Pearl Jam tours, just to give the new music a test and to see how they went down with the crowds. Nathan recalled: "They're all over YouTube. The cat's out of the bag. That's done fucked up the whole world of playing new material live and having it not get out. We played four or five on the Dylan tour and on the Pearl Jam tour. Shit, if they like it, they're gonna buy it and if they didn't like it, they're not gonna buy it anyway, so who gives a shit?"

A new-found sense of perspective was settling into the band, it seemed – both in their music-making and their partying habits. "[Fame] sidetracked me," admitted Caleb. "I've got to be honest, I was out of hand for a few months: sometimes that was the drink, but also the things I read about myself on the internet. I could get upset about it, then go to do a show and be crap company. After a few days my brother Nathan gave me a dressing-down. He said, 'You can't let some idiot who writes terrible things about you get you down. Look around you and see what's happening – everybody loves this band'. The bigger the band gets, the more shit we get to deal with. We realise that."

"We've all calmed down," added Jared. "I would say that most of us drink as much as we used to, but we don't party as much. It's become more like hidden drinking." Nathan added: "I think we've learned to keep what we do a little more private. At first, it was all about the sex and drugs and rock'n'roll. It was great, it got us in the tabloids and got us noticed. We used to come to London and stay in little hotels. We didn't want a hotel with a good bar, because we wanted to go out and get trashed and be seen. But then we thought, 'Do we really want to be socialites?' It started fucking with our creativity. It got to the point where we had become a rock band that was known for everything but music, like actors or actresses that are known for being on the scene but you can't name one good movie they've been in. Now we'll stay in hotels that have a cool bar, have a few drinks then pop back to our rooms without making fools of ourselves."

Success was coming the Kings Of Leon's way, then – and in a huge way. This seemed to match the Followills' ambitions, fortunately: as Caleb put it, "I've always been scared of us getting real big, but now I'm getting a little scared that we're not gonna get any bigger. What I definitely don't want is for Kings Of Leon to be remembered for a genre of music, or for a look, or for a story. I want people to think of us as a big band that did something great and that influenced young bands to come. I want to challenge people to make better records; I don't want us – or even this generation – to be remembered for the pop music that's being made right now. It would be nice to sell lots of records, if only because that would allow us the freedom to do what we want, to continue changing when we want."

Jared summed up the band's position after two hit albums, saying: "There are no drugs these days, but I feel confident in saying that, between the four of us, we could fill 1,000 swimming pools with the alcohol that we've drunk over the last five years. And that is not an exaggeration."

Nathan, always the spokesperson and the band-member with the most accurate perception of the band's history, pondered: "It sucks that we never really got the chance, as a band, to go and have five horrible shows and get our legs. I mean, the first publication we were in was *Rolling Stone* and, y'know, you're kinda fucked when that happens, because every show we do someone important is there expecting some sort of great thing that they read in *Rolling Stone* or they read in *NME*. So it kinda sucks as a band to not be able to have horrible shows and fuck up. But on the other hand, it's great that we came out of the gates rockin'! And everybody's diggin' it. But, y'know, we take it all in stride and every good review is just as good as the worse review we just read, so we try not to get big heads."

The last couple of years had been exhausting for the band, despite the many high points – one of which included an after-show party on the U2 tour. "We got pretty hammered at a party; Bill Gates, Bono and Eddie Vedder were there," recalled Nathan. "We tried to get Bill Gates to streak but he wouldn't. The sad thing is he would have made $5 million while he was streaking…" The rest period had been most beneficial to the new, as-yet-untitled album, he added: "We've been touring [*Aha Shake Heartbreak*] forever, it feels like. Luckily for us we have fun playing the songs. We try and think of that when we're recording. We're gonna play these songs for the next year and a half, so we try to make them challenging enough to keep the interest. We actually start the third record as soon as we get home. This is the last tour for *Aha Shake!*"

Asked about the album, he enthused: "Ah man, the third album is gonna be great. We're excited! The songs are amazing and you can tell that we're rested. You can tell that we actually had a chance to take a breath and, you know, sit back and look at the kind of record we want to make and go for the sound we want to go for. This album is going to be a lot bigger sounding."

Caleb recalled: "Going out with U2 really opened our eyes. Hearing their songs – song after song after song after song – and seeing them play every night in these huge arenas, it was just amazing that every one of the songs sounds so good. We wanted to make a record where it would come across playing in arenas that big. That was one of our goals for this record, to make a big-sounding record that would sound good in a club in front of 200 people or in Madison Square Garden."

Nathan added: "U2 was a very big part of our headspace going into this [new] album. That tour is where we tapped into some of the layered sounds and effects. They opened our eyes to new guitar sounds and vocal effects. They were definitely very influential, not only musically but they kind of mentored us. Touring with them was great."

"We did have fun," Caleb concluded. "We're ambitious, we want to grow and we want people to notice. We don't want to be forever known as every band's favourite band, but nothing else."

If nothing else illustrates the point that the Kings Of Leon were at a tipping-point in their careers, his statement of, "Right now it feels almost like the beginning" surely does. Whatever lay around the corner, it was going to be big.

CHAPTER 6

2007

You might reasonably assume that the Kings Of Leon felt on top of the world in 2007. Now a respected live and studio band with two hit albums behind them, the Followills were becoming idols for a whole generation of music-loving kids with a taste for unconventional Americana.

However, there was a seam of insecurity in the Kings – most evident in their frontman. "I don't want people to ever think we're arrogant or we don't appreciate what we have," mused Caleb Followill in May that year. "There were a lot of years where I felt bad about playing music. I realise I'm in front of multitudes and I know we're sinners. I know we're far, far from anything that's right. But at the end of the day, I still want it to be a good message that we're putting forth."

With statements such as this, it's difficult to know whether Caleb, and perhaps the other Followills, find their religious convictions a blessing or a burden when let loose on the lecherous, drug-addled world they had inhabited for the past four years. Christian rock'n'roll has never enjoyed the best press, primarily because rocking out and proclaiming the gospel seem to be polar opposites for most people. The Kings Of Leon were managing to do both, but not – it seemed – without some internal conflict. Maybe Caleb found a solution by viewing his crowds as congregations: as he put it, "I like to do a little preaching... I like to dance and shake my ass and point my finger at people."

While the band deliberated about their place in the creator's grand scheme and album number three rested dormant in RCA's vaults, the faithful were beginning to get up something of a head of steam about the Kings' next move. The album would, it seemed, be huge: the question was only when it would finally appear. The Followills, who rarely stopped doing press this year, goaded the masses by dropping hints that the record sounded rather different to its predecessors. This tied in, it was apparent, with a sense of renewed confidence.

"I'm trying to get back to the way that I was when I first wanted to be a songwriter," Caleb said. "I want to be able to tell a good story. 'This is what I'm sayin'. Turn my vocal up.' I want people to hear me. I'm not scared any more... We took so many risks [this time] that we never would have taken in the beginning. We knew we were going for something anthemic and very fist-in-the-air."

The band were eager to give the new songs a proper airing as part of a headline set, Nathan added – even though the new material would be more challenging to play. "We're a live band, that's our bread and butter," he declared. "We like to get up there and put on a good show... I'm sure we'll be kicking ourselves in the ass for recording such hard album parts that we're going to have to play live every night."

This burst of creative energy manifested itself both on stage and in the rehearsal room, Caleb explained. "Lately, during soundcheck, it's hard to get us off the stage," said the frontman. "We're constantly trying to make each other smile, and we only make each other smile when we're doing something right."

This was coupled with a strong desire on the part of the band to update their image with the public. A wiser, more versatile group by this stage, the Followills knew that their look – basically a combination of downhome country boys and fashion clotheshorses – needed an upgrade if they were to retain credibility.

"We were really tired of what people thought Kings of Leon were about," said Caleb. "So when we got home, it all just poured out of us. We wanted to write a record that was very personal and very emotional. We've always had this thing with the press, with people wanting to get in too deep, and wanting to know about the things they shouldn't know about. So we said, 'Fuck it, if that's what you want, we're going to give it to you, as honestly as we can'…although it's probably not something my mom's gonna want to read, or my grandma's gonna want to hear me saying."

"We wanted to go for the sounds that we were hearing in our heads," Nathan added, "because your record represents you as a band. But when you're young, as we were when we made our first two albums, we didn't know that." In sessions leading up to the third Kings album, a new sound had evidently made itself heard – a different approach that added clarity to the band's lo-fi tone and announced a fresh, more easily digestible direction. "I think we touched on something the other day that no band has really touched on, which immediately gave me chill bumps," reflected Caleb. "I think I saw a vision of where Kings of Leon are going next. If we can do it, we're gonna skip ahead a few generations."

This would be most evident in the vocals, he added. "I never really expect people to understand what I'm saying. I know the way I phrase certain things, people aren't necessarily going to get it… on the last record, people would try to guess what we were saying and they'd make us sound like idiots. You're never gonna be confident about [your music]… you're always gonna expect to fall on your face, but you keep working through it. Eventually, you're either gonna know that you're bad, or the people around you are gonna convince you that you're good."

Longtime Kings fans might find it strange that after all this time, Caleb still lacked total conviction about the quality of his band's music, but it's not an unusual frame of mind for any singer who has experienced unusually quick success. The pressure on him to deliver remained constant, from a songwriting and performing point of view as well as from the press who wanted interesting, soundbite-heavy interviews from him. This wasn't helped by the sluggishness of the American public to accept the Kings Of Leon, which was beginning to mystify the Followills after two albums. Nathan shrugged: "With the sound we have, I guess one would expect us to be bigger in the States. We played London last night and fans over here just kind of think of us as their band, which is awesome. America's always been more of a gradual grassroots thing for us, but fans there keep getting better. And we're happy with the pace of our band in the US."

The new album might help the Kings' Stateside following expand, the drummer noted. In the run-up to its release, he and his bandmates dropped several hints indicating that it featured a new, more expansive sound that would transcend anything they had done before. For example, Nathan observed, "This was the first album where all four band members contributed equally and had a say-so in every song," and Caleb clarified: "Because we were trying to make a different-sounding record, we had to sit back and listen to each other a little more."

It was also revealed that the new album – set for release in April – began with an unusually epic composition. "We figured if you can stand the seven-minute opening song then you'll be well-prepared to hear the rest of the record," remarked Nathan. "It's definitely not a barn-burner. We decided against starting the record off with one of our 'boogie and sweat' songs…"

The new era in the Followills' career was ushered in by a far-ranging tour schedule. Consider the following itinerary – and how meticulously it was planned to take the band into the deep, B-league markets. The year kicked off in February with a short trip through Britain's provincial and metropolitan cowsheds, starting in Lincoln and ploughing through London (where shows at the legendary 100 Club were packed out), Swindon, Blackpool, London again and Birmingham. The Californian Coachella desert then beckoned for a set alongside the Red Hot Chili Peppers, Arcade Fire, Arctic Monkeys, Amy Winehouse, Interpol, Rage Against The Machine, Lily Allen and many others. In June the Kings were booked to play club shows in Boston, Philadelphia and San Diego before heading north-east to Toronto. Other midwest shows took place before and after a third outing at Bonnaroo, where an eclectic bill featured acts as diverse as The Police, Tool, Franz Ferdinand and White Stripes. The European festival circuit was next, before dates in Germany, the UK and US – including an appearance at Minneapolis' famous First Avenue club, made famous by Prince's 1984 movie, *Purple Rain*. A Lollapalooza outing and other festival slots preceded a US tour in September and October, before yet more British and Irish shows until the end of the year.

On April 2, 2007, the album finally appeared, named *Because Of The Times* after the church festival the Followills attended as youths – but the title also had another, although not necessarily deeper, meaning. "It's kind of an excuse," chuckled Caleb. "No matter the success, no matter the failure, whatever. Because of the times. It was actually a church conference that we used to go to every year as kids… But [the title is] an excuse more than anything. Why did it work? Why didn't it work? Why did you change your look? Because of the times."

The look to which Caleb referred was his newly short haircut, a fashionable combover job that he retains to this day, which was sleeker and less contrived than the asymmetrical long locks he'd sported since the band's arrival in the UK. "We've seen a lot of the world now and that's opened our eyes," he explained. "When I got my hair cut it was a shock for the band, but then suddenly I was getting my picture in magazines that had never written a word about us. You need to be open to these things; I don't want to be 'the boy from the hicks' all my life."

Because Of The Times begins with that seven-minute song: it's called 'Knocked Up' and deals with the unexpected subject of fatherhood. "I don't care what nobody says / We're gonna have a baby," intones Caleb in a clearer, less obscure vocal style than in the Kings' previous songs. A heavily delayed guitar line from Matthew encouraged the first of literally hundreds of U2 comparisons in terms of pure sound, although the subject matter itself was generally not thought to be derivative. "We definitely wanted to make a record that was a step above what we've previously made," said the singer. "Shit, starting the record off with a seven-and-a-half-minute song about getting a girl pregnant… Getting a girl pregnant, that's very Kings of Leon, but [a] seven-and-a-half-minute song, that's not Kings of Leon at all."

An atmospheric, mesmerising song of great depth, 'Knocked Up' came – like all the Kings' better-known songs – apparently out of nowhere. "That song started with the melody and it started chugging along," remembered Caleb, "then the first thing that came into my head was, 'I don't care what nobody says, we're going to have a baby'. Everyone just looked at me in the rehearsal room and I threw my hands in the air and said, 'I don't know what to say – it just came out'. I think the reason I talk about having a baby is because of my fear of an actual relationship.

I can actually see myself having a kid before I can see myself getting married, and I know that goes against everything we were raised to believe, but the whole marriage thing... I don't know if it really works these days, which is unfortunate. It just seems divorce is inevitable. So for me talking about having a baby in that song, it's like the glue that might keep things together, or at least an excuse to make it last a little longer." Nathan rapidly defused any rumours that the song might have been based on reality when he joked: "I'm not an uncle. At least not that I know of! The lyrics are definitely fictional. That's often the way Caleb writes. He's always been a storyteller and 'Knocked Up' is one story he felt he needed to tell."

'Charmer' follows – and immediately demonstrates that even if the Kings were looking for a more mainstream sound, they weren't ready to introduce it so early in the album. "It was an experimental song that ended up being a lot cooler than we thought it would," said Nathan. "I played the drumbeat backwards just to fuck with the guys, and they hated it. They said that there was no way we'd ever be able to work out how to play it live, but after playing it 10 times we kinda figured it out."

"On our first album, I just played straight 4/4 because I was scared to death and had never made a record," he added. "On the second record, I stepped out and expanded a little. But on this one, we'd played the songs a lot at soundcheck before we recorded them, so it was probably a natural progression, and also me wanting to show that I can play a little more than just a two-and-a-half-minute barn-burner." Jared noted, more prosaically: "Caleb just squirrelled out [the lyric] one night and we're like, 'Shit, that was cool'. So, he did it again and did it every time, and we turned the drumbeat around backwards, and the next thing you know, we have a very good tribute to The Pixies."

Nathan's offbeat pattern isn't the only strange thing about the song. Caleb's line, "She's such a charmer, she's always looking at me" comes in halfway through each bar, and there's little melodic harmony anywhere. Add to this a weird yowl that the singer executes every few words and it's an odd beast indeed. "He only just learned how to do [the scream]," Nathan chuckled. "He got his prostate checked three weeks ago... Nah, I'm joking. He's always had it in him, he's always had a hoarse, shrilly voice... I don't know how he does it. For him it's pretty easy."

Because Of The Times' release was preceded by a single, 'On Call', which follows 'Charmer', even though it too is far from immediately accessible. It does have a memorable hook – the two-note melody at the end of each line. Caleb explained its confessional nature, saying: "I think there's always two sides to your personality, be it when you're drunk or sober, or at home or away, or whatever. Our song 'On Call' is about the grounded part of you. It says, 'And when I fall to pieces, Lord you know I'll be there waiting'. You could take that in a biblical sense. The Bible says that David, or Daniel, or one of those guys, was a man after God's own heart. But he was quite a messed-up person. So if he's the man after God's own heart, well, maybe when you're at your roughest moment, that's when He's watching over you and smiling."

'McFearless', named by Jared as he wrote the distorted bass-line that opens and anchors the song, is the most easily digestible song so far on the album, opening out into an anthemic, stadium-sized chorus. 'Black Thumbnail' is another droned song, beckoning the listener in without any apparent effort, but the album receives a definite boost when 'My Party' begins. It's another bass-heavy song and a rock number of considerable power, based – Caleb revealed – on his fondness for the actress Rachel Bilson.

Angelo Petraglia and Ethan Johns co-produced the album, and between them pulled out a handful of studio tricks that enhanced the songs no end. One of them is the distortion placed on Caleb's vocal in 'My Party', which lends his voice a slightly unhinged tone – a little like Tom Waits at his most confrontational. Another is the layering of the guitar effects in 'True Love Way', another song with a deliberately bigger, fists-in-the-air sound and structure for the large venues that the Kings were about to play over the rest of 2007. 'Ragoo' is next, a slightly unusual song with a prominent, stop-start bass-line that comes and goes without leaving much impact: however, when Caleb intones, "All of London sing / 'Cause England swings" in 'Fans', a homage to the UK, the message seems both heartfelt and enduring. After all, without the Brits the band would have suffered a much longer and more uncertain rise to prominence, if at all.

'The Runner' is a much more thoughtful song, in which Caleb addresses his Christian faith. While a certain number of Kings Of Leon fans appreciated its sentiments, most merely enjoyed it for its haunting melody. Caleb once observed that this devout song struck a chord even among people with no religious beliefs, saying: "I have atheist friends who always want me to play 'The Runner' to them. They're like, 'Play me the Jesus song!' And they don't believe in Jesus, they just believe in what I'm saying, that longing for something that you can hold on to... I remember when I used to get all hopped up on cocaine. Whatever hotel room I was in at the time would turn into a church. There were all these people around me having fun on cocaine, and me and my cousin Nacho would bring the whole vibe down by preaching to people. We'd be shouting at them, 'You don't believe there's a life after this?' and our eyes would be bulging out of our heads because of all the coke."

Played in 3/4 time, the song has a dusty, church feel that suits the lyrics perfectly, but despite the religious overtones, Caleb explained that the song was inspired by his own misbehaviour: "I had done something really stupid on tour a while back – been drunk and an asshole, and pissed off the whole band, like I do sometimes. Our equipment was all set up for our soundcheck and it was like an hour until we were supposed to do it. I went up there with a guitar and I started playing this riff, and all the security workers that were in there turned around and looked at me. I started singing, 'Our time as we go, we know our time will change. I talked to Jesus, Jesus says I'm OK'. As soon as I sang that, I got chill bumps and everyone in the band gave me the look. It was me forgiving myself, because I knew it'd be a couple of days 'til they all talked to me."

He continued, "It was one of the first songs I've written where I actually talk about Jesus, but it's not religious. The song is about being centred. It's about being a son of a bitch and really having issues being the centre of attention. That's why I think that song's so special. It's like a song for everyman. We have a lot of people that work with us that are Jewish. They don't believe the way we believe in Jesus, but they walk around and the only thing they sing is 'I talked to Jesus'. It's one of those real ballsy lines to say in a rock'n'roll band."

'Trunk' is a beautiful song, all echoed vocals and deep spaces behind a hypnotic bass-line and a gentle drum pattern, while 'Camaro' amps up the riffs and tempo for a suitably raw-edged paean on the subject of

Seventies America's blue-collar vehicle of choice. The Americana theme continues until *Because Of The Times'* final song, 'Arizona'. Asked why he'd written a song devoted to his home country's most arid state, Caleb replied with the perfect blend of rock'n'roll and romance. "I hold that place close to my heart. I love the desert and always have," he explained. "But the story behind that song is kind of bad. I can't really get into it. It's about when Nathan and I went to Arizona, and... well, we had quite a few different substances in us, and we decided to go to this brothel. I guess I am telling you now, aren't I? This really is a heartbreaker. We walked in and I looked around, and there was this one girl who was so beautiful that all I could think was, 'What happened in her life that could bring her here?' as opposed to me thinking, 'Yeah! I'll take that one!'... I took an ugly one. I knew why she was there." The song builds to a crescendo and fades away in a blur of guitar echoes, part Sergio Leone, part Steve Reich.

As many had hoped, *Because Of The Times* debuted at the top of the British charts, their first number one in this country, but the band were – understandably – focusing more of their attention on the US, where the album entered the chart at number 25. "These songs are so much bigger, this band is so much better," crowed Caleb when the new album began to make an impact. "There was a growth that people thought they heard on *Aha Shake Heartbreak* from *Youth And Young Manhood*, but there's no comparison this time out. I think it's pretty evident when people hear it."

"We wanted to make a record that was really close to home, like really American," he added. "Every vehicle I mention on the record is American-made. It wasn't something that was conscious. It just came out that way. We made the record at home in Nashville. We'd drive from our own house to the studio, actually slept in our own beds. I just wanted to go back to some good old storytelling. The way we tell stories now is a little more hidden than maybe the first record, but we wanted it to be natural and very anthemic."

Early reviews of the album focused on its new, expansive approach. Caleb's vocals were clearer and wider; many of the guitar figures were heavily delayed for a ringing, echoed sound that was wide enough to fill arenas; and the production focused on big drums, uplifting sheets of sound and dynamic arrangements for maximum drama. Nathan reacted to these observations with the words: "A lot of people now want to know why our sound has changed. They want to know if the shift that was… *Because Of The Times* was intentional. The answer is no. We were just growing musically. This is the first and only band any of us have ever been in. What you are hearing is us getting more comfortable with ourselves and our instruments."

As for the bigger feel of the songs, a lot of this came with the vocal melodies and Caleb's willingness to enunciate the lyrics with greater clarity, in itself a result of greater confidence in his abiliities. "I started writing some of these melodies and I thought they were beautiful," he said. "When we got in [the studio] and everyone came together and started playing, I didn't want to be the missing or the weak link. I felt like these songs were good songs and I wanted them to be heard the way they should be."

He added: "Because I felt the songs were so strong, I wanted to take the opportunity to actually sing them and showcase my voice in a way that I never have before… I always used to feel intimidated and tried to hide what I was saying in case people didn't like my opinions."

"We're the kind of band that we try to change from album to album," Nathan said. "We try to do things that we haven't done before. So after three albums, you look back and there were things that you'd done that you just barely kind of dipped your toe into the water, as opposed to really just diving in. And that's something we tried to do with this album and something that we tried to do with every album."

One notable quality of *Because Of The Times*, which reveals much about the Followills' modus operandi, is the songs' lack of overproduction. The band wanted to be able to play any song they chose from the album without sacrificing layers of sound to do so. As Caleb insisted, "We refuse to go to most concerts, because we know what we're gonna walk into. We'll be completely disappointed and, as opposed to leaving there saying, 'I like the record better', I'll leave there saying, 'I don't even like the record now'. It's like it's all fake to me." In typical fashion, Nathan likened it to a female celeb, saying: "It's like meeting someone that you admire and when you see how much of an asshole they really are in person, you're like, 'Wow, you totally ruined it. I wish I never even met you. I always had this fantasy in my mind that you were this cool, gorgeous supermodel and you're a fucking crazy bitch'."

The new sound allowed for greater expression, of course. Previous Kings songs had been emotional, but never quite as atmospheric as anything on *Because Of The Times*. Nathan described some of the recent songs as possessing "a real looming feeling of sadness and longing" and added: "The first two records are pretty live, pretty gritty, pretty dirty. We obviously don't want to make the same record over and over. We try to challenge ourselves enough to where it's different, but not so much so [that] people won't recognise it... or say that we're trying to make that huge record that everybody wants [us] to make, and it's not the Kings Of Leon. That's the last thing we want. We've got quite a few songs on the new record that you can hear and know immediately that's us. But then there are songs that might take three or four listens, and then you get it."

Although the rest of the Followills' career (or at least, the part of it covered in this book) would be dogged by criticisms about their supposedly sudden switch to a new, more mainstream sound, the truth is that the band were basically feeling their way forward by instinct. There was, they insisted, no megabucks-centric gameplan. As Caleb shrugged: "When we made our first record, we didn't know what our second record was gonna be. When we made our second record, we didn't know what our third record was gonna be. I still don't know what the fuck our next record's gonna be."

Now their task was to convince gig audiences of the quality of the new songs – a job they were keenly anticipating, given the convincing nature of the new material. Far from delivering a set of homespun country tunes with Caleb hiding behind the mike stand, the Kings could use the new songs to grab audiences by the throat, using techniques that would expand the music to fill the largest venues.

"Oh, Lord. We're excited," said Nathan as the tour dates approached. "We started [this album] last April. It came out a year and one day after we started it. So we've been sitting on it for a while – it's kind of like sitting on a big old bag of popcorn that sits on the bus, and you're just holding your breath. And it's out there now, and it's being well received, from what we're hearing. So man, that's great, we're so thrilled that people are enjoying the fruits of our labour."

Explaining why *Because Of The Times* had waited a year to be released, Nathan explained; "It's all about the quarters with our label. First quarter, second quarter, third quarter, fourth quarter and the last thing we wanted to do was be competing with Beyoncé and Justin Timberlake. We're like, 'Fuck it – we'll compete with Yanni and Kenny G when they come out in the second quarter, and we'll kick their ass!'"

Despite the big, big sounds of *Because Of The Times*, there were deep emotional reserves in the songs – and not necessarily the jubilation and exuberance that you'd expect. "We love the road," explained Caleb when asked about the forthcoming tour, but he added: "We go out on tour, get sick of the road and hate the road, so we go back home. Then we make a record about missing the road. The vibe of this record is almost melancholy. We came home from this great tour of England and went straight into the studio. You love being at home, but you're also wondering what's going on out there while you're there. There are songs that are kind of melancholy, but a good melancholy. It's kinda like when I listen to My Morning Jacket's *At Dawn*. That record sounds so lonesome, but they were at home making that record. I guess at home people feel more comfortable to cry."

The alternative rock band My Morning Jacket was an appropriate reference for the Kings: the Kentucky quintet's music has attracted a large following for its quirky, observational nature, a trait in which the Followills themselves had specialised. Nathan added: "*At Dawn* didn't leave our CD player for probably five months. It was just one of those records where every song reminds you of five different things. You experienced every single emotion on pretty much every one of those songs. You felt happy, sad, lonely, loved, whatever. It's so amazing. It's a feel-good record, but there are songs that'll rip your heart out. But you don't mind that your heart's being ripped out because it feels so good, so natural. It pretty much hit on all cylinders on that record, and that was very influential in our headspace for our new album."

Asked how the songs on *Because…* had come together, Caleb explained: "It goes in different ways. Every now and then I'll sit down with a guitar and be like, 'I got a song, guys. Here it is'. For the most part, it starts with one person at a soundcheck playing a riff or a drumbeat or a bass-line. As soon as that happens, we all kind of smile and play along with it and realise it's getting somewhere. After that, we'll chug it out for 10 soundchecks in a row. I'll be doing dummy lyrics and making people laugh. Once I realise it's getting close, I'll sit down and write the real lyrics and try to tie it all together. Then we'll go back and try to write a bridge and shit like that. Hell, half the time I don't even tell them the lyrics. I just go in there and record them. They ask me what I said, and I'm like, 'You can't hear what I'm saying? Well, that's good 'cause I'm talking about you." Nathan observed: "You can always tell when it's gonna be a good [song] because we'll all walk around humming the same melody for two or three days straight... Finding inspiration isn't hard," he added. "Life itself is always tricky, no matter who you are, yeah? So, as long as you don't bore yourself with tales of your life, and draggin' all the stuff that's happening to people and the world around you, then there's always going to be ample stimulation for writing... I don't know why we seem so prolific, but I guess we just work together so well. We just love recording, and we love doing what we do."

Not for the last time, the frontman revealed that the songs sometimes took form without him fully realising what was happening – as if sent by a higher power. "I don't know if it's the way that we work," he pondered, "if it's that we work quickly or that sometimes I'm a little inebriated when we're working, but on several occasions it's been two and three years down the road and I've been onstage and I sang something – and it was the first time that I actually realised what I was saying. I got chill bumps. Like, 'Wow'. It's almost prophetic in a way. It's like you don't realise what's going on until later on, and it's like, 'Oh, I get it now'."

Amazingly, the band found some time for self-analysis among the chaos. Caleb reflected on the special bond that he and his elder brother shared, explaining: "Me and Nathan have the most fun together. We watch each other. If one of us wants to get fucked up before a show, we both get fucked up. There is no him or me with us. If he knows I'm doing something without him, he gets pissed, and likewise with me."

The drummer was emerging as the most serene Followill, neither plagued by Caleb's creative demons nor too young to comprehend the speed of the band's progress, like Jared and Matthew. "I'm loving life at the moment," he smiled in a short break between dates. "Here I am, sitting at home for the first time in ages having a bit of a, I guess, breather. It's nice just to be doing nothing for once, you know? I mean, for the last week or so, all I've been doing is lying on my couch doing absolutely... fucking... nothing." Asked how he regarded the band's surreal progress towards stardom, he laughed: "I guess it has been pretty amazing. I suppose that the way this band has grown up in the spotlight has been pretty strange. There's not too many bands who kick off when they're as young as we were, and get to the point of releasing a third record. Along the way we've had a blast. It's the only way to do it... I never thought I'd get to do some of the things we've been able to enjoy, but this band has opened doors most people wouldn't even dream of being able to open. I thank my lucky stars every day that we're able to do what we do, and that people dig it. I mean, shit – it's the rock'n'roll dream, isn't it?"

On the subject of the big new sound of the band, he attributed it squarely to the huge bands the Kings had supported in 2005 and '06. "Supporting bands like that," he recalled, "we'd be soundchecking to a massive open space, and we had to basically step up. That definitely seeped into the writing period again, and we'd find ourselves writing these songs that felt huge and ponderous to play, and we loved doing it. I mean, the way we recorded this was pretty relaxed, and playing together felt really good, having Ethan [Johns] there, it felt totally natural to take the band down that path. It's darker, it's bigger, and yeah, it's stranger."

Not only were the Kings' elders and betters inspiring them to greater heights, he intimated, but the Followills' own maturing process was a major part of it too. "We changed a lot between the first and second records, and then again between *Aha Shake Heartbreak* and this record. We've grown up a bit, I guess, and musically, we totally wanted to push ourselves, and try shit we hadn't really tackled yet. We did that, and *Because Of The Times* is just that, I reckon. It's completely about the times we had making it, what we were going through... I mean, what's the point of all this, of being in a band, of travelling the world, if you can't have a few drinks with your best friends and really enjoy it. How does a King Of Leon woo a lady? Well, you gotta be smooth, but entirely respectful. It's all about the charm."

This new-found confidence had paid dividends in the band's willingness to aim high with their songwriting. "We took the limitations off of ourselves," said Caleb. "We went into the studio with an open mind, thinking, 'Let's do whatever it takes to get these songs to the next level'. Because we really have a lot of music inside of us and a lot of different places we can go." Nathan added: "We weren't scared to try anything. I think that's the difference between this album and the last. We weren't timid at all. Every song showed us something we had inside of ourselves that we didn't know existed, which enabled us to be even bolder on the next song."

2007 was a pivotal year for Nathan in personal as well as professional terms. He had met a songwriter, Jessie Baylin, at the Bonnaroo festival two years previously, and struck up a relationship with her. As she recalled in an interview, "It's really romantic for us coming back to Bonnaroo, because we met here two years ago in front of the ice-cream man's truck." In July he proposed to Baylin at her parents' New York restaurant, and she accepted – to Caleb's initial horror. As the singer told James McNair at *The Independent*, "I bought them a bottle of Cristal [champagne], then had a long hot bath and just wept."

"It's always hard when big brother starts devoting time to a girl that would normally be devoted to little brother," explained Nathan sympathetically, while Caleb went on: "If he doesn't get a pre-nuptial agreement, he's an idiot. Me and him have a lot invested in each other. We started this band. We've bought land and houses together. We've been best friends since we were little biddy boys. I don't want him to make mistakes… we have friends in bands who are married, and their songs start being watered down because they're all about the same girl. I mean, Nathan's not writing the lyrics, but still... I'll have girls come to the show who are beautiful and are in love with me, but as soon as I let them in, they start to try to change me. They don't like me going to this party, or being seen taking pictures with that girl. But that's what I do. This is my life."

Despite his new-found monogamy, Nathan wasn't averse to dropping the occasional frat-boy quip such as, "Oh man, you can not believe how cool we think [New Year's Eve in Australia] is. We all love Australia, and yeah, that's why we keep coming back. I mean, the weather, the food, the people – and yes, the ladies – it's all perfect, isn't it? Spending New Year's down there is going to be huge; it's going to be one massive party, trust me." Nevertheless, he was entirely serious about his relationship with Baylin, even betting Caleb the frankly unnerving sum of $100,000 that he would never have sex with another woman.

For her part, Baylin was smitten with Nathan, writing a song about him called 'Tennessee Gem' and even hinting that the pair might one day make an album together. "We maybe want to make an old country music record, but really lo-fi. He's an incredible singer. We might just make it for ourselves more than anything. It would just be fun to do." Truly, the times were a-changing in the Followills' world, with a new sound, a new confident attitude and now an outside allegiance.

What next? Accusations of selling out?

CHAPTER 7

2008

The end of 2007 and the beginning of 2008 was the most crucial period in the Kings Of Leon's career to date. A burst of unexpected creativity, plus the chance to headline one of the world's biggest rock festivals, led to a new album, shortly after the last one – even if the new songs were defined by a near career-ending injury.

Although Nathan Followill and Jessie Baylin were now living together, the Followills often convened at their rehearsal room for practice and also for partying. One of these sessions ended badly when Caleb and Nathan, the closest and also the most volatile band members, angered each other to the point of a fist-fight.

It turned out that Caleb had been prone to injury for many years. As Nathan explained, "Caleb's always been double-jointed, and it got to the point where his shoulder kept popping out all the time because the tendons were worn down. He went a whole year and a half where his shoulder would pop out five or six times a day. He couldn't swim, he couldn't ride a rollercoaster – all the things we liked doing."

"My arm would come out of its socket," remembered Caleb. "It got to where it was just popping out. I'd wake up at three in the morning, drunk in a hotel room and my shoulder would be out and my security guard would have to pop it back in."

This didn't seem to stop Nathan from fighting with his brother from time to time, though. "We were really drunk," recalled Caleb regretfully, "and one of us said something really deep and hurtful, and that was it. Our assistant shuffled people out the door when he knew it was about to go down, and once the house cleared, it was like they let two dogs off their chains – we went crazy. Just a good old Wednesday night in Nashville…"

Nathan added: "I don't think we even knew the next day what the fight was about. It was a drunk fight. They normally happen when we get the grill at one of our houses and top it off with a little too much sauce – then we'll end up grappling."

As the two Followills lurched around the room, Caleb slammed his shoulder into the doorframe. Feeling his arm pop out of its socket, he shouted at Nathan to back away, before pushing his shoulder back into position. History does not record what happened next, but it's a safe bet that the night ended then and there.

As it happened, Caleb had been planning to undergo an operation to secure his shoulder in its socket for some time. "I had put the surgery off for a whole tour," he explained. "Every three days my shoulder would come out of its socket and have to be popped back in." Now he had no choice, and the operation was successfully carried out.

As he was recovering from the surgery, with his arm in a cast, a call came from the Kings' management that the organisers of the Glastonbury festival had offered the band the headline slot for 2008 – a hugely prestigious offer for any band. After accepting the festival's offer, the band began to consider their set list. *Because Of The Times* had been recorded in 2006 and released in '07, and therefore couldn't be considered new: by the following year, its songs might be showing their age a little. "I was going to get surgery on my shoulder and then go to the beach for six months," Caleb sighed. "We were going to take a load of time off, but then we got the call about [Glastonbury] and we were like, 'Fuck, we should probably be putting out another record'."

The decision was quickly made to write new songs. "I went for surgery and the doctor said he didn't want me playing guitar for nine months," laughed Caleb. "Three days later, I took off my cast and we started writing…"

Of course, the singer couldn't move – much less play guitar and sing – so soon after the operation, and was prescribed large doses of painkillers. "The amount they were wanting me to take? They would kill a man," he marvelled later. "But they definitely made me want to go different places, because I felt so pretty. So I wanted to sing pretty, I guess."

Caleb understood that the Glastonbury headlining slot might be perceived as controversial, saying: "We know there are people saying Kings Of Leon don't deserve to headline Glastonbury. But we've put in our time and we've definitely paid our dues over there [in the UK]... Arctic Monkeys have headlined it, and the Killers. I mean, we've put in a lot more time than those bands. When we leave there, people will be saying, 'Yeah, they kicked it'. We didn't ask for it, we didn't even expect it. As a matter of fact, we'd just played the last concert of our tour in New Zealand. We were going to take six months off, and that day we got a call about Glastonbury. We were like, 'Fuck, we've gotta do this'."

Asked if he felt under pressure with the forthcoming Glastonbury date and a new album to deliver, Nathan said with typical laid-back confidence: "There's no pressure, really, when it's your fourth record. They say you have your whole life to write your first record, six months to write your second, then the third is make or break! So, by the time you've done four you can tour as much as you want to, even if you don't want to make another record... plus, we didn't want to get too overweight and bald-headed before we had the chance to play the Pyramid Stage."

Caleb was a little more circumspect, saying: "We always put pressure on ourselves, but I think we knew what we were going to do on this album and we didn't really care what people thought. We wanted to have a couple of big songs – well, one to open Glastonbury with – but then the rest of the songs fell into place."

Most of the above took place by the end of 2007. With the new album release on BMG's autumn schedule, 2008 began to take shape for the Kings. In January they played shows in Australasia before heading back across the Pacific for US dates and the return to the studio. In June there was the small matter of the Glastonbury festival alongside Jay-Z and The Verve, before the usual round of European summer festivals and American and British dates taking them all the way to the end of 2008.

By the start of the new year, Caleb had a set of songs ready to go. He insisted that he didn't remember writing some of them, a side effect of the pain medication having wiped out parts of his memory. "My lyrics would come at home, high on my pain meds," he recalled. "I'd wake up the next day and see my songbook open, not even remember writing and look at it and be like, 'Whoa, this is really good'…"

Nathan added: "Caleb would call me, saying, 'Dude, you gotta come over and check out this song I wrote'. I would go over, listen, and say, 'OK, cool, when did you write that? It's amazing'. He's like, 'I have no idea. I just woke up and my songbook was open. I guess I wrote it last night'. They'd put him on Vicodin and he was like a vegetable."

Caleb went on: "They were pretty serious meds. The prescription said I should take a lot more than I was taking, but I just couldn't do it. It was too much. But whenever I was taking them, I felt good. As soon as I started to come down, I was supposed to take another. After a while, I felt trapped. There was nothing to do and everything was kind of boring, so I'd just write songs and, in the process, I really expanded my mind."

It's interesting to note for the record that this marked the first instance of publicly aired dissension within the band. In response to Caleb's account of his medicine-addled songwriting approach, his cousin Matthew – who rarely said much in interviews – retorted: "I don't know how much of all that is necessarily true, since I think [Caleb] likes to make things seem awesome. We'd just come up and he'd be like, 'I wrote these lyrics down last night and I don't even remember them. Thank God I wrote them down'. We'd just say, 'Oh cool man', but supposedly that's what happened. Everybody gets inspired by different things, and I guess while he was hopped up on goofballs he wrote some cool songs."

"It's always this huge deal with Nathan and Caleb," he continued. "I won't say they are liars, but they are extreme exaggerators and it kind of gets to the point where you can't believe anything they say. I think it's because we know them, and we're brothers and cousins, and they just get so excited."

Despite this minor difference in perspective, the recording sessions for the fourth Kings Of Leon album went smoothly. Once again the band had decided to record 'at home', which meant Blackbird Studios in Nashville. This time, one major development was that the Followills had decided to bid an amicable farewell to their longtime producer Ethan Johns and strike out on their own, using the engineering and production skills of Jacquire King and Angelo Petraglia. The former spoke to me about the experience for this book, and remembered that most of the songs were in reasonably complete shape when the Followills arrived at Blackbird.

"The band mostly write on tour, at soundcheck," King says. "That's where they come up with bits and pieces of the music. They bring those small things to the group and then they develop lyrics and melodies. When they came into pre-production, and they had a few songs that were complete, and much of it was in the 75 to 80 per cent range. Their front-of-house guy records all of the rehearsals and soundchecks and shows. It's a very good way of working because they're together in that atmosphere. It's an easy thing to do, and they feel inspired to play and mess around."

Of the band's decision to work without Johns, Nathan explained: "We knew this record was definitely gonna be our bold attempt at trying to make a record that wasn't necessarily obviously Kings of Leon. And with the first two records with Ethan, as soon as you heard the first note of any song, you could tell it was definitely a Kings of Leon song, just based on the sound that Ethan got. So, going into this record, we knew that we wanted to step away from that sound. We just realised that not very many bands ever get the chance to make the fourth record, so we might as well have fun with this one. And man, we had a blast making the record – got all the sounds we wanted, and the songs were recorded exactly the way we wanted them. So we really feel confident about this record, because it's the first one we had our hands in [from] beginning to end."

He went on: "Each record you want to make not only better than the last, but different enough to where it doesn't feel like people are buying the same record over again. We could have easily picked one great thing about those first three records and made four songs with each of those in mind, and basically released a record that we knew would please any fan of Kings Of Leon. But *Because Of The Times* pushed us in the direction we were headed as a band."

Nathan rhapsodised about Blackbird Studios, saying: "The studio we made this record in is the most amazing studio in America, maybe the world. They've got this lighting system and you can set the mood, make the room any colour you want it. On [the song] 'Cold Desert' we made it dark and blue, and tried to set the tone of what it would be like to be in the desert when it's just going pitch black. We threw all the conventional ways we used to do things out the window and started from scratch: 'OK, we're gonna make the record we want to make, not the record anyone else wants us to make. We're not going to make… a greatest hits compilation and call it our fourth record. We're going to make the record we feel needs to be made'."

The results spoke for themselves, Caleb said: "We had to depend on each other a lot more this time, because we were taking a big risk by not having the trusted producer team. We had to be our own support group. We'd hang out in bars pretty much every night, have cook-offs once a week… it was a totally different vibe from arguing about girls all the time. There was no, 'I saw her first', 'Well, I shagged her first', on this record."

Once again, Petraglia and King had earned the band's gratitude. As Nathan put it: "Man, they're great. They're a great duo. They work really well with us, just in the sense that Ethan is so good with all the technical stuff, and he just knows his shit… once he gets the idea down, and [he knows] the kind of record you're wanting to make, and the kind of sounds you're wanting to get, it's his mission to get exactly what you're hearing in your head down on tape."

It was important for the Followills that they were allowed to pursue their instincts on their fourth, and inevitably most mature, album. After all, by this stage in their careers they knew more or less how a studio album is assembled, and were able to experiment more. "We stepped out a little bit on our own," commented Caleb. "We were having fun – we had more fun making this record than any of the other ones, because we didn't really hold ourselves back. As soon as we got there we were mixing drinks, having fun, playing wall-ball, just because we knew the material was there."

Referring to Petraglia and King as "producers willing to set their egos aside", Nathan said: "They let us go in and fuck around with sounds and didn't think it was a waste of time. The record is exactly what we wanted to do," while Caleb concluded, "We're really proud of ourselves for getting in there, rolling our sleeves up and doing things differently.

It's the first Kings Of Leon record we've really put our stamp on. It's the way we've always heard our music. We didn't let our record label or even our manager hear it till it was done."

In late May 2008, the recording and mixing sessions were completed and the Kings were free to rehearse their Glastonbury set. It's a measure of their confidence that they chose to open with 'Crawl', a brand new song that no-one in the 120,000-strong crowd could possibly have heard before.

A couple of days before the show, the band's record company made the official announcement that the Kings Of Leon's fourth album would be released in September and that its title would be *Only By The Night*. The Followills were immediately asked to describe it: Nathan told one interviewer that it represented the pinnacle of their evolution to date. "When we first started out, we were so young," he admitted, "and the first two records were pretty much us going in there and doing the best that we could do, as far as the writing and the production and all that. And this record was a result of just being a band for five years, and growing from day one. It's the first band any of us have ever been in, so we've had the luxury of growing from day one."

Come the day of Glastonbury, one member of the Kings was almost overcome with stage fright. "It was the biggest honour because it [Glastonbury] was the first festival we ever played," said Caleb. "Going back to headline was overwhelming… That day, I couldn't look anyone in the eye, I was so nervous, but when I walked onstage there was a peace that washed over me… As soon as we started the set, it was like, 'Wait a second, this may be Glastonbury, the biggest festival in the world, but right now this is a Kings Of Leon concert with a huge drunk audience'."

"I was throwing up all day," he added. "When I walked onstage, everything went quiet. I knew people were cheering and I could see their hands flailing, but everything was quiet, like in that Kevin Costner movie [*For Love Of The Game*] where he walks out to the pitcher's mound… It was amazing. Halfway through the first song, it was my show. The one thing I can remember is going backstage and taking a drink from a Corona. I've never had a sip that tasted so delicious."

The band were on peak form, probably because they had given themselves an early night the previous evening – despite it being Nathan's

29th birthday. "We flew our mom over because it was my birthday the night before, which sucked," he said, "because I couldn't go crazy [as we had] the show the next day. But if ever there was a moment to die after a show, that would be the one. Look at the bands who have headlined it in the past, and there we were – three brothers and their cousin from Tennessee."

Jared added: "When I walked onstage I felt a rush of emotions. I almost felt like I was gonna cry. It wasn't even because I was so happy or nervous [that] I wanted to cry. It was just that all those emotions came at once… it felt great. Well, it felt like we did as well as we possibly could, as a band. But then, what may be a 10 out of 10 for us, wouldn't even be a seven for a band like Radiohead. We did the best we could, and the fact that people appreciated us was great because we couldn't have performed any better… It was an absolute milestone. It was one of those few moments where we felt we'd really made it." Meanwhile, Nathan was relieved by the crowd's reaction to 'Crawl', saying 'Some said it was a ballsy move to play an unknown song, but it's a good, memorable rocker and people seemed to love it," and adding, "We're going to play the whole record three times in a row, every set – that's all you're going to get!"

Glastonbury caused a wave of publicity for the Kings Of Leon that lasted for the rest of the summer, boosted immensely on September 9 by the release of the first single from *Only By The Night*. The song was called 'Sex On Fire' and has become the biggest-selling Kings song to date by virtue of its huge, anthemic chorus and attractively filthy theme. The single went on to be the UK's most downloaded song of all time and a permanent staple of the band's live set, despite the fact that it very nearly didn't appear at all.

It emerged that Caleb, the song's writer, had come up with the music and the primary melody lines before coming into Blackbird Studios to record. His usual method for writing lyrics was to begin with a set of joke lines that he would fit around the music, before going away to complete proper lyrics later on in the recording process. This time, however, inspiration for 'real' lyrics wasn't forthcoming, reports producer Jacquire King: "'Sex On Fire' in particular was a song that was encouraged to be developed in pre-production, because Caleb had the guitar riff and the melody, but he wasn't taking the lyrics that he had seriously. At first he didn't want to sing the lyric – but we all encouraged him, because it was such a great melody and such a fun song."

Caleb was plagued with questions about what, and who, 'Sex On Fire' was about, with its provocative line of "head while I'm driving". He told one interviewer, "It's about a great sexual relationship with hot, hot sex that you remember forever," adding, "I can't believe the label picked it [for release] because the lyrics are pretty in-your-face sexual. I think my girlfriend hopes it's based on her. Maybe it is my girlfriend, because we've had some good times together... but I'm not really sure."

Celeb-watchers take note: for some time Caleb had been squiring the model Lily Aldridge, the daughter of photographer Miles Aldridge and sister of actress Saffron Burrows. However, it appears that she is not the inspiration for that line in the song. Caleb was quick to add, "I did put in that line about 'head while I'm driving' [but] that's never happened to me before – I'm a very good driver, and I'd be very scared to drive while getting head."

The singer didn't take the song seriously even after he'd written it, he said. "When we had too many songs for the album, we were all taking out picks as to which songs shouldn't make the [final selection]," he recalled. "'Sex On Fire' is the song that was my first pick! So it was crazy that it ended up being the biggest song we've ever had. It's just lucky that I got voted out. It's funny... I kind of wrote it when I was drunk, but... I didn't want it to be too clichéd and too corny, so I actually rewrote those lyrics probably six times in my songbook. You know, I knew the hook, so I wrote one song about two people that hated the sight of each other, but the sex was so good that they couldn't stay away. And then I wrote one that was just way too explicit. I don't know. I just kind of tried to find a happy medium there somewhere."

The rest of the Followills were surprised when Caleb came out with the chorus line. Matthew remembered, "I said to Caleb, 'Did you just say 'sex on fire'?' I don't know where it comes from. For me, it was all about the melody." The singer himself remained mystified by the success of the single, remarking: "I started to look at it like a Weezer song, something that shouldn't be taken too seriously. I don't want everything in our career to be so serious. I wasn't trying to save the world with that song...

I wanted to get rid of it, and now it's the biggest song we've ever had. It shows how much I know."

"I just had this melody and I didn't know what to say," he continued. "One day I just sang, 'This sex is on fire' and I laughed, and the other guys are like, 'What are you laughing at?' I thought it was terrible, but they were like, 'It's good, it's got a hook'. There's an element of sex that's expected in our songs, so I tried to wrap it all up in one song. If you read the lyrics you'll find it's got some quite visual lyrics in it. It's a pretty sexy song, actually."

'Sex On Fire' was a watershed in the Kings' career: they'd enjoyed hit songs before, but nothing on this scale. It became ubiquitous in late 2008 thanks to Caleb's long, radio-friendly wail of "Yeah!" and the accompanying video, a strange bit of film in which he was pictured in the throes of sexual ecstasy, Nathan writhes under a shower of water and Matthew eats fried chicken. The band were now obliged to consider the nature of fame at this level for the first time – and with their resolutely small-town mentality, this was quite a mental leap. "We once toured with The Strokes and I thought those guys were the coolest men," pondered Jared. "But a week later I saw a picture of them chatting with Justin Timberlake and I thought, 'What the fuck?' But now I completely understand. We're all young men, or even kids, making music and trying to make it to the top."

With a clearer world-view enabled by their decision to quit drugs, the band were finally getting a sense of where they stood in the rock pantheon. "I feel good, man," said Caleb. "We had a chance with this album to actually get a little rest. I know it's just the calm before the storm, but we put in our time, so now it's to the point where we're getting to do big things. In order to do that, you have to prepare yourself for it, so you get a big break like this every now and again, and that's good. But right now, I'm ready to get back out there, especially in America, because all too often we'll just end up touring overseas."

Jared was also keen to get on the road, explaining that the larger venues in which the band were now playing were a wholly new experience: "It's very different, mainly to do with the sound. It sounds better in a smaller venue, but you feel more self-conscious having people stand so close to you. Actually, it's much more fun playing in a smaller venue.

You feel intoxicated with that many people so close to your face. On a larger scale, I have to admit, it's much more fulfilling to sell out Madison Square Garden!"

Matthew explained that the band's more sober lifestyle was its own reward, saying, "Pretty much all we do now is drink. Nobody does drugs like we used to. It's not nearly what it used to be. It was crazy. We have more important things to do. We can't be wasted all the time any more," adding, "We used to party really hard, I'll tell you that: I remember back to the 2004 Big Day Out, staying up with The Strokes until eight in the morning and there was no telling what we were doing. We've settled down now, man. We're pretty much only on the alcohol and we do celebrate, but not with models and all that."

He went on, obviously feeling a sense of responsibility: "There's just so much more on our plates and so much to think about now. There's really no time to be carefree, and it's fucking non-stop these days. Before, when we used to party, we'd play one show and then we'd have nothing to do for a week! Obviously it is a fun job, but a lot of people don't realise the stuff that goes into it."

As many journalists had reported incredulously, golf was now a major concern for the Followills. Matthew confirmed the story, saying: "I play golf all the time now, and I love golf… they got me to come play one day when it was a beautiful day and there was nothing going on. It was one of those things where I had beginner's luck and kept up with the other guys who'd been playing for a year, so since then I've loved it."

On September 22, 2008, *Only By The Night* was released. Asked about the relatively short period of time between the album and its predecessor, Caleb ruminated: "I don't think we ever really have a schedule in mind. I think usually we just come off the road and it'll come pretty quickly… y'know, we're in Nashville where the scene isn't so exciting to where you get lost in what's going on and where you forget to make music, so we always try to make music. But I think on this one we had a little bit of pressure because of the success of the last one. We had a lot of festivals and big concerts and things calling, to where we knew that if we were gonna go back and play these places we would want to have some new songs and some new material to play. It ended up [that] we finished the record – we didn't realise we were gonna do it so quickly, but it came pretty quickly to us."

Of the album's title, borrowed from *Eleonora*, a poem by Edgar Allan Poe, Caleb explained: "Actually, in his poem it says 'only by night', not 'only by the night'. I had it memorised, but it was great. It was talking about something like all these people that live in the daytime and they miss certain things that you can only find by the night." Jared added: "It took us forever to come up with the album title. We had probably five or six that ended up in the short list, and we thought about it throughout the entire writing of the record [and] throughout the entire recording, and it was just something about our record… we kinda like night-feeling stuff, you know, vampires and *The Lost Boys* and cool stuff like that. We're all into that, so there was just something about [the phrase] 'only by the night' that felt edgy and what we thought this record felt like."

It was pointed out by a few interviewers that all four Kings Of Leon album titles to date had five syllables. Informed of this, Caleb laughed and explained: "[With] *Youth And Young Manhood*, we didn't think about it like that. And as soon as we knew [the next one] was going to be *Aha Shake Heartbreak*, my little brother said, 'OK. Well, the next one has to be *Because Of The Times*'. And that was years ago. And then one day someone did the math and it was like, 'Wow, everything's five syllables. We want to stick with that'. And that was actually the toughest part of this album. I mean, we had the music and we knew it was good. Or at least to us. Every day we'd go in there and record and it would come out great, to us, but we would still have our heads down. Like, 'What the fuck are we going to call the record?' Because we had all these great titles, but none of them were five syllables…"

The cover of *Only By The Night* was a composite portrait of the four Followills with elements of an eagle's face inserted into it. This tied in, they revealed, with the band's fascination with American Indian heritage, and their own biological links to the culture. Matthew explained: "We just write about things we love, and I was actually just having a conversation with Jared about all the things we all really like. It's always Christmas, fireworks, vampires and Indians. We've always loved that kind of stuff and it's weird that certain things make us feel really good. It's our fourth album, so we've gotta find something to write about. Caleb took everything we liked – vampires and Native Indians – and put it in the record to create this fantasy world."

Nathan added: "We wanted a nocturnal feel to the artwork and asked for some animal to be put over our faces, so they did that and it looks awesome. I think we're an eighth Native American, but I think I am more because my grandmother's great, great, great, great, great grandpa was an Indian chief. She always tells the story, so I've always been kind of inspired and loved that whole Native American thing. I think she told me we're Chickasaw or something like that."

The sales trajectory of *Only By The Night* differed sharply from that of the Kings' previous albums. While *Youth And Young Manhood*, *Aha Shake Heartbreak* and *Because Of The Times* had all peaked and fallen as expected before becoming respectable back-catalogue sellers, *Only...* peaked at number five in the US chart before falling and rising again (making number four this time) and then hanging around the top reaches of the charts for several months, refusing to go away. In the UK, the album debuted at number one and became the biggest-selling digital album ever released in this country. With this album, the Kings truly found their niche – a niche supported by millions of album sales and shows at the biggest venues in the world. Worldwide, the album has sold over seven million copies at the time of writing – a huge achievement in the era of filesharing.

So what's all the fuss about?

The album begins with 'Closer', an ethereal, haunted-house cluster of reverbed guitar and slow drums. Loaded with atmospherics and distant, wailed guitar lines, the song builds slowly, focusing on Caleb's wide-open vocals. It's a beautiful song and has – predictably – been used on several TV programmes in the past couple of years. Memorable as it is, 'Closer' is effectively a precursor to the heavyweight 'Crawl', which the Followills had deployed as the opening song at Glastonbury three months before the album's release.

Although the media had a field day with the sentiments of 'Crawl', which alludes to the state of the American nation as it approached the November 2008 presidential election, it was generally agreed that the song neither transformed the Kings Of Leon into a political band nor made *Only By The Night* a particularly politicised album. It was merely the sound of Caleb looking around him, realising that the world outside America wasn't especially enjoying the Bush regime and deciding to comment on it.

As he explained: "I think [the song] just came from us being a band that pretty much grew up in Europe, and we couldn't really enjoy the success that we had, because every time we went to a restaurant, everyone looked at us like we were these people that came from a country that supported war and supported all the terrible, terrible decisions and mistakes that were going on in America."

Not that he wanted to jump on the anti-Bush bandwagon along with so many American bands. "Everyone in fucking country music and Green Day and all these other people were writing songs about America," he sighed, "so we refused to write anything political. But I always knew if I wanted to ever do it, I was going to do it like Rage Against The Machine – it wasn't going to be some ballad. If you really believe in something, you should be able to scream it from a mountain. But all of my songs are about five different things, usually. It's just talking about how someone can just come in and fuck everything up and then they're gone, and everyone else has to deal with the consequences."

Anchored by Jared's heavily distorted octave bass-line, the song refers most notably to "the crucified USA" and "the red and the white and the abused" – incendiary stuff for a band from the Southern states. "In prophecy, it says at the end of days there will be wars and rumours of wars," Caleb explained. "Look at all the hurricanes and earthquakes and everything that's going on, to me it's almost like what has been done in America has brought on the feeling of a religious war, and along with that a lot of other prophecies are coming to pass. It scares me."

This is understandable – even though Caleb had revealed himself to be a Barack Obama-supporting Democrat, four years of touring in Europe during George Bush and Tony Blair's War On Terror had left him feeling that America was being unjustly portrayed. "We're not really political. We never have been," he said. "But we're just sick of it now. Politicians do all that stuff, and we have to pay the price. Truth is most Americans didn't have anything to do with it. I would say that probably not even 75 per cent of Americans vote, and the ones that did didn't get the president they voted for. Everyone's so looking forward to getting a new president in the White House, and at this point we don't even really care who it is. Something's got to make this better. I just want to get some intelligence."

Nathan sighed, "There's been a lot of unrivalled stupidity in politics lately... We travel the world and meet all these people who don't like us because we're American, but we didn't do all that shit," and Jared described the song as "prophetic... like the fall of Rome, America is losing its global empire".

Caleb went one better, insisting: "My little brother came over here [to Europe] when he was 14. We'd go out, cruising around, and people would cuss us. What could he have to do with what was going on out there? What could any of us have to do with it? It's not the first time I've wanted to say something politically, but it's not about George Bush. It's about other countries and how they treat America. It's still a great country, you know. But we didn't have a TV growing up. We didn't know what was going on in politics. I don't like politics, but we have to do our part... When I say 'the crucified USA', what I mean is that we're a band that has basically grown up in Europe. But when we got here we had to hold our heads down the whole time because everyone looks at Americans in a certain light. Back then, we weren't even voting. There's all this evil going on in the US, but all Americans are looked at like they're a part of it."

Nathan was equally incensed, recalling: "Back in 2004, we had to hang our heads. We were touring Europe, where America was being hammered. We hardly left our hotels. We were in Paris on election day and every single question was about Bush, and why was America so stupid." Jared took the wider view, saying: "There are very smart people in America, and yet we are represented by a guy who can't complete a sentence. You shouldn't look at a country as a whole. I mean, sure, with Bush's second term, he was voted in on a majority. But the majority are older people who are out of touch with the times, and who are easily tricked into believing anything they see on Fox News. Something bad about Obama only has to be written in an email for people to believe it. It's sickening. If you're young, please vote!"

Although Jared probably didn't win the Kings Of Leon any new fans in the over-50 demographic when he said this, it seems that the band as a whole understand that it's possible to be isolated from politics – since that was their own experience as teenagers. "When we were growing up," remembered Caleb, "our parents didn't talk about politics, and they never voted because they were all wrapped up in the religious life. The family listened to nothing but gospel music and didn't own a TV, so when we got to the UK we were like: 'Wow, so that's what's been going on out there!'"

After the heavy pontification of 'Crawl', the lightweight, singalong vibes of 'Sex On Fire' are a relief. The song's most notable features are Caleb's clean vocals, his least attenuated yet. He explained his desire for a cleaner singing style on many occasions, notably when he said: "While we were making the record I was listening to Radiohead's *In Rainbows* a lot. It's got beautiful melodies, and Thom Yorke sings the ass off it. It was the first time I looked at my voice. I've always held back with my singing, to be cool or whatever. In the beginning I tried to make it so you couldn't understand what I was saying, and people thought I was 50 years old. This is the first time I've been confident enough to actually sing. When I used to go to church I was the singer and I sang pretty. On this record I really sing again, and you'll notice it, you actually can understand what I'm singing about."

One other notable aspect of 'Sex On Fire' is its big drum sound – perfectly suited for stadiums. "That's one good thing about Jacquire King," said Jared. "He's like a total drum fanatic, a freak. We'd be like, 'Fuck man, what are we going to cut today?' and we'd talk about it and he would then go and spent two hours tuning the fucking drums! We'd be like, 'It's fucking drums, what are you doing in there?' He's really crazy about that, so by the time he got the drums right, we'd all be drunk [and saying], 'You've sacrificed the rest of the band for the drums!'"

The power drumming was aided by an unexpected inspiration from the American stoner-rock scene, Caleb added. "The drums are really powerful on this record. Nathan started working out for this. In the last festival cycle we did, we were playing a lot of the same days as Queens Of The Stone Age and their drummer [Joey Castillo] is a gorilla. He's massive and hits them so fucking hard, so we'd be going to Nathan, 'Look what he can do'. So Nathan actually got a trainer for this album. He's pretty buff now. I have to start watching my mouth when I get drunk now, because I reckon he could probably take me pretty easily!"

Even months after writing the song, Caleb had difficulty believing that so many people took 'Sex On Fire' seriously. He marvelled, "When I wrote 'Sex On Fire', I didn't feel as though it was a composition that would especially help us break through in the US. Sometimes the popularity of a song can take on ridiculous proportions. There I am singing this song, and suddenly a grown man stands straight in front of me and screams, 'Yeah, your sex is on fire!' That's, er, something else… It was honestly not what I intended when I wrote the song!"

And yet 'Sex On Fire' isn't the most stadium-friendly song on *Only By The Night*. That goes to 'Use Somebody', a genuine arena anthem complete with highly singable backing vocals and a chorus that pulls off the trick of being bittersweet and uplifting. The Kings were – perhaps uncomfortably – aware that they were entering highly commercial territory with this song: when an interviewer told Caleb that 'Use Somebody' reminded him of Arcade Fire, he retorted, "I'm glad you said Arcade Fire and not Coldplay..." Nathan, with his usual relaxed demeanour, concurred: "I could hear some Arcade Fire-esque stuff on there, but this is just us spreading our wings. All these new sounds and this new direction that it might feel like we're going in, this is where we're going naturally."

The genesis of 'Use Somebody' was, like most of the Kings' biggest songs, fraught with uncertainty. "I've always been scared of songs being these big crossover hits," admitted Caleb. "Like with 'Use Somebody', I wrote the melody and all of us related to it, it felt like this big song, so I kinda pushed it under the rug. Then we were making *Only By The Night* and Matt kept saying, 'Where's that song about using somebody?' I would act like I didn't know what he meant. I knew the song he was talking about, but it scared me."

Scared of what, though? Major success? Possibly – after all, Caleb had admitted to feeling pressure from his band's rapid rise to prominence. "I felt immediately that it was a big song, and it scared me away," he mused. "The meat of the song was written on tour… When I came up with 'I could use somebody,' I didn't know if I was talking about a person or home or God… finally, I went, 'All right, we'll do it,' and as soon as we started playing it, the producers looked up and said, 'Whoa, that's a good song'. I was like, 'OK'."

It certainly wasn't easy for Caleb to write a song as confessional as this one – he'd been obliged to dig deep, he said. "It's kind of like you feel good," he remarked, "but it's the kind of good feeling that brings about sad emotions... I hold a lot in. I'm not the kind of guy that cries, and stuff like that. Not that that's a good thing. But, you know, after I've had a few drinks and I have a songbook in front of me, a lot of times I'll kind of talk to myself a little bit, and point a finger at myself, and usually that's the most emotion that comes out of me. I mean, I'm going to open up one way or the other, but I think it just happens a little quicker when you have something altering you to give you the confidence to do so."

'Use Somebody' caused dozens of reviewers and interviewers to ask the band if they'd been listening to a lot of U2 while they were recording the album, a question that the Followills rapidly tired of. Still, Matthew's reliance on a heavily delayed guitar sound (one of U2 guitarist the Edge's standard tricks) lent some justification to the claim, especially as the next song, 'Manhattan', takes this approach to its logical conclusion. In this song Caleb is referring obliquely to the fate of America's dwindling population of native Americans – "the unfortunate story that has happened that's kind of been pushed under the carpet", as he described it.

"No-one really likes to talk about it," he went on. "But yeah, the beginning of the song's about the beauty and the freedom of the way that it was, and then by the end... it's all been taken away. And you still have the hope that, even though it's been forgotten somewhat, I like to think that some of us still have that spirit inside of us. You know, as far as living your life with a smile on your face and wanting to go and dance and enjoy all the beauties we have... it's kind of me trying to pardon myself [for] my party lifestyle."

Once more, then, Caleb's guilt about his profoundly irreligious life choices was a songwriting inspiration. 'Revelry' continues the idea, at least superficially, although the song is much more introspective than its title would suggest. Referring to drinking, smoking and wondering if an unnamed person "was ever around" (God, perhaps?), the song is one of the better downtempo tracks on the album – and a complete contrast to the one that follows, '17'. With its bizarre, Christmas-themed introduction and midsection – complete with bells – the song is a paean to an unknown 17-year-old female, with one of its primary features Jared's question-and-answer bass playing.

The rest of the album is less fiery and more pensive than the fireworks at its beginning and midsection. 'Notion' is an unusual song, based on a droned bass and guitar line that lopes thoughtfully along beneath Caleb's impassioned vocals; 'I Want You' is a slow, bass-heavy ballad; 'Be Somebody' is more urgent, but full of spacious echoes; and the closer, 'Cold Desert', is a sign-off of great power. "Jesus doesn't love me, and no-one ever carried my load," calls Caleb, a line he explained – with scathing honesty – with the words, "There's still lingering guilt, and once I start to drink you don't want to be around me because there's a level of brutal honesty, if not just pure meanness. In a way, I lash out at everyone else because that's when I start to point fingers at myself. And that's when I write lyrics.

Not an easy album, then, but one that thousands of listeners reacted to immediately – enticed by the bigger, more digestible songs into examining the darker, less obvious tracks. *Only By The Night* isn't a pop album with instant hooks: it requires an investment of time on the part of the listener, as Caleb well knew. In a moment of confidence, he declared, "We took some risks and we did some things that could potentially lose some of our fans, but at the end of the day you have to make a record you're pleased with. You can't worry about anybody else. Come on, four albums in six years? Any naysayers can kiss my ass!"

The Followills were delighted with their new album: the recording had apparently felt right, as well as sounding good. "We were good friends again on this record for the first time in a while," enthused Nathan. "It really felt right for this record, the way we were and where our heads were at… We had a lot of fun making it, and when the work day was finished we went to the bars at night together and hung out. I think *Only By The Night* was a proper statement for this album. We were back!"

Its delayed release in the USA was, Jared revealed, the result of record company caution. "It's pretty much suicide for a band like us to release an album in the fourth quarter in America," he said. "[It's] bullshit, really. Every big act releases their record around Christmas time, so we would be going up against your Destiny's Childs and your fucking Britney Spearses and all that bullshit. You can't really do that. But over here [in the UK] we can actually compete. We had the number two slot behind Robbie Williams or something."

The progress of *Only By The Night*, already a major hit after one single, was boosted still further when 'Use Somebody' – like 'Sex On Fire', a huge, arena-filling single – was released as a single in December. Jacquire King, who co-produced the song, explains its impact: "That song made a huge difference here in the US as well as in the rest of the world: I knew in pre-production that that song, in terms of what it could do in the US, was great. The band are on the radio quite a lot now, and the general public is becoming aware of them. They've been playing in front of tens of thousands of people and they've headlined a lot of festivals and their record went platinum."

"This was the album where I felt the songs were too pretty to fuck them up," laughed Caleb, although Matthew didn't agree that *Only By The Night* represented a particularly extreme change in the Kings' sound. "It wasn't a deliberate change, to be honest," he said. "But everybody says it sounds different. We weren't saying, 'Let's make a hit record'. We actually thought it was going to be a flop. I remember Jared calling me and saying, 'This is going to be our worst record'. But it didn't work out like that."

It didn't work out like that because the songs sounded so big and contained such catchy hooks, you might well surmise. Of the full-fat production of the songs, Caleb explained: "We wanted it to have a more professional feel than anything we've ever done. We've always thought that, you know, the music that we write, it all feels big to us but the production styles that have been used in the past, when we come out of the studio the songs felt smaller than when we were writing them. So this is the first record that we literally rolled up our sleeves and said, 'All right, man, we're not going to come out of here again and have a song that can't get played on the radio because it's so lo-fi that, you know, people can't put it up next to other music. We want it to be bigger'. And I don't mean popularity-wise. I mean, we want it to feel bigger and more professional."

"We didn't want to have one song on *Only By The Night* that wouldn't stand up against the rest of the songs on the radio," he continued. "We've always felt we're a lot better than most bands live, and we've even felt that we do things with our music that is better than other bands, but we've always dumbed down our sound in the studio, to where you could hear it on the radio [and] our song might be better than the other songs, but the other songs had better production. So we wanted to change that about this record, and have a more professional sound."

Angelo Petraglia had played a major role in the new approach, he added, describing their longtime partner as "literally... the fifth King of Leon. We don't hold back in any way, shape or form with the way that we talk to him and vice versa... the comfort level also contributes to how immediate it sounds." He thought that the Kings Of Leon's fan base would be able to withstand their change in direction – or at least most of them would. He pondered: "Whether or not our fans are ready, we just felt like if we don't record it now, we're never going to, so let's go ahead and try it. Then, when we put the new stuff up to the other songs, they fit and it didn't feel forced. There are a few people getting scared and thinking that our sound is going into something different. I think it always will go into something different from album to album. If people get scared and think that they don't like something about what we're doing right now, it's not like this is gonna to be the way we make music forever."

It was interesting to note that Caleb also made statements such as: "It's like asking somebody who works at a computer company, 'Would you like to be Bill Gates some day?' Everybody wants to be at the top of their game, if nothing else than for their family's pride. If we can do this on our own terms and continue making the records that we make, but be able to ride our own ticket and choose where we play, then yeah, of course." He had no need to excuse the more commercial nature of the songs; his fans bore that out – but it's revealing that he seemed to feel some inner conflict about this deliberate step into more mainstream territory.

He was supported by Nathan, however, who reasoned: "If we're going to get big, by now we should be thinking about trying to take it to the next level... for our fourth record, the time was right for people to actually understand what's being said," and added, "On the first listen [*Only By The Night*] seems like a slower record, in the sense that people are used to us comin' out of the gate and knockin' your front teeth out.

'Boom, here's the Kings Of Leon with a new record. Let's go fuck shit up.'"

It wasn't long before interviewers began to ask questions about the new sound in slightly underhand terms – implying that the Kings were seeking success with a cynical change of approach. Matthew took exception to this, insisting: "I don't think we've ever sat down and said we have to write a song that sounds like this. That just never happens. The songs just kinda come together. You always get these questions, like, 'Did you guys try to make this record more poppy, or whatever?' And it's like, no, we literally wrote 12 or 13 songs and recorded them and put them in sequence for the record. That's just the way it goes."

Nathan added: "I don't think that we ever want to make a decision as a band based on what we think someone else thinks about us. We don't plan stuff, ever. That's why it's never taken us more than six weeks to make a record. And two of those weeks are us jacking off and being stupid. It's like going to school – in the first week of school you don't do shit."

Some support from on high came when Pearl Jam singer Eddie Vedder phoned the Followills at home to offer them his congratulations on the success of the new album. "He was just telling us how proud he was of us," reported Caleb, "and he said, 'Now you guys are playing on the same stages that we were playing on together [in 2006]' – it was amazing."

The Kings themselves were back in Australia before the end of the year, where a vast Kings fan base had grown in the previous year or two. Remembering the Pearl Jam support slots, Caleb laughed: "I can remember walking out on those stages in Australia and, even though there were hardly any people there when we were playing, it was still amazing. Here we are a couple of years later and we're playing the same places. Hopefully a few more people should turn up this time."

"When we played [in Australia] with The Strokes a few years ago, they walked onstage and it was as if they were The Beatles," he added. "There were the loudest high-pitched screams from girls, and I was thinking, 'Holy shit, man, this is just insane'. We have the older women who scream for us; maybe they'll hit those high-pitched levels if we ask nicely!"

"Australia's an easy place to tour when you have the opportunity to leave a cold winter for sunshine,' continued Caleb. "And when we heard we had three songs in the charts at the same time, it blew our minds. You hear stories about The Beatles doing that, and you think, 'I guess those days are gone'. But when we heard we'd achieved it, I thought, 'Wow, Australian kids are pretty cool, aren't they?'"

"They're the ones who come to the shows and buy the records, basically giving us our living, so we like the relationship we have with our fans," Nathan added. "In fact, I think we should keep this same relationship for, oh, the next 50 to 60 years, at least…"

A lot was at stake with this album, it emerged – nothing less than the good name of the Followills, at least in the USA. "I think we had a reputation for things that weren't related to the music," said Caleb, "so it's been a goal of ours to prove to America that it wasn't just hype." Success in their home country was now important to them after so many years in the relative wilderness of Europe and the UK, added Nathan: "The first three records didn't do what we thought they would – in America, anyway – so we were hoping for the best but expecting the worst."

When the album was a huge hit Stateside, therefore, the band were doubly pleased. "We never imagined this," gushed Caleb. "We'd hoped it would do better than our other three albums, but we had absolutely no idea it would do what it's done. I mean, we're still scratching our heads, thinking, what did we do right this time, you know?"

Towards the end of the year, it emerged that some of the new songs were being recorded at live shows and shared via the internet, which irked the band no end. "You don't wanna play all the new songs live, [because] with technology these days, there'll be someone out there with a recorder and it kinda spoils it for us," said Matthew. Caleb added: "There are a lot of people online that say, 'These guys have a wonderful life, screw them if they don't want me listening' – you don't know what it's like! Literally, sometimes I jump out of bed at three in the morning and go and write something down because I just had a dream and I thought of something. You don't know what goes into writing a song, let alone an album. It's not a day at the office – you're putting your heart and soul into something, and for people to not respect that, that's crazy. But when you have people that do it the right way – that's pushing your art form."

Despite this minor irritant, the Followills knew that they should appreciate their success. An appearance on the cover of America's biggest rock magazine impressed them greatly: as Caleb observed, "It's the cover of *Rolling Stone*, man. You dream about that when you start a band. It's definitely one of those things... that I'm pretty sure will sink in down the road a little bit, and we'll be like, 'Holy shit, what happened?' I mean, I still have a *Rolling Stone* magazine that says 'Kings Of Leon' on the front of it. And to me, that was like the pinnacle."

"I don't know what made this album bigger than the rest," said Nathan, looking back on the success of *Only By The Night*. "I think it was a series of events, between [appearing on the US TV show] *Saturday Night Live* and headlining Glastonbury. Glastonbury was big, because it was us, Jay-Z and, I don't know, Coldplay or Oasis or one of those bands. And I think that got America's attention, like, 'Holy shit, these guys are headlining the same festival that Jay-Z is?' Between that and *SNL* and [playing] Madison Square Garden and 'Sex On Fire' being the first song that really has ever done shit for us on the radio, I think this was the record that America was finally like, 'All right, now we finally get it'."

"Every record you put out," Caleb went on, "you hope it's going to be the one that pushes you over the edge as far as getting the credit you feel you've worked so hard for. This was the first record where the stars kind of aligned. It just had that underlying tone of, 'This could potentially be a huge year for us'. We were definitely mentally prepared... There is no masterplan to *Only By The Night*. Funnily enough we were trying to reach a larger audience with our previous album, *Because Of The Times*. *Only...* is very diverse and lighter on subject matter. Everyone is trying to write songs about war, politics and crisis, and then there's us with a song that has me shouting at the top of my lungs, 'Sex is on fire!' That's a bit of a different note, you know? There is no message to it; it's just about having a good time with a beautiful woman. That's what people want to hear about now."

When they were at home, the brothers were spending their spare time acquiring motorbikes, recounted Caleb: "I'm scared to death of them. I'll get a moped, or something that won't crush me when it falls on top of me". Home time also gave the Followills a chance to take care of their investments, which were said to be largely in Nashville real estate. Of the band's other face – businessmen rather than rock stars – Nathan explained, "It humanises you. When we're back home and we aren't the drummer and guitarist from Kings Of Leon… we're just Nathan and Caleb Followill. It's a good way to make money when we're not on the road, and it makes you realise how much fun it is to be making records and playing music."

So far, so homegrown and relaxed. However, Caleb revealed that his restless nature hadn't been diminished by success and recognition. Talking about his love for the road, he observed: "It's strange because, when I'm away from it, I can't wait to go home. Then, when I get home, I'm twiddling my thumbs after a week or two, and my girlfriend and I are booking a vacation somewhere. It's going to take children to make me want to be there every minute, to watch them grow."

In fact, this inner division in his personality could cause problems at times. In late 2008 the *Sun* reported that Caleb and his bandmates had fallen out over his lifestyle. A source was quoted as saying, "The others have warned Caleb over and over again that they weren't happy about his drinking, but he carried on regardless. The lads have always fought, but they usually sort it out the next morning. Things are completely different this time. The label is deeply concerned that if they don't sort out their differences the tour won't go ahead." The report also cited a quote from Jared that ran, "The only time we fight is when Caleb's drunker than he's ever been so it's not really him. He wakes up and he doesn't remember any of it".

Despite his on-the-road trials, Caleb's love for performing never left him. Asked how he felt about playing on stage, he was more enthusiastic than ever. "It absolutely feels like a gift, something that's handed to you," he said. "I've been absolutely blown away to where I can barely even sing, because you see something happening out there in the audience, something bigger than what we're doing, you don't know if you should keep going or jump off the stage and see what the hell is going on out there… When we're on the road, the loneliness is gone. There's not that deep longing for something new. When we're writing songs, it's almost as if we're buying ourselves some happiness. For me, it's a momentary resolution. But those deep issues, I think they will always be there. And, whenever they go away, I would hate to hear what kind of songs come out."

By now the Kings Of Leon were attracting praise from celebs of all stripes. Sir Elton John and the Followills' heroes, Radiohead, had uttered encouraging comments, for example, and the bevy of minor actors and indie musos who flocked around them on a regular basis was growing almost daily. However, not everyone shared an enthusiasm for the new musical direction that had begun with *Because Of The Times* and had expanded on *Only By The Night*.

One notable critic was the ever controversial Oasis singer Liam Gallagher, who told *Rolling Stone*: "I like the Kings Of Leon, but I don't know about this fucking new record. I like the old stuff... I like his voice, you can always tell his voice when it comes on." Tellingly, he went on: "But it seems to me they've gone for the bucks, man. When they first come out I was going, 'Who the fuck is this?' They were cool and now they've all got their sleeves cut off."

The killer comment came when he said: "And I'm not dissing them because I fucking really like them, but it's like they've got this U2 sound and you can do better than that."

This remark was something of a watershed in the Kings' story. Though Liam has never been one to mince words, for him to come out and make a statement like that in public had to mean something. Clearly the road that lay ahead of the Followills would not be entirely smooth, no matter how successful they had now become...

CHAPTER 8

2008–2009

The criticism the Kings Of Leon faced from certain of their peers after the release of *Only By The Night* may have stung, but it didn't deflect the band from their trajectory towards 'biggest alternative rock act in the world' status. It still hurt, though: Matthew Followill, whose recent experimentation with delay pedals made him a target for accusations of sounding like a certain Irish guitarist, retorted: "Some people would say, 'You sound like [U2 guitarist] the Edge'. To me, there aren't that many guitar players that *don't* sound like the Edge these days. If you use a pedal or any kind of different sound, you're going to sound like the Edge. I hate when people say that, though. All I did was start using pedals. If I had [played] the same guitar parts without the pedals, they wouldn't say anything." He continued in obvious annoyance: "I get flak sometimes from the band. They'll say, 'You can't have guitar parts like that any more. We don't want to hear any more U2 comparisons'. I'm like, 'Dude, *whatever...*' All of those people that say we sound like U2 aren't really listening, and they don't really know music."

In any case, the Followills' detractors couldn't argue with the simple fact that the Kings Of Leon were now powerful enough to play the UK's very biggest venues, and some respectably large sheds elsewhere too. The summer festival shows benefited immensely from the valley-filling width of songs such as 'Sex On Fire' and 'Use Somebody', with crowds in Scotland, Ireland, Spain and the USA responding with loud enthusiasm. A headlining summer and autumn tour in the USA was held in largely mid-sized halls such as San Francisco's famous Warfield Theater, and took the band through to the first Kings show at London's giant O2 Arena. Dates at Wembley rounded off a stunningly successful year for the Followills.

One notable date took place on July 10 when the Kings headlined the T In The Park festival in Scotland. Reviewers wrote that Caleb elicited huge cheers by swigging from a bottle of spirits while toasting the crowd with the words, "If there's anywhere where it isn't frowned upon to drink, it's here, right?" and adding, "I hope I don't fuck this up,' before launching into the intro to 'Sex On Fire'. The band dedicated their set to Nacho Followill, who had just had a baby daughter. Matthew played his guitar with his teeth and Caleb closed the set by saying, "Everybody having fun? I've been looking forward to this for a long, long time. It's good to be here – come on, let's have a party tonight... This is one of the festivals that we look forward to the most. We're home, right? We love you guys very much. We love you because you guys have made us... Kings Of Leon. And guess what – we're gonna be here forever."

Perhaps this slightly rash confidence stemmed from the band's more relaxed lifestyle, and the significantly reduced pressure they were under as a result. Caleb explained that he spent his downtime taking it easy with the rest of the band: "We have a farm out in the country... I just go out there and ride on my four-wheeler and I do a lot of cooking. We all have little hobbies. My cousin Matt buys cars like every day, and Nathan works out. We're not used to having time off, but it's a good chance to try to catch up to normal life... we don't have shows but we have so much going on right now."

He added that even when the band weren't touring, they stayed as ready to play as possible: "It's really strange right now. This record [*Only By The Night*] is getting the most attention of anything we've ever done, so that's why we rehearse... We're just trying to keep on our toes, because every day we hear new information about opportunities that are coming open. And, you know, we like to play. We like the sound of our own voices."

Caleb's relaxed state of mind could have been due partly due to the experience of recording the album at home once again. "The comfort level is just such a different thing," he enthused. "You know, we've recorded in LA and all these places, and it really feels like you're at work. But when we're home it feels like we're home. We know where we're going at the end of the night. We know what restaurant to go to, or you have the luxury of cooking your own meal or sleeping in your own bed. And besides the work, it really gave us all a desire to get in [to the studio and record] every day... I think the amount of comfort is evident when you listen to the music, because we were going in there pretty buzzed every day and recording, as opposed to trying to keep our composure fully. It was a hometown vibe, and everyone there lived in Tennessee. We weren't the only people talking with a country accent, and I think that helps."

The release of *Only By The Night* had been accompanied by a series of video clips streamed on the Kings Of Leon website and at YouTube, and had caused much hilarity among the press and fans. The clips showed the band rehearsing and recording the album, making music with friends and family and generally fooling around behind the scenes and at home. In true *Jackass* style, there are a few practical jokes and gross-out dares as well, notably a scene in which the Kings' drum tech, Dan, snorts wasabi sauce up his nose. "He was saying that he had some bill he had to pay and he was $100 short, so we said, 'If you snort the wasabi, we'll give it to you'," recalled Caleb, adding: "We gave it to him. It was a valiant effort."

"We still document on a regular basis," he went on. "I think we have 23 clips and then some already down, but you know we still try to make some changes and approve and improve them. It's actually fun, man. It's a weird thing. At first you're really nervous about it, but then when you see it it's like, we feel we'd be missing out on some good stuff if we quit now."

Some of the most interesting footage showed the Kings jamming on songs before they recorded them. The dynamic between the band members had evolved after so many years into an almost telepathic understanding of where the songs were going and what they needed in order to come together. This is not to say that there weren't obvious tensions between them: at one point Caleb barks at Nathan, "Come on,

Nate, or we'll never get anything done!" and Jared is the butt of some half-serious piss-taking. The total picture is one of a band at the peak of their powers, however – a fact that Caleb fully understood, saying: "We're pretty quick when we get in there working. I would say it takes a little longer into the day before we start recording, just because there's not that pressure on you. You don't feel like you're spending money in a studio. It's just [that] we would go in there and we knew the material was there… so we were all about getting the right headspace and going in there and recording. But we've never taken longer than six weeks to record an album."

Caleb also revealed that the band liked to jam on cover versions while rehearsing – some of them from unexpected sources. "We did a Pretenders song for a VH1 special," he said. "And we play a pretty good version of Joy Division's 'Transmission'… Somebody suggested we do [Lynyrd Skynyrd's] 'Sweet Home Alabama' at Madison Square Garden – I told them to fuck off! When I heard that My Morning Jacket and Eddie Vedder did The Band song 'It Makes No Difference', I literally wanted to die. My Morning Jacket always do stuff right before we get a chance to. I was like, 'Damn it, they got us again!' For the last two years, I've been listening to *The Late Great Townes Van Zandt* non-stop [and] The Band's *Greatest Hits*. It's full of untouchable songs. When I hear them, I think, 'I'm starting back at zero. I haven't fucking done anything compared to anything they've done'."

As always, however, the Followills were seriously considering how best to make the same inroads into the US market as they'd carved in the UK and elsewhere. Caleb explained, "Our first European tour was sold out, and every tour since has been sold out. Over there, some kids have been trying to get into our concerts for five years." Jared added: "We can go to the UK and play all of England, literally the entire country, and it'll sell out. And then we come back home, and people are like, 'You guys are nothing'… Over there, they just seem to be more susceptible to liking rock music. Rock music is for them what hip-hop is over here. [In the USA], it seems that anything hip-hop, it's easier to be popular with that… We don't worry about it, but you think about it. We have to think about it, because we're from America. It's not for superficial reasons that we want to be big here, it's just for respect reasons, you know?"

The bassist went on:"I've been telling [Caleb] to really use his voice for three records now and he's finally started doing it," and Caleb admitted once again that a basic insecurity lay behind his earlier, mumbled vocals. "I was trying to hide my lyrics and what I was saying," he explained. "Mostly that was because I thought journalists would say I wasn't intelligent, you know, I was from Tennessee and didn't graduate high school. So I always just tried to hide what I was saying."

Despite this recent tendency towards good behaviour, the Followills were still partial to the odd spot of debauchery. Despite being warned by Nathan not to repeat a certain story to a Scottish interviewer ("or we'll never be allowed back in St Andrews"), Caleb recounted: "We arrived at this hotel at 4am, thinking there was no way we'd get to see the Oklahoma Sooners, our college football team. But not only did the staff rig up the game on TV, they laid on snacks and gave us all the beer we wanted. And how did we thank them? By peeing in the wind. The restrooms were three floors away, the game was real exciting, so we went outside and peed on the world famous St Andrews golf course, actually on the 17th fairway… though we stayed in the rough at all times. We're very sorry."

While the band were off moistening hallowed ground, some of the figures behind the scene were emerging. One of these was Ethan Johns, who had watched from a distance as the Followills opted to produce *Only By The Night* without him – and been delighted with their progress. He remembered the Kings' early days in an interview, saying:"The noise they made together as a band was there right off the bat. They were a stunning unit within two months. The level of commitment to mastering their instruments and putting their emotions into their playing – they were just complete naturals… The biggest thing that's influenced the material on this album is the fact that they'd been writing a lot of it during soundchecks in arenas – [there's a] big sound, the tempos are slower, things thematically are bigger."

A feature of the 'new' Kings Of Leon sound was the bass, which Jared Followill had developed into a half-melodic, half-supportive role. Johns laughed as he recalled the struggles he'd had with the bass player when they were trying to get the mix right on the previous album, *Because Of The Times*: "I don't think bass is ever gonna be loud enough for Jared, but if he's happy with it, then he was definitely right. He's a force to be reckoned with, but it's great energy to have in the studio – it's full-on. One of the most special things about [the Kings] is their ability to allow a spiritual elevation to occur during a performance – getting something going and feeling it and creating that elation of spirit… when they hit that, it all makes sense."

Jared himself recalled: "On one song, I was like, 'I just need a little bit more bass,' and you could tell that Ethan was pissed, and he told the assistant, 'All right, turn it up 1.5 decibels' to teach us a lesson, because it was obviously gonna be way too loud. And he did it, and everybody listened to it, and everybody was like, 'Yep, it's great – that's it,' and we kept it there."

When Jared's bass parts combined with Caleb's deliberately widescreen songwriting and Matthew's delayed guitar sounds, the Kings' new songs were bound to possess a bigger feel than their previous work. Matthew was obliged to dismiss U2 comparisons in more or less every interview he executed in the latter half of 2008, telling one interviewer, "We put about as much weight into that as we do taking out the trash… Going into this record, I don't know if we necessarily set out to make a record that would sound good in stadiums or arenas, but we had the fortune of touring with bands like U2, Pearl Jam and Bob Dylan, and we got to play to crowds that were much bigger than we've ever played before, especially in America."

He admitted that finding the right balance between being influenced and being original was difficult: "I think it's [hard] not to subconsciously go to that place, when it comes time to start the process of making a new record. We definitely wanted to keep it in mind that we would still be playing to smaller crowds in America – as opposed to the crowds in Europe, Glastonbury, all that stuff – so we didn't want to make a record that would alienate our audiences over here [with] songs that are way too big-sounding for the size of the room we're playing."

Asked what had led him to add so much Edge-style delay to his guitar sound, Matthew came up with the rather unconvincing excuse of: "I don't know what happened. I bought some pedals that had a bunch of stuff on them. We would rehearse and I would play the parts without the pedals. Then I would plug them in, and it would always sound better.

I was like, 'I'm bored. I might as well start using the pedals'. I get to be creative, so it's worked out."

"We just listen to music – whatever we like," he went on. "Caleb likes one kind of music, Nathan likes another, and so on. It all comes together. We have different elements in our records. *Only By The Night* has 'Revelry', but it also has 'Use Somebody' and 'Sex On Fire'. All three songs are so different... if you're going to stay recent, you have to change. You can't ever really stay the same. That's just the way we've felt – we have to change with the times. That's why we called our [previous] album *Because Of The Times*. We knew it sounded different than the other stuff, but we thought it was necessary to move in that direction with a little bit more of a modern sound. Before that album, we sounded a little older."

Jared had an interesting view, too, saying: "It's a lot of things – growing musically, growing personally, listening to a lot more music, getting turned on to a lot more music. Once you're in the music industry you know everything six months before the records come out. So we've just become friends with a lot of bands, and once you become friends with a band you kind of take on their style of music – bands grow together. A lot of the people that we tour with, we end up sounding like. And when we see them next, they'll tell us that they feel like they're ripping us off... they'll say, 'Yeah man, I feel like that and I hope you don't mind'."

Caleb added: "On our first record it was obvious we were going to have this Southern thing, because we're from the South and we hadn't exactly escaped it at that point, you know? We were still there. So I thought our first record sounded more like Tom Petty. And I thought I tried to rip off Bob Dylan by trying to sing that way a little bit. But definitely on the second album, we had seen the world a little bit. So even though we were still writing that record in Tennessee, in our house, in our basement, I called cigarettes [the British nickname] 'fags'... We used to be crazy. You could tell by our outward appearance, you know? We used to look the part. We were a band that dreamed of being a rock'n'roll band, and so we were going out, falling off of tables and getting crazy. Now usually it's us and the opening band, and we play pool and drink spritzers."

It emerged that the Kings had been looking for a new sound for some time. Even before they recorded *Because Of The Times* they had considered using a new producer: as Jared told interviewer Austin Scaggs, "We talked about everybody. We went to dinner with Dave Grohl, and met with Brendan O'Brien." However, Ethan Johns' understanding of how the Kings worked was just too important to discard – hence his presence for one more record.

"We've learned you can make albums that sound just as good in a 15,000-capacity arena as on a record," added Nathan. "Those tours we did with high-profile artists taught us to be a little more classy and considerate of the bands you play with. Because you never know when you might have the next Dylan, U2 or Pearl Jam opening for you. Touring with them also taught us that we all started at the same place; it's just that some people get there a little quicker. We appreciate every opportunity we've got. And, hopefully, we'll get to keep doing what we're doing."

Interviewers often asked why the Followills felt the need to explore new sonic territory, having already established a sound of their own with their first two albums. The answer lay, of course, in the musicians' unorthodox backgrounds – a cultural vacuum that has influenced them to this day. "Growing up, we weren't allowed to listen to U2, so an album like *The Joshua Tree*, we just discovered that two years ago," Natahn explained. "If we were a band that had grown up listening to U2, we'd be a hell of a lot more scared than we are. But what we do take from U2 is the realisation of how great it would be to be a band for 20 years. We can only fathom how great we could potentially become as long as we keep our heads on straight and don't get married and divorced two or three times."

Caleb added: "A lot of people start a band after they've been listening to Radiohead for 10 years. We've only just listened to Radiohead for the last two or three years, and we've been working our way up the whole time... But due to the fact that we haven't had the influences that everyone else has, there's something about our music that people will feel is fresh... it's just that every trend that comes back around, we're just slower than everyone else, so by the time we get somewhere it's like, 'Oh shit, that's cool!'"

Caleb Followill embracing the Kings' all-grown-up image and music at the London Astoria in 2007.
(Simone Joyner/Getty Images)

On the roof at the House of Blues. *(Mick Hutson/Redferns)*

Matthew and Caleb laying down the riffs. *(Mick Hutson/Redferns)*

Jared, previously the quiet one of the band, had become something of an alt.rock icon by 2008. *(Paul Bergen/Redferns)*

Don't try this at home, kids. *(Mick Hutson/Redferns)*

Drunk on their own success, and who can blame them? *(Mick Hutson/Redferns)*

The Kings Of Leon with engineer Jacquire King (seated) and co-writer, producer and mentor Angelo Petraglia at Bluebird Studios in Nashville.

blackbird studio

Date: 4·23·08

2806 azalea place, nashville, tn 37204 (615) 467-1487

Song Title: SEX ON FIRE

Tape #: 5 Take:

Tempo: 21☐ 16☒ 8☐

Calibration: +6 > 185 HzB NR Type: —

Tape Speed: 15 IPS SMPTE Rate:

Song Start: Song End:

Artist: KINGS OF LEON

Producer: JACQUIRE & ANGELO

Project: LP #4

Client: RCA

Engineer: J. KING

Assistant: L. REYNOLDS

1 BASS DI	2 BASS AMP	3 KICK	4 SNARE	5 TOMS LEFT	6 TOMS RIGHT	7 OH	8 RIDE
	U47	52/F42/NS	57(THSS)	E225	E225	251	77
9 HAT	10 MONO ROOM 1	11 MATT GTR AMP 1	12 MATT GTR AMP 2	13 CALEB GTR AMP 1	14 CALEB GTR AMP 2	15 VOCAL	16 MONO ROOM 2 CHMB
77	U67/44	57	U67	57	U67	3M2	44/SF12
17	18	19	20	21	22	23	24

The blueprint for the Kings' breakthrough, in black and white – studio notes for 'Sex On Fire'.

From hayseed curiosities to bona fide rock gods in four short years. You couldn't make this story up if you tried. *(Jo McCaughey/IPC Images)*

Caleb with Lily Aldridge. *(Sipa Press/Rex Features)*

Nathan with his wife Jessie Baylin.
(Sipa Press/Rex Features)

Jared and Alisa Torres at Heathrow Airport,
followed by Nathan and Jessie. What, Heathrow
doesn't have a celebs-only arrivals lounge?

Matthew Followill and Johanna Bennett.

(from left) Matthew, Nathan, Jared and Caleb win Best International Album at the 2009 Brit Awards. Backstage fighting not pictured. *(Dave Hogan/Getty Images)*

The Kings Of Armani: a long way from Nashville. *(Jim Smeal/BEI/Rex Features)*

On top of the world in 2009. Where do the Kings Of Leon go from here? *(Dean Chalkley/IPC Images)*

He added that Kings Of Leon fans of different ages had different perspectives: "It's getting to a level where things are changing, but 15-year-old kids are the ones that are commenting, 'That fucking sucks', or, 'I can't wait to marry him' – it's like all these things, but then you have the older fans, who are just fans of rock'n'roll, fans of music; they're usually the ones that point out every great thing about your music, and when the younger kids don't realise what's going on, they're like, 'Well hey, I've been listening to this kind of music for generations. You can't come in here and hear one thing and dismiss the band as a [bad] band, because you don't like what they're saying or you can't relate to what they're saying'."

After this many years at or near the top of the music industry, the Followills were starting to get a clear perspective on how different their upbringing had really been from that of most people. "We [used to] come into town," Nathan recalled, "and there would always be all these girlies around us. So every church we went to, we had to convince the guys not to whip our ass. The girls would be talkin' about us, and the guys would be like, 'Hell, no! You're not coming into our church for one week and taking all our women'."

"We got so used to saying goodbye to people because we were always travelling, but that's also why we're so close," he went on. "We're all we've got. We get asked a lot about our fights, which make headlines, but it's just me fighting with my little brother. That's what brothers do."

"We knew it was a different kind of upbringing," added Jared. "Looking back, we think it's kind of cool that we did that. We're not ashamed or anything. It's something that makes us unique. We don't feel like we were held back from anything in the world… My dad used to listen to old rock stations, and you'd hear stuff like The Band, Tom Petty, Neil Young, Bob Dylan, that kind of stuff. It wasn't a big part of his life, it was just stuff he'd listen to to pass the time while we were driving."

"We were in our own little bubble," Nathan added. "We would pull into a town on a Monday or Tuesday. Church services would be from Wednesday to Sunday. Then we'd go to the next town and do it all over again, all year round… It all took its toll on [our father Leon]. He stepped down, and kinda faded out, rather than burned out. We had grown up living by rules all our lives, and then boom! That's all gone. It's every man for himself. That's when we started discovering who we were."

A key revelation occurred when the elder Leon Followill fell from grace in the mid-Nineties, said Caleb – the Followill most affected by the event, or at least the most open about it. "Once I heard the Stones and Dylan, I thought, 'My God, why should we be held to our own experiences? Why not do like our dad did as a preacher?' Every day, he saw something that inspired him and told a story about someone different. I had to put myself in other people's shoes… I had once wanted to be a preacher, but I got burned by a lot of people in organised religion. But we're spiritual; I pray and thank God for everything I have every day."

"Our parents' divorce shattered the whole mirage of this perfect little existence [which] the outside world couldn't touch and couldn't pollute," Nathan admitted. "We realised that our dad, the greatest man we ever knew in our eyes, was only human. And so are we. People are gonna fuck up. They're gonna want to experiment with drugs, have premarital sex. This whole new world was open to us."

The 'new world' was, at first anyway, based on downhome country music – a universe away from the stadium glamour that now enveloped the band. Looking back, Caleb marvelled about the nature of the Kings' first ever gig at a drinking hole in Atlanta: "That was one of the scariest moments of my entire life. We walked in and saw all the cowboy hats, and I literally said to the guys, 'You fucking country it up. Tonight, these songs will be alternative country'. And we fuckin' went out there and people were takin' their cowboy hats off, goin' 'Whooo!' and fucking lovin' it, even though we were dressed like The New York Dolls. When the curtains closed, it was like a *90210* moment, we all gave each other high fives!"

This is the key to the whole Kings Of Leon conundrum. With their bizarre roots, it's little wonder that the Followills wanted to shake off their original country sound and explore new territory – and why couldn't it be U2-shaped territory? While it's understandable that more than a few critics and fans found this change of direction confusing and even alienating, some of that reaction might have been due to the simple fact that modern country music is usually safe and predictable.

In any case, the Followills were happy to mess with people's prejudices: as Nathan sighed, "In the UK, people think we come from a fantasy world. Like, we all live in a house together in the country with no running water, and we all have long hair and beards and drink moonshine and don't wear shoes. I think they were fascinated with how our lives are the total opposite of anything they'd ever seen. It's the same reason the Stones and The Beatles were so big in the US – their long hair and their simple ways."

Behind the pretty clothes and haircuts, though, the Kings offered an attractive fatal flaw to their fans in the shape of Caleb Followill, whose propensity to share his darker concerns through his songs has always made the band more than just another bunch of partying longhairs. Referring to his early songs about those classic middle-aged man's fears – baldness and impotence – he stated: "If all people want to talk about is, 'The Kings of Leon do drugs and hang out with models,' I'm gonna give it to them straight. You want to talk about how you saw me doing blow with such-and-such supermodel? Well you know what my rebuttal is gonna be? 'I couldn't get my dick hard that night'."

"You see people that find the perfect girl and start writing these songs that are too happy," he added. "Where does inspiration come from? That's my biggest question in life. A lot of the problems we have that are brought on by our vices – like drinking too much and our egos – are what inspire us. Could I be happy if I had a different lifestyle? I don't know. You need to shake things up and have these experiences, even if they're fake."

This sense of discontent and neediness in the Kings' songs is what has kept the band interesting – especially to music consumers who require more from their idols than mere good looks and song hooks. Caleb's alter ego, Rooster – a certified idiot who emerged after spirits had been consumed – used to be a genuine problem in the band's early days. "Rooster is a dick. I hate him,' as the singer told *Rolling Stone* in 2005. "I'll wake up some days and the guys will tell me what Rooster said to them the night before. And I'll be like, 'Oh, my God. That was the meanest, deepest, darkest thing ever'. The other night in LA, Rooster was at a table at the Rainbow Room with Drea [de Matteo, actor] from *The Sopranos* and [porn star] Ron Jeremy. He got so fucked up that he had to be carried out!" Nathan explained this astutely, saying "[Caleb] doesn't really do that much talking when he's sober. He does a lot of shit talking when he's drunk… He's my brother, I've grown up with him, but his songwriting is a part of his personality he really doesn't let out. He's kind of a reserved guy."

The Kings' demons are enduring ones, then – although Rooster was eventually knocked off his perch permanently when Caleb quit drinking whisky. What remained was a desire to keep the band's audience attached, with new music in an updated style that would carry them along with the Followills' progress. "Most people who buy albums listen to the first 30 seconds of a song, and – if it doesn't grab their attention – it's on to the next one. You can listen to the whole record in six minutes," Nathan noted. "We wanted to show people that [*Only By The Night*] might not be the typical Kings Of Leon album they're expecting. It's something some of our fans may not like, but we were willing to take that risk to maybe get fans we wouldn't have gotten [otherwise]. As a band, you should want every show and record to be better than the last."

Fame was beginning to catch up with the Followills by this point, even in the USA. Endless magazine covers and music TV had made them commercial property, and they were often pursued by the public for photos and autographs. "There's a huge difference now," exhaled Matthew. "We were in New Orleans yesterday and I was taking pictures with people, and that was just so weird to me – having people want my picture in America. But I'm really glad that it's happening here because it means we can [play gigs] at home more… If we were always gone and then lived in London or something like that where we're kinda popular, I would just be miserable. I mean, I definitely would've gone crazy by now… But it's great, we go out to the farm and ride dirt bikes and four wheelers and stuff, and that really helps us to stay grounded. To be able to go home and just feel like a normal person for a while really helps us a lot."

Caleb added: "It's getting crazy going home to Nashville now. I'm having to sell my house because they've put it on some celebrity homes map. There are kids from the UK who go to Nashville and leave me presents. My cousin, who looks after the house, hides them from me – he said I'd be scared. The other day I was there and left the house for a second, and when I got back there were four playing cards, four kings, with all of our names on them in the door. There's an apartment complex across the street, and there are people renting the place out and watching." Nathan added, "We've got a farm in the middle of nowhere. It's so hard to find. But we pulled up and by the mailbox were two girls in go-go boots, little outfits, just waiting…"

Perhaps because of their newfound fan base in their home country, some elements of the American press had decided to start giving the band a hard time. Nathan remarked, "When we say something in the UK, the Nashville press repeat it and take all the jokes and sarcasm out. They don't get our sense of humour. We make some joke, then the next day in the Nashville paper it will be, 'The gross Kings Of Leon watch each other have sex'. They didn't realise we were being sarcastic. We've got a Ricky Gervais-type of sense of humour. Very sarcastic. Some people just don't get it."

The success of the Kings had made them especially popular in their home town, Jared sighed: "We are one of the first bands from Nashville who aren't country artists to have become famous. Everyone recognises us, but they just hate us. The local papers always put a question mark after Nashville when they're writing about us, like we're not really from there. But now we're so unpopular at home it's becoming cool to like us. It's gone full circle."

A dose of normality was important in the Kings' world by this stage – they had seen so much excess that they understood the price of fame only too well. Nathan observed, "We had friends in bands that came out and sold four million records with their debut [album] and that's amazing. Then they come back and sell three million on their second, and it's considered a failure. The bar gets set so high, you have so much pressure to replicate what was so successful about the other one, which kind of sticks them in a rut." He added that he felt that his band were lucky "to get a record deal where the label was willing to grow with us, let us take our bruises and figure out the kind of band we were and the band we wanted to be".

In spite of the band's neuroses and the pressures of fame, they were still growing and having fun at the same time. Nathan pointed to their more efficient intra-band dynamic ("I definitely worried the most… I mean, that was my 14-year-old brother; we're in Hamburg, Germany, and he's out with God knows who. Now it's definitely democratic. Every decision we make, we all four sit down and talk about it") and Caleb highlighted the Followills' more confident recording approach. "We spent six weeks doing [*Only By The Night*], and out of the six weeks the most we spent was two hours [recording] in one day," he said. "We'd drink and play wall ball. Most people would record, then reward themselves by taking a break. We play wall ball, and reward ourselves by going in and recording… [This is] the least cringeworthy album that we've made. I'm pretty proud of these last two records we've made; maybe there's a little more professionalism than previous records. Maybe it's because we're stronger musicians and I feel as though I'm a stronger songwriter."

Nathan clarified this point, saying: "When we made *Youth And Young Manhood*, Jared was 15 years old. That was the first music we'd ever made in our lives, and that was the only kind of music we knew how to make. And then *Aha Shake Heartbreak* came along and we were a little more comfortable with our instruments and ourselves, so we upped the ante a little bit. Then, with *Because Of The Times*, we had toured with U2 and Pearl Jam and Bob Dylan and got to play in these huge arenas, we started thinking, 'Man, we need to start making music that's gonna sound good in a sweaty club for 300 kids but will also sound great in Madison Square Garden or wherever'. That became a factor in the music we were making, and this record is just us not being scared to try anything – any sound, any tempos, any vocal effects. We really felt like if we never make another record, out of the four records we've made, this will be the one that either gets the job done or it doesn't."

The band were now doing well in America. Not, you understand, to the point where they were selling out venues the size of London's O2 Arena, but well enough so that they would be invited to play on the best TV shows, for example. 'It's a relief, for sure," said Nathan, "because you want to be accepted in your home. Obviously, the UK and Europe have a lot to do with the Kings Of Leon still being around. If it was based on America, record sales and airplay, we probably wouldn't have got to make a third record, let alone a fourth record! But it does feel good to get recognised in the grocery store by somebody other than your mom or your fiancée. We're stoked."

The critics on both sides of the Atlantic weren't spending so much time talking about the Followills' back story these days, even if the band's unusual background was still on Caleb and Nathan's minds from time to time. "It's a good day, you know, now that people talk about the music," said Nathan. "We spent our whole beginning of our career – hell, not only the beginning, but the beginning and the middle and all that stuff – and after a while you feel like you're [just] a story, and you're not being recognised for what you're actually out there sacrificing everything for."

The fluke success of 'Sex On Fire' – which had bothered the band a lot, it being a song that they didn't rate highly – was also less troublesome now that some time had passed, perhaps because the 2009 UK tour had sold out a reassuringly long time before the song was released. The band were beginning to appreciate the single for what it was – a fortunate accident. As Nathan put it, "That's the beauty of music, you know. I don't like to overthink stuff. So many people do it… if you overthink something and it ends up being a hit, then you're going to spend the rest of your career trying to repeat that, and I don't want to do that. That's the beauty of accidents, because it's like, 'Well, we did that. We'll never be able to do that again, so what's next?'"

He wasn't overstating the importance of the song, either. Where Caleb had previously split the Kings Of Leon's fan base in half – those who liked the band and those who liked 'Sex On Fire' – Nathan went one better, nominating a third category, "[There are] those die-hard fans that refuse to cheer or sing on 'Sex On Fire', to show us that they're not fans just because of that song. There were these two girls at our show in Vegas, and they sat there and honestly, just crossed their arms and were shaking their heads back and forth and refusing to sing when we got to [that song], but then sang every word to every other song the rest of the night. It was pretty funny."

"I've gotten a couple of farewell e-mails from fans," Nathan added, "saying that it was a good run but that we're to the point where they have to share us with too many people who don't like us for the 'right' reasons. But those same people sent me e-mails two months later, acting like nothing happened, and they're back on the bandwagon… If everyone liked you, it wouldn't be any fun, so it's good to have that variety in there."

"It's funny," he added. "The lyrics 'sex is on fire' were just dummy lyrics. But after playing it over and over, we just realised we probably weren't going to find anything that fit any better than that, so we ended up keeping it. But after we heard the finished product, we were like, 'Aww shit, what have we done here?'… We had no idea in our wildest imagination that it would propel the band as much as it has. If you would have told us while we were making the record that a song that talked about sex and fire would win us a Grammy and all this crazy stuff, we would never have believed you. We're just thankful that we're getting the opportunity to reach a broader audience than on the first three records."

The fame the band were experiencing wouldn't change the Followills as people, promised Nathan, who said: "We're all normal guys. The way we grew up and the way we were raised, I think we all had certain things instilled in us: no matter what's going on in your life, it shouldn't affect how you are. We hear a lot of people say, 'You change when you get famous'… it's not so much that you change, it's that everyone else changes around you because they expect something out of you – they expect more from you. But I don't think you're going to see any of us getting cocky or arrogant or anything like that. We realise definitely [that] as quick as it came, it can be gone. We're just trying to enjoy as much of it as we can and try to keep each other grounded. No matter how famous you get, if your brothers are in the band, they're always going to tell you how stupid or ugly you are."

This consistency extended to the band's religious beliefs, which many observers had expected to disappear (or at least diminish) as a result of several years of debauchery. However, the Followills continued to fight the good fight, Nathan insisted: 'We're all definitely men of faith, I would say. The older you get and the more you live and the more you stay in the world, you realise that certain things that you were taught when you were growing up were a little more fear-based, as opposed to reason-based. But there are parts of our lives that'll never change. We'll always want to be good people and be kind to others… we took all the good we could from that lifestyle and cut off all the gristle. And yeah, we've got a little prayer and a chant we do before every show."

By the beginning of 2009, the Followills were beginning to look forward again. Fame was a pleasure as well as a burden, of course, and incidents such as a meeting with Ringo Starr proved that the band were still fans at heart. "I got to meet him when we did a TV show in England," gushed Nathan. "He was very quiet, very reserved. It was kind of weird – what do you say to a Beatle?... My brother Caleb talked to him, but I kept my mouth closed. I probably should have said something, being a drummer, but, 'Don't speak if you don't have something to say'. I probably would have said something stupid."

Asked how the band were feeling about their forthcoming string of arena shows, Nathan exuded positivity. "I think the crowds will be a little bigger," he chuckled. "I think it will be a little more fun, more our type of a crowd. With the U2 gig we were forced to win over a crowd of angry U2 fans every night. With our own tour it's better to be able to have people dig us for our own stuff... You want every record to be the one that takes you to that next level, but for us it was always a little difficult because we were always big in Europe and the UK and in Australia, but we would go home to America and we would have to step back a year and a half as far as our progression... *Only By The Night* really took off for us and put us on the map in America, and we're just stoked and so appreciative of fans from Australia and Europe [because they] kind of made Americans jealous and made them realise they've got a band from America that they don't even embrace, but is embraced all over the world – but they're finally catching on. It's great to see we've got these fans that have been there from day one and stuck with us. [The fans] actually gave us a chance to grow into the band we are, and hopefully they feel proud and a big part of the success we are achieving."

By now the Kings were also being quizzed about a possible fifth album, probably because their output had been so prolific in the recent couple of years. "For us songwriting is kind of weird," Nathan shrugged. "We'll get inspired at times and we don't even realise it. You tour and have memories and have all this shit that's happened to you, and you don't even realise it happened until you have time to sit down and collect yourself and reflect. A lot of [the new] songs are things we did or wanted to do, and didn't get to."

As with the Kings' previous albums, any Southern or country sounds that they contained were natural rather than forced, he insisted: "I guess if we're going to be labelled as a Southern band it's good that we're the new definition of Southern rock. We thought it was funny that we could be labelled as Southern rockers and not even know any of the typical Southern rock music. The Allman Brothers Band came to one of our shows a few years ago in New York City and thought we were a British band... We've pretty much run the gamut of going from the epitome of Southern rock to arena-sounding songs, so I think there's going to be a little bit for everyone."

He went on, "We're about seven or eight [songs] deep and we're pretty stoked about it, man. We're all in a good head space and enjoying the success we're experiencing, and not getting too cocky or too conceited. We're considering it a blessing as opposed to us being God's gift to music. Every band says their next record is going to be the best work they've ever done, and it's kind of a cliché, but we really do feel the songs we've got going right now are pretty special. The kids are really going to like them."

A pivotal point had been reached. With their new, lustrous songwriting and confident performances making their old music look like the work of an entirely different band, the Kings Of Leon were risking the loyalty of their old fans while attracting many more new followers. This approach has led to disaster in the past: would the Followills survive with dignity and credibility intact?

CHAPTER 9

2009

2009 was shaping up, just like 2008 had been, to be the biggest year that the Followills had yet experienced. The obvious peak was a series of dates in the summer at London's O2 Arena, one of which would be filmed for a live DVD release. "This is the best year we've ever had, and all the hard work we've had to do has come good," said Nathan, appreciatively, adding, "This record [*Only By The Night*] did a lot of good things, but we've been putting in a lot of work for a long time. It's nice that people are starting to give us credit for it."

Caleb, who had become known for stage fright – a factor that would inevitably come into play at such a huge venue – commented: "When you get an opportunity to play the O2 in London, you have to realise that there will be people who have never seen us before. There are two types of people – 'Sex On Fire' fans and Kings Of Leon fans. A lot of people only know us from that single, but it's great the tour sold out before it was released."

Note this crucial last point: Caleb wanted it to be noted for the record that, even before the huge impact of 'Sex On Fire' – a song he had never rated particularly highly – the band were riding a wave of popularity. The success of the Kings Of Leon, he reasoned, couldn't easily be attributed to one fluke single – even if 'Sex…' did scupper this argument slightly when it netted the band a Grammy in February.

"It's unreal," commented Nathan. "As songwriters we've tackled a lot of different things [including] politics and religion. Then we write a song called 'Sex On Fire' and it's Grammy nominated. Of all the songs I've put my heart into, that wouldn't even be in the Top 10." Once more Caleb attributed the song's winning hookline – surely the primary reason for its recognition – to the pain medication he was taking at the time, saying: "I was cooped up in my house as a one-armed man, and writing a lot of things that required me to sing pretty melodies in a higher voice than I often do."

Rolling Stone magazine reported that Caleb only found out about the Grammy nominations when he checked his cellphone after a night on the tiles in Birmingham, of all places. The 50 congratulatory text messages on his phone unnerved him a little, he insisted. "It was a huge shock," he said later. "I didn't even think we had a chance." When the band's victory over luminaries such as Radiohead, Coldplay and AC/DC was announced, they could barely believe it. "It was star-studded, A-list, but we just started jumping up and down and yellin' and screamin'," recalled Caleb. "Everyone was looking at us thinking, who the hell are you and what the hell is going on?… I don't know how the hell that happened. And of all the songs for it to happen with, I never would've thought 'Sex On Fire' would beat a Radiohead song."

"We were definitely the youngsters of the lot," added Nathan. "I think we got away with one there, for sure."

As well as 'Sex On Fire''s Grammy for the snappily titled Best Rock Performance By A Duo Or Group With Vocals – one of two nominations it had received, along with Best Rock Song – *Only By The Night* was also placed on the shortlist for Best Rock Album, although it lost to Coldplay's *Viva La Vida*. Several British (and tellingly, American) magazines placed the album on their end-of-year lists, but *Only By The Night*'s most prominent achievement outside America was undoubtedly the two awards it received at the UK's BRIT Awards ceremony in February.

The Brits show was eagerly anticipated by the Followills. Caleb said: "We always knew the Brits was the Grammys of the UK. So we basically knew that was our Grammy. It was always the biggest shot that we had. And I hear the gift bags are much better at the Brits… It will be fun to perform. Playing a concert is one thing, but performing in front of loads of jaded artists is different. Hopefully, they will be into it. I can't wait to see U2 and Coldplay perform. I want to see if our sound stands up to the big boys."

The band were up for two awards – Best International Band and Best International Album – in competition with four other acts: the Killers, Fleet Foxes, MGMT and AC/DC. In terms of sheer presence on the world stage, only AC/DC outstripped the Kings, but the Australian act lacked the edgy cool that the Followills exuded – and no-one was really surprised when both gongs went to the Followills.

No-one, that is, apart from the Kings themselves. Jared had said in the run-up to the show, "I worry we're going to jinx ourselves if we plan an acceptance speech. But if we think on our feet, we'll probably fuck it all up." Caleb added, "I don't think any of us are great public speakers so it could be funny. It will be YouTube-worthy." Nathan, always the joker, remarked: "It really depends on how much alcohol is consumed. I hear there are tables full of booze at the Brits. That's what I love about the UK. At the Grammys you have to sit there in a suit with a flask… I just want to see Girls Aloud."

After accepting their awards and performing 'Use Somebody', the band left the venue – but that didn't stop a cloud of controversy from descending afterwards. The next morning, rumours flew that the Followills had been involved in a backstage altercation. The *Sun* quoted a source as saying, "Matthew's always the last one to be asked for an autograph. He hasn't been feeling part of things, especially at big events like the Brits. Caleb was annoying him up all night, unintentionally, and all of a sudden something snapped and they just went for each other. It was like a proper old-fashioned bar-room brawl." Another rumour insisted that Jared's female companion had thrown water over a backing singer from Alesha Dixon's band.

All this juvenile rubbish doesn't leave any of the band looking very dignified, but the rumours illustrate perfectly how much the Kings Of Leon had become a favoured topic for the lowbrow mass-media. In any case, Nathan explained that the truth was completely different, saying:

"In reality, we'd already gone when a guy came busting into our dressing room, drunk. Our security is like, 'Whoa, you can't come barging in'. This guy stormed off, and he's about 6'4", a decent-sized guy, and he comes back and punches our tour manager right in the face. And our tour manager is like, 'Is that all you got? Seriously, a guy your size?' Security drag him out and they bumped into a girl as they were dragging him out. She spilt something on her dress, turned around and saw our tour manager and thought he was the one that had done it. She threw her drink in his face, and then his girlfriend got in *her* face."

The Followills understood only too well by now that the press weren't there to do them favours and any story about disorderly behaviour, true or not, was likely to get printed. Nathan concluded: "The press can take anything and blow it so out of proportion. We've learned now that it's pretty comical, some of the stuff you read is hilarious. When our family reads stuff that is horrible that didn't happen, we can be like, 'Honestly, do you really think that something like that would happen?' But it's also good because you [can] tell a couple of fibs during an interview... 'Do you really think that I would say that?'"

Despite all the glittery award ceremonies and column inches, there were more important things to think about in early 2009. A massive tour schedule lay ahead of the Kings, for starters. It was just as well that Matthew pronounced: "I can't see us coming off the road any time soon. In the last six or seven years, the longest break we've had was four months long. Even then we were calling each other to book studio time. Some bands will take a year off: I feel like we'd go crazy if we did that. I'd end up being 300 pounds, eating all the time and never leaving the house!"

Once again the band were converting the world to their cause, one arena at a time. American, European, Australian and New Zealand dates were set to be followed by a slot at the New Orleans Jazz & Heritage Festival, an unusual event for most rock bands – but one at which the Kings fit perfectly, thanks to the profusion of blues and country acts on the bill. More US dates were booked after that, before a series of festivals all over the world – the KROQ Weenie Roast, Sasquatch, Hurricane, Heineken, Werchter, Oxegen, Lollopalooza and Benicassim events among them. The band were then booked to co-headline the UK Leeds and Reading festivals with Radiohead, before more North

American dates, including the Austin City Limits get-together for music biz professionals, before they headed off across the USA and Mexico to end up with an October mega-gig in Abu Dhabi. Quite a schedule, you'll agree.

And that's not even the whole picture. Between those dates the Kings Of Leon squeezed in as many American and British shows as possible, including the three dates at London's O2 Arena and another slot at T In The Park. A slot at the MTV Movie Awards piqued their interest, as it made a radical change from the music-related shows they normally performed. Matthew sounded his age when he enthused, "We're excited, it should be awesome. I always watch that stuff on TV," while Nathan added a dose of sarcasm, remarking: "Hopefully we can break into our acting careers. Maybe an agent or something will come up like, 'Hey, you look pretty good up there, wanna be in my movie?'"

As with any tour of this magnitude, there were setbacks. Two shows in Spain were cancelled in February because of stomach upsets caused by an out-of-date prawn dish; as Caleb recalled, "I was in a restaurant and I looked at this *gamba*, and he looked right back at me. I knew it was bad news, but my eyes were bigger than my brains. I have never been as sick as I was from that one measly shrimp. Maybe he was avenging the deaths of all his sea mates! It's the first time I had to cancel two shows because of physical problems...."

More seriously, cracks began to show when Caleb lost his temper at the T In The Park concert on July 10. The headliners experienced some problems with the sound – although it was reported that nobody detected this from the crowd – and the frontman did the unthinkable by smashing his Gibson 325 guitar, the instrument he had used for years and on which he had written every hit the band had released. After throwing the shattered instrument into the crowd, he stormed off stage and into a huge shouting match with his bandmates. A "source" (unnamed, naturally) told the press, "He was livid about the sound and took out his anger on stage without considering the consequences. His guitar is now ruined. The crowd were oblivious to the sound difficulties, but the Kings want every show to be perfect... When they came off stage, tempers flared and they were effing and blinding at each other. It was really nasty before their tour manager stepped in."

The significance of the destruction of Caleb's Gibson shouldn't be underestimated. It was practically a part of the singer, his sole instrument of choice for years. Purchased for him in 2002 by Angelo Petraglia on eBay for $900, the 325 had supplied Caleb's signature sound on all four Kings Of Leon albums and, as any guitarist will know, had become like a fifth limb to him after so long.

"I would never, ever dream of doing anything to that guitar," insisted Caleb regretfully afterwards. "It's moments like that where you realise you need a break… I got a bit angry after T In The Park and broke my guitar, so I have to get a new one. We have zero reasons to complain, but I do blame me breaking my guitar on being overworked."

However, the pressure didn't relent just because of one broken axe. A similar catastrophe occurred a couple of months later, this time after the Reading Festival on August 28. More sound problems led to more frustration, but this time Caleb didn't take his anger out on his guitar – he made the mistake of aiming it at the crowd. He'd started the set with some typical Kings banter ("I know I say this every night, and I don't want anyone to think I have a problem, but I want to get drunk and party") but towards the end he shouted, "I know some of you are sick and tired of the Kings Of Leon, but we've worked really fucking hard to get here!"

Unusually, Nathan – the mellowest Followill by far – added fuel to the flames by adding a disappointed tweet to his Twitter account the following morning. "Reading? What the fuck?" he wrote. "Zero love for the Kings. I know it was cold but holy shit, y'all were frozen. I can only hope Leeds is in better form." Fortunately, the Leeds leg of the festival was just that, leading Caleb to proclaim from the stage, "We're only five songs in and you've blown Reading to hell… This is the last show we have booked in England for a long, long time, so I'm gonna get my buzz on. We're gonna miss you guys – we'll see you next year. When we come back, it's gonna be bigger and even more beautiful." However, his most revealing statement at this show was, "This is for all you people who didn't come for two songs…", a transparent comment on the changed nature of the Kings' fan base.

Anyone who has been on a tour bus for more than a few days at a time, let alone the months on end that the Kings Of Leon were enduring this year, will understand the tensions that touring brings – and it's clear that the Followills, and Caleb in particular, urgently needed some time off. Even Jared, who was usually a meek character, complained at one point: "The whole thing makes me tired. I feel like it's five in the morning and really it's 6pm."

Add to this the profound boost in profile the band had enjoyed in the previous year or so, and their problems become understandable. The Kings Of Leon had already been a well-known act before 2008, but since the release of *Only By The Night* and the singles 'Sex On Fire' and 'Use Somebody' (the "two songs" Caleb had referred to snootily on stage in Leeds), their position had been enormously elevated. The world lay at the Followills' feet, sometimes inconveniently so – as we saw when Nathan complained about fans turning up uninvited at the band's remote rural farm.

Apart from the incessantly high profile of the four musicians, the men were also passing through what is usually a pretty complex time of life. In 2009 Nathan turned 30, causing Caleb to quip to one interviewer, "We're about to Menudo his ass", a reference to the Mexican boy-band whose management recruit new members when the existing singers get too old. Caleb himself was 27, Matthew 25 and Jared 23. Things were different when the Followills' age range extended from their late teens to their mid twenties, when life is simpler – but now the band were at opposite ends of their first decade as adults. For proof, take a look at how the two major motivating forces in their lives – their religion and their family members – were beginning to redefine themselves.

"For 20 years of my life, [religion] was put into my head, and there are things you hold on to," Nathan mused. "That was a totally different time of our lives, and you realise that the majority of it was fear-based. But there are morals we will always have." As for the influence of his extended family, the drummer dismissed some of them with the words, "White trash, that's basically what it is", while he clarified: "We have relatives that are pretty crazy. Got one uncle that just got out of rehab for crank a week ago. Half of them don't even realise [that we're successful], though they're coming round, now they've seen us on TV. Up until six months ago, they didn't know what the hell was goin' on."

Nathan looked back at the band's roots with a rueful wisdom that only several years at or near the top of the rock tree could bestow. Of his childhood, he sighed: "I didn't hear John Bonham until I was 23 years old. I started playing with ink pens in church until I ruined about four of my mom's dresses. Then I switched to straws. The only influences I had were nameless, faceless church drummers all over the Southern United States. We were in a different church every week, so I'd get to see a different drummer every single week – and I'd watch the drummer the whole time. It was always fun to watch them snicker when this little eight- or nine-year-old kid would walk up to the drum set and get up there and kick their ass. They'd buy me pizza after church."

"The church we went to was way too strict for anybody," Jared recalled. "United Pentecostal makes Baptists look like Sodom and Gomorrah. No drinking. Guys can't wear shorts. It was like the Amish on vacation!" Nathan added: "No smoking. The women have to wear dresses, no make-up. We heard no popular music growing up, it was a big taboo. Have you ever seen the movie *Footloose* with Kevin Bacon? That was the kind of lifestyle we had, where rock'n'roll was the devil's soundtrack. Our brains were such sponges that had never been touched. It's impossible for us not to get influenced by music we have never heard before; it's just we were exposed to them so much later in our lives."

As for the Followills' entry into the sinful world of rock'n'roll, Caleb knew full well how the band's religious background had benefitted them from a purely cynical marketing point of view. Commenting, "It's kinda awkward. They stick you in a conference room with a bunch of people in suits saying, 'Give me a reason to give you a record deal'," he added: "But they were so mesmerised by our story and our lives, that we just talked to them about real stuff, and they were shitting their pants. They couldn't believe this had been thrown into their laps… It didn't occur to us until we were older and had stepped out of that lifestyle. Looking back on it, I can see how people misconstrue it and think it's something else. But that's the way we were raised – that shaped us into who we are, and that's great. I wouldn't trade it for anything. We were either 'Southern boys' or the 'Southern Strokes', or 'Southern rock's great revivalists'. At first it got on our nerves. We gave memorised speeches as soon as they went into the Southern thing. It really doesn't bother us that much any more."

Despite the marketing suits' eagerness to exploit the Kings' back story, the record company turned out to be useful allies, Nathan recalled. "Before you know it, we had a record deal and they were ready to put our band together for us. We were like, 'We wanna buy our 15-year-old brother a bass. He's never played before, but he's gonna do it'. And they laughed. Then we said we were gonna get our cousin, who's 16. 'He's gonna get a guitar, move in with us, and he's gonna play guitar.' And they laughed again and said, 'OK. We'll see you guys in a month'. And then they came down a month later and we rocked their asses off in our garage. And they have never given us any shit, man. They're like, 'Good work'."

While the band's preacher-boy background had indeed been a PR exec's dream, Nathan didn't feel that it had worked to the Kings' detriment – even though it had caused the Followills to be painted in a slightly surreal light at times. "It's one of those things where we don't mind that you have to live with something for a little while before you truly get it. That's the way we are," he concurred. "At first look, with the first record especially, you see these hairy boys with huge hair and tight pants. That's what everyone expected on the second record – for us to be a little ballsy and come out and really show our Southern heritage and take command of our Southern rock scene, or whatever the fuck they call it. But, no, instead we did the opposite. We're brutally honest… and talk about shit that most bands are too scared to ever admit: that they had a bout with impotence with a supermodel or that they are going bald. Most bands want to write about sweethearts."

He also recalled the Followills' years of debauchery, saying: "One thing we've kept and been able to keep was moderation. We're not gonna be stupid. I mean obviously there is a bunch of shit to do out there, and we've got all the time in the world to do it. We saved that for after our first record, then we went fuckin' buck-wild crazy. I can't share any of that. 'Buck wild' means not being able to talk about it with a tape recorder on…"

Not that the fun had stopped, by any means. Caleb said of *Only By The Night*: "On the last album, a lot of the songs were about my dick. This new record, not so much… Come to think of it, my dick's all over this record, too. No doubt it is." He too had gained a clear perspective on the Kings Of Leon's place in the rock pantheon, warning: "You can think you're a rock star, until you get on U2's plane and see how much bigger their security guards are than your security guards. It was an ego check. We put a lot of pressure on ourselves – it's how we're wired. And to have Bono or Eddie Vedder find something worthwhile about our music only adds to the pressure. To have people like that looking over our shoulders to see if we're going to do something with this band is nerve-racking." Looking back at the drug years, he admitted: "Shit got out of hand there for a while. I think we caught ourselves in time, though. And I came home and looked at some of my friends on drugs. They were ugly. They looked funny. I don't know how I got laid, sweaty and chewing on shit."

By now the band's profile in the US was rising rapidly: at the time of writing, it looks as if they'll be selling out O2 Arena-sized venues Stateside with their sixth and perhaps even their fifth album. "It seems to work itself out," agreed Jared. "It's like we cover all spectrums. We go to the UK and it's this huge thing, we go to America and it's just kinda big, we go to places like Australia and Japan and it's kind of in-between, so it evens itself out… It's weird because we'll play B-sides from singles and stuff like that over here and people will be like, 'Man, I love your new song,' and we'll be like, 'Yeah, we recorded that a long time ago'."

"I think our story was worth a lot more over there [in the UK]," Nathan added. "In the UK, there's always been a fascination with the South. To someone from New York or Arizona or California, three brothers and a cousin, all from a very religious background, making music, that's not as enticing as it is to someone over there. And luckily for us, the story kept their attention long enough for our music to creep in and take over the story… People connected to the idea of country kids playing two-minute rock songs who didn't know shit about shit going on in the world. We worked hard, but I think without 'the story' we would have had to work a lot harder." Like the others, Caleb was amazed at the band's level of success after a mere five years in business, saying: "I don't think we ever expected, and we still don't expect, to be playing Madison Square Garden every time we play New York. We just kind of wanted to spend more time in America, and it's hard when your success is bigger in Europe. You spend more time there, and for us, I think we're just a little homesick. The more that people know about us here, the more our demand will be."

Of the Kings' recent rise to prominence, he added: "It's always seemed weird to us that you'd put together a band and sign to an indie label and [not] want to be popular, just play clubs forever. Anybody who plays music and takes it seriously wants to move to the next level. Yeah, I guess I don't mind admitting that it's a good feeling when more and more people like you, and you get bigger and bigger."

Matthew, too, had gained a sense of the big picture, observing: "When we first started, we were just kind of nervous, sort of punks, scared of other bands. We tried to be as raw as we could, as rockin' as we knew how. Over time we got more comfortable finding own sound, our own thing musically. We were so young. I was 17. Jared was 15. You could argue there's a big difference [now], and not only in the songs… When we started, it was a matter of what we were able to play. After a while, it became, 'I want to play that', so we figured out how. I don't know if you ever knew a preacher's kid, but they're always the super-rebellious ones. We really started rebelling, if you wanna call it that, at 14. And we've always kind of liked it. To say 'fuck' in a song, we thought it was cool."

But no longer: there was now much more at stake than simple youthful rebellion. The Kings were playing the long game, it appeared. Caleb confided: "We look at it in a smart way. We know our time could be short, or we could keep going on. You've got to strike while the iron's hot," and Nathan admitted: "We're the biggest little secret about. We may be playing to 100,000 people at Glastonbury, but because we haven't had a huge hit or anything, people still think of us as the cool band they discovered. There's a drastic difference now when we play in the States than there was on the first two records. We'd come home from playing to 80,000 kids in Glastonbury and arrive back at the airport where our mom was the only person that knew us. People used to laugh at us with our tight pants and moustaches, but it's got to the point now where we're playing some big, big venues we'd never dreamed of playing at – let alone headlining."

"We've got to a point where we can play for 3,000 to 5,000 kids in any city in the world," he went on. "Japan, South America, Australia, anywhere, you name it, we can fill the venue. I don't think we'll be touring as much in the future, though. If any band toured as much as we have for another 10 years, then someone is going to get killed or go crazy! We'll be doing this for a long time, though, and we always want to be creating good music for our fans as long as we are able and hopefully one day Dylan and U2 will be opening up for us."

Caleb added: "It's just a strange thing for us, because we've had success in the past, but a great majority of it hasn't been in America. And when it starts to happen in America, you turn into a wild person again. 'Oh, let's party!'... we can consume more alcohol than any other popular band that actually works. As soon as we say 'thank you' and 'good night', that means it's time for us to have fun. We're sober in the mornings. Most mornings..."

Amid all this retrospection came the news that the Kings Of Leon had taken a step up to another level by designing their own clothing range. Always fans of high-level designer wear, the Followills had teamed up with a French fashion house called Surface To Air to create a line that would include initially leather jackets and checked shirts. This is hardly the average career move for the common-or-garden guitar band, signature clothing lines usually being the province of the well-to-do hip-hop performer, but then again the Kings were in a different league by 2009. Sales of their four albums had topped 28 million units – a mighty feat in the era of filesharing and CD-burning – and the expectation from critics and fans alike was that their profile should continue to climb, accidents and unforeseen developments aside. "I heard people saying that after you headline Glastonbury your career takes off," noted Caleb. "I'm sure it's happened to bands before, but I don't think it's gonna happen to us. Literally since that festival, though, it's been a fucking whirlwind."

A new level had been reached with the summer 2009 dates at the O2 Arena, he accurately noted. "[They're] one of those things where we have the biggest smiles on our faces," he explained. "We agreed with everyone that we didn't deserve to headline Glastonbury last year. When we got the call, we asked them which stage they wanted us to play! We still consider ourselves to be growing as a band. But when we come back this summer it's going to be great. Last time we played the O2, I had a massive smile on my face and ever since then I've had a grin. So next time we come back, we're just going to bring even more to it and hopefully we'll have something special. Something that people have never heard."

The Kings' set at Glastonbury the previous year had been prefaced by the release of a new album, and the band were prepared to put in similar preparation for the London shows. This time, the Followills would be playing around with their usual set list for maximum value and commemorating it with the DVD. "Now we're at a level where we're playing these big places," pondered Caleb, "we have the opportunity to play multiple nights. When you're doing that, obviously you have to switch it up a little. We've been trying stuff that we haven't played in a while and pouring old songs out. It's amazing – like riding a bike, you know? We have old songs we've been so scared to play, because I knew we would fall on our faces when we attempted them, but it just comes right back to you… as long as they don't try to cut us off, I think we'll probably try to play one of the longest sets that we've ever played."

Faced with the pressure of delivering the goods to tens of thousands of people, the Kings Of Leon were now operating with a level of professionalism that almost, but not quite, forbade the on-the-road debauchery for which their previous tours had been renowned. Caleb remarked, "We hit a wall… and it got to the point where we forgot what we wanted to achieve with this band. We were wanting to quit the music so we could enjoy the drugs more. Well, we weren't rich enough to do that," and Nathan added, "We've got a lot to answer for. Because of bands like ours, you can pick up a magazine and read about a musician fucking up and no-one is talking about the music: it seems to be OK for folks to have drugs careers." However, Jared confided: "Don't believe what you hear. The other three are still fuckin' crazy. I'm still so fucking hungover from playing [the show] last night but every single one of those guys got up this morning and started drinking. Look at them now, they're drunk. It's been a four-year hair of the dog for these guys. In fact, they're slowly turning into dogs."

Still, the essential work ethic of the band was there, reinforced by the scale of the opportunities that had been offered to them this year. "We've figured out the formula," said Nathan. "The harder you work, the more successful you get. The more you party, the shittier you feel and the less you wanna work hard. We still enjoy drinking, but we realise that the harder we work while we're young, the more we can party when middle age hits and the band is over." Caleb revealed that a change of habit had done the band good, saying: "When I quit drinking whiskey, I'd say 80 per cent of my anger went away. I still drink wine, though. This life would be much tougher if I didn't drink."

"It's not all sex, drugs and rock'n'roll any more. It's like, sex, work, drugs, a little more work… and then rock'n'roll," quipped Nathan, adding: "When you make a record, you know that the next 24 months are going to be taken up by recording, then promotion, then the record comes out, you gotta do a tour to support the record, you then set out on another tour to hit all the markets you didn't hit on that first tour, then you've got to do another tour of the major markets because your last show sold out."

It was just as well, given the mighty scale of the upcoming shows, that the new *Only By The Night* songs had that essential stadium quality. Without songs like 'Use Somebody' and 'Sex On Fire', the Kings might not have been able to fill the giant O2 Arena. As Jared put it: "People think that being big-sounding isn't 'cool' and you're somehow getting away from what you once were. But all the biggest bands in the world, from The Beatles to Led Zeppelin, sounded fucking huge. We don't want to sound 'vintage' any more, we don't want to be a novelty band… We always try to make the best-sounding and biggest-sounding record we can. The sound that we have now is what we've always wanted to sound like, it was just that on those first two records we weren't good enough to pull it off."

Caleb added: "I've always felt that we had the potential to have big songs before, but the fact was that I was always self-conscious and didn't want to make it known what I was saying. In a way I was holding the band back. And these songs were so big that I didn't want to be the reason that they didn't go anywhere. I've always been able to sing. On those first records, I just didn't have confidence in the lyrics or the songs."

By now, the frontman had learned how to interact with crowds big and small, and also that it was impossible to judge an audience member simply by their appearance. "One time we had two skinheads in the crowd," he recalled, "[with] tattoos covering them, they were full-on, hardcore – and they were jumping around, singing every song. I felt for sure they were taking the piss, but I found out they weren't. Our security guard kinda looked at them and told them to settle down, because they were pretty aggressive with all the people in the pit. And the guy went off: 'Man, you see me with my tattoos and my bald head, and you're gonna watch me all night and make sure I'm not doing things'. And really he was absolutely having a good time. I see a 60-year-old couple out there dancing, you meet little kids, and you see grown men singing 'Sex On Fire' – it's crazy, I don't get it, but it's cool."

Now that they were on top of the rock world, the Kings found that sections of the press who had supported them beforehand were withdrawing some of their support. To the band's credit, this didn't seem to bother them unduly: as Matt said, "It's weird how they like you and then they hate you. I've never disliked a band just because they got popular. I listened to The Killers for what seemed like forever, before they were even heard of, but I didn't really change my opinion of that first record just because they had a hit single." Caleb added. "I go through phases when I read [what's written about us]. For us, in Nashville, most people don't recognise us and the people that do, don't like us. So you walk around and you get that kind of attitude all the time. Every now and again you have to boost your ego, so I'll go home and read some stuff. Most of it's bullshit. It sounds cool but it's not real… Bob Dylan was very positive about us in the media and so was Bruce Springsteen. Looking back, it's good that we took four albums to get where we are. Bands like R.E.M. and Pixies also had to take that road. Success is a wonderful thing, but it moves me far more when my idols and the people I respect say positive things about me."

Still, the act of playing for so many people in summer 2009 obviously unnerved the Followills slightly. "We're playing for 28,000 [people] in three nights in London," marvelled Nathan. "We couldn't do that anywhere in America, I don't think. We're to the point now where we can play for a couple of thousand kids in any city in the world, not just America, but in the world. And that's all any band could ever ask for, to sell enough records to keep making records, and to sell enough tickets to make enough money to keep touring."

For those who didn't make it to the London shows, the *Live At The O2 London, England* DVD – released in November – reveals that the Kings delivered an effortless set of 22 songs to a baying crowd, from 'Notion' via the obvious big hits through to a triumphant 'Black Thumbnail'. To their credit, the band dug deep into their catalogue for songs that didn't often get an airing: a refreshing change for the musicians as well as the audience. "My favourite [songs] are usually not necessarily the ones that come from me," said Jared, who delivered the bass parts at the O2 in deep concentration, barely cracking a smile. "I feel connected to the ones that came from an idea I came up with, but there are a few that I like, like 'Crawl' [and] 'Manhattan'. I like a lot of the songs that aren't big songs, like '17'. The songs that people aren't necessarily fans of tend to be my favourites."

Events such the O2 tour series led to renewed creativity, the band revealed. "We stopped soundchecking for two or three tours because we just really didn't need to," explained Jared, "[but] that's where we wrote most of the stuff. We just started soundchecking again, and we've been coming up with new songs every day now… Everything sounds completely different from when we first start writing it to where the song ends up, because you overthink things. That's why we like to record things quickly and early into the process: songs tend to get a little too polished when you overthink them, and we like the ideas to be more raw and off-the-cuff."

As 2009 passed, it seemed that nothing could go wrong for the Followills, with the huge arena shows executed without a hitch, a DVD en route that seemed bound to be a hit and new songs on the way. However, in an interview with the *Daily Star* it was revealed that all was not well behind the scenes.

The problem centred, of all things, on money – and specifically how it was divided between the band members. In a quote that (in hindsight) should probably not have been uttered within hearing of a tabloid journalist, Jared fumed: "We started seriously writing the [new] songs when we got back home from tour. I got a call from Caleb going, 'I'm sitting here writing the next album by myself'. And we're like, 'Oh no, you're not!' We ended up going to his house so that when the record comes out he can't go, 'Dude, I'm getting 70 per cent of this shit'." Matthew was quoted as saying, "We basically go [over] to his house for the royalties," while Jared added: "Everything that I thought was charming about us, he [Caleb] wanted us to lie about." Most damningly, the bassist said: "In every song there's something I wish I could change. If I wasn't involved, I can't imagine liking us a lot, just because I only control 25 per cent of it."

While this raises serious questions about the nature of the musicians' personal and business relationships as well as the nature of the Kings' forthcoming fifth album, the royalties argument didn't seem to get in the way of one Followill's personal life at least. On November 14 Nathan married Jessie Baylin in a wedding that was refreshingly free of the tackiness that characterises so many rock-star nuptials. The event took place in Brentwood, Tennessee with a posse of celebs in attendance, actress and Baylin's schoolfriend Scarlett Johansson among them, frothed the gutter press. The morning after the wedding, Nathan tweeted, "I woke up with a married woman in my bed this morning. Luckily she was mine."

Nathan wasn't the only Followill doing some romancing. Caleb and model Lily Aldridge were a permanent fixture and Matthew had hooked up with singer Johanna Bennett. Meanwhile, in November Jared (who had been engaged to a model, Alisa Torres) was photographed in New York with *Twilight* actress Ashley Greene, causing the tabloids to go into a frenzy of speculation. "They were immediately attracted to each other the night they met at [the Kings'] show in Vancouver," a wisely unidentified source said.

All this had deeper implications for the Kings. At the beginning of Nathan's relationship with Jessie Baylin, Caleb – always the most vulnerable member of the band – had commented, "I didn't like the fact he had a woman, because me and him, we lived in the same house, we rode in the same vehicle, and everything we did had been together. I was very dependent on him and needed him to watch over me." With all four Followills now focusing outside the inner circle, would the band continue to be as close-knit as before?

CHAPTER 10

2010–2011

P ress duties for *Only By The Night* continued for two full years after the album's release, and by 2010 the Followills sorely needed some time off. "I'm going to sit on my couch and cry tears of joy, sitting in my pants with a tub of chocolate-chip cookie ice-cream," Nathan told Q. "Then it's onto the golf course, a bit of fishing and some camping in the wild. Cooking your own meat under the stars, that's the way to reconnect with something real after a year of immigration lines at the airport…"

It was time to let someone else do the work for a change, and the Kings had wangled this by commissioning a set of remixes of their songs for release as an album. Thanks to the band's heightened profile this year, remixers of a certain calibre were queueing up to be involved. Whether the band themselves would enjoy the retweaked versions of their songs was a matter for conjecture: perhaps Nathan put it best when he said, "It's amazing to hear your song played by these people who are so creative. It's neat to have these people, whom we would have jumped at the chance to work with ourselves, coming to us before we even get a chance to ask them" – but then adding slyly, "Most of the time it takes me two or three listens to even wrap my head around, 'Oh, man, that's our song'…"

Jared, as the youngest and most musically literate Followill, was more educated about dance music than his older brothers and was enthusiastic about the project, gushing: "I love it. I've always been into electronic-based music and I was very excited about the whole idea. It started with a few people making some remixes for us. We talked about maybe just doing a five-song EP, but then everybody else started sending in their remixes and cuts of our songs, so we just decided to make a record… We've got a lot of cool, good bands doing things for us like M83 and CSS and Lykke Li and the Presets, Justin Timberlake, Pharrell… it's really, really cool. It's a different take on the same songs that people have heard before, and it's interesting to hear our music with an electronic side to it."

The best-known musician involved in the album was, of course, Justin Timberlake – in many ways the Kings' cultural counterpart in the pop world. A fashion icon who moved in the most prestigious circles, had Timberlake made guitar music instead of lightweight pop for the masses, he might have qualified as an honorary Followill. Furthermore, it emerged that he and the Kings shared common turf. He commented: "I met Caleb Followill and the boys and we hung out. I never knew, but some of them used to live out in Middleton, Tennessee, a few miles from where I grew up playing baseball… I don't know if it will see the light of day but I did a remix for them of 'Use Somebody', which is really cool, so maybe you'll get to hear it." As of mid-2011, this album is yet to appear.

Given the Kings' remarkably prolific work rate, expectations were rising that the band would also come up with a proper studio album in due course. It was no surprise, therefore, when Caleb announced that new songs were coming together thick and fast less than a couple of years after the release of *Only By The Night*. "We've already been writing!" he declared. "We've finally earned a year off, but we're liking the buzz of this album, so we're jumping back into it. There's such an edge to what we're doing right now. Actually, right now we're writing pretty fast songs and some pretty hard rocking songs. Then there's a lot of the slower songs that are really unique from anything out there. A lot of them don't even have a chorus. It feels so good, we just keep going and going and then we just stop, you know?"

With the 2010 summer festivals taking bookings up to a year in advance, might the Followills repeat their 2008 performance and come up with a new album in order to showcase the material to the biggest crowds of all? Possibly, the singer hinted. "I don't want to get anybody's hopes up, but obviously for us it would be a thrill to be able to go up there and play something new at all of those big shows," he observed. "We're once again at that weird spot where we're literally having to lock ourselves away and not have guitars in the dressing room, just because we're writing music so much right now."

The band had made much noise in the past about how they liked to change their sound from album to album, and the first question was what the new music would sound like. Nathan dismissed any fears that the Followills might soften up just because they were hooked up in apparently serious relationships, saying: "[We won't] do the clichéd 'Go to rehab, come out, get fiancées and write a sappy love song record to show how we've found ourselves. We'd just say 'Fuck rehab!' and go write another *Youth And Young Manhood*"."

More revealingly, their sometime engineer and recent co-producer Jacquire King told the author: "It's so hard to speculate, but they might want to do something a little more like *Aha Shake Heartbreak* – in that it's rough, and fun, and edgy, but their songwriting is developing, and they have a grasp of melody, which came to the forefront on their last record – so I think it's gonna be kind of a combination. And they're also playing really big rooms now, and that influences the way they feel their music."

Jacquire said elsewhere: "Part of what happened is over the course of their four records they began with a production aesthetic that was very simple. It was straight performance-based, and it was live. By the third record the band had grown and wanted to experiment more with production. They wanted to take a little bit more time in the studio. They wanted to have an opportunity to layer on some things and do some editing of arrangements after the recording. The role of the studio was changing as well. It became more than just a place to document, it became a place to experiment."

He went on: "Most of Caleb's vocals on the first three recordings were sung as part of the basic tracks. He is an incredible singer, but one of the things we wanted to explore on [*Only By The Night*] was being able to fine-tune, and finesse, his vocals over the basic track a little bit more. Everything was going down at once, and in hindsight Caleb wished they happened a little different. To correct that on these sessions, we didn't record any vocal more than three times, and what it then came down to was what take we wanted to use."

Most revealingly, the producer said: "The growth you are seeing is the band wanting an opportunity to experiment on this record. They are becoming sonically adventurous, and I think their best work is still in them. Based on their track record for the past four albums I feel they are in a position to take a big step after this record. I have seen them grow, and I can tell you [*Only By The Night* was] tremendous. They just keep finding new things within themselves. All of that rings true. The Kings Of Leon have greater records to make."

King vehemently defends his namesakes' recent, more expansive sound: "They got a lot of flak for this record: a lot of people say they're selling out and they wanna be like pop stars, but everybody wants to be successful at what you do. No-one wants to be a failure at what their dream is. These guys did certainly not set out to change their music and have it be something that is consumable: I know people think that the music's different because *Only By The Night* was popular, but it's not. It feels and sounds, at its core, the same: 'Sex On Fire' is a classic Kings Of Leon song in its feel and its approach. I think that they will be having a little bit of a reaction to all these false accusations: they'll probably on purpose try and make things a little bit less consumable. But I think in the end it still will be the same great music."

Hints at the new music's nature came from the band on occasion. Matthew explained, "We're touring until the end of this year so we can't start until 2010, but it'll come out probably fall of 2010," and Jared added: "The next album that we make, that we're already working on, I can assure you, is one that I'm the most excited about. We haven't really got down to lyrics yet but [we have] a lot of good stuff. It's cool."

With his usual perceptiveness, Nathan knew (even though no-one had specifically framed the question yet) that fans would be asking if they could expect another 'Sex On Fire' or 'Use Somebody'. He remarked, "We're not stupid. We know that there are people out there who are only interested in hearing 'Sex On Fire'. But we're doing something different. We've got eight to 10 songs, none of them like *Only By The Night*. We'll never put a song on a record that couldn't stand up on its own as a single."

Despite all the behind-the-scenes activity, Jared was looking forward to some rest and recuperation, saying towards the end of 2009 that in a few months from that point he'd be "probably on the beach somewhere. I might go to Mexico for a little while or something. Six months from now… I don't know where we'll be. We could be writing the new record at that point, so we'll see. I don't know where we're gonna do the next one… There are a couple of ideas floating around, and we were thinking of maybe going to an island somewhere and doing it. I'd rather do it in Nashville or LA or somewhere familiar, you know?"

As the new songs evolved, more details gradually emerged. Pressed for information, Nathan revealed that the sound was "all over the place. There's stuff that sounds like Radiohead, there's stuff that sounds like Thin Lizzy, there's stuff that sounds like The Band. We're pretty much to the point now where… we can be experimental and try stuff we would've been scared to death to try on the first couple of records. Now we find ourselves being a little more adventurous."

As always, Caleb was full of excitement about the next album, stating that the band were in the best possible creative place. "We're on cloud nine," he said. "And to be able to share all this with your flesh and blood is the best thing." Interestingly, he dropped the first hint that he might one day step outside the band, saying: "We have a lot of fun, uptempo songs. We also wrote one of the prettiest country songs I've ever heard, and if it doesn't make the album, I'll use it on a solo album."

Asked about the new music, he explained that the old influences remained the same. "Great production doesn't mean a ton of extra fancy stuff," he observed. "To us, great production is like Steve Albini or Brian Eno… old Pixies records or *Nevermind* and stuff like that. That might not be what most people consider to be great production, but we wanted it to be classy and classic, with the right space and balance. The Stones, the Beatles, Pink Floyd, the Beach Boys and Zeppelin – they all wanted to make the best-sounding records possible. They wanted to have timeless albums. Now, some people are trying to dumb down their sounds, so they sound like they came out in the 70s. We kinda did our first and second records that way, but the time we came around to [our third] record, we had bigger ideas."

Most of the fans and writers who had witnessed the Followills' rise to prominence were looking forward to the next album – most of them. It should be noted that not everyone appreciates the Kings Of Leon. Snide comments along the lines of the Followills being fake hillbillies and mere clotheshorses have been directed at them since they first emerged from Nashville and bought their first designer suits. A critic in their hometown called Ian Cohen was particularly scathing, reviewing *Only By The Night* with the words "Dropping the transparently hayseed act, the band could have turned an artistic corner... What if Bono got lost in the Blue Ridge Mountains and was replaced by a local yokel? (Suggested band name: Y'All2)... these are the same clunky Kings Of Leon songs, just now presented in an incredibly weird context. It all starts with Caleb Followill's never-ending need to play to type, and if you've kept up to this point, you know the drill – though his band has toured the world several times over, dude can't see past his own dick."

It didn't stop with reviews: some writers for *The Spin*, a Nashville blog, were swiftly removed from the Followills' aftershow celebrations. They wrote afterwards: "Apparently the Kings Of Leon can't take a joke. Midway through Friday night's sold-out Sommet Center homecoming performance, before more than 15,000 fans, singer Caleb Followill addressed their Nashville detractors who 'talk shit' about and criticise them: 'If any of them are here, I just hope they know how hard we work,' he said. Could he really have meant little old us? A few hours later, as we were being forcibly removed from their after party (presumably at the band's request, or their management's) by security, who relayed the message, 'Don't think that you can write the shit that you write and then come down here and pretend like everything's cool' – it became abundantly clear just how thin Followill skin is."

Still, from most people's perspective the Kings Of Leon don't seem overly affected by negative commentary. As Jared said, "We're open to criticism, and we'll listen to it. There are some [people in the press] who obviously don't like us, which is fine. There are some indie websites who will never like us. You just take it with a grain of salt. Oscar Wilde said it best when he said, 'The critic educates the public, and the entertainer educates the critic'." Not a bad cultural reference for a kid from the country...

In a revealing interview with *Q* magazine in 2009, the brothers revealed that their relationship was as tempestuous as ever. Caleb and Nathan in particular were still prone to fighting, with Jared marvelling: "In two beers they will go from completely cool to death threats. The next day they're best friends again. I'd definitely say that their relationship is abnormal. They're the weirdest dudes in the world." Nathan recalled the time he'd injured Caleb's shoulder, with regret – even though it led, via strong pain medication, to their most successful songs – saying: "We still fought for a good five minutes after that. When I saw that he was really hurt, it immediately clicked over and I wanted to be the protective brother, even though I was the one who inflicted the injury."

Caleb said of the brothers' intense relationship: "I didn't want to fight but [Nathan] was coming at me with smoke coming out of his nostrils. There have been times where anyone else would never have talked to their brother again. We can't seem to do that, we seem to know that we need each other. I depend on Nathan and Jared and Matthew. Making music, I need people around me that love me because I'm the most negative person. They make me cooler than I really am." Nathan mis-paraphrased the Eagles when he concluded: "Being related, we're like the Hotel California. You can check in any time you want, but you can never leave."

Jared and Caleb also come to blows from time to time, with the former commenting on an occasion when the singer pulled out a chunk of the bassist's hair: "Real manly fighting skills. We wouldn't have security guards if it wasn't for Caleb. More than anything, they protect us from each other... It was like the fucking *Matrix*. The only time we fight is when Caleb's drunker than he's ever been, so it's not really him. He wakes up and doesn't remember any of it."

Booze was, in an increasingly obvious pattern, responsible for much of Caleb's worst behaviour. "If I stopped drinking I wouldn't be able to take it, the pressures that get to me," he sighed. "If I couldn't reward myself with something, I would have to walk away... I hate it, man. Whenever there's the word Rooster [the name of his drunken alter ego] involved you can wake me up and I think life is great and have zero memory of what happened."

Still, Caleb's relationship with his girlfriend Lily Aldridge helped buff off the roughest edges of his character, he said. "She gave me a lot of confidence. She pointed out a lot of stupid things that I was doing, just being a prick and having a bad hairdo at the time. Not that it's much better now. She says that I have a warped opinion of myself and I agree with that pretty much. I still every now and then think I should probably be doing something else. I always felt that I should follow in my dad's footsteps, but I know in my heart of hearts that this is something I was called to do…. Most of the time it's me saying thanks rather than getting on my knees and asking for something. I don't really want for much. I mean [I get] drunk and stuff like that, but I consider myself to be a pretty good person. Better than a lot. If there is a heaven, I hope that'd get you in."

The frank interview covered a lot of ground, including details of the Followills' business interests: Nathan explained, "Me and Caleb and Jared have a corporation. We have three or four commercial properties three towns over and a couple of rental properties." Asked about his stepfather, Tom Murphy – their business manager – he said: "He's been a businessman his whole life. He sold Elvis Presley the insurance for his pink Cadillac." Elsewhere Jared – the only Followill still apparently engaged in playing the field – said: "You can have sex every single night if you've got no standards. I always tried to get the cream of the crop, but that didn't work out sometimes when I was drunk. Matthew was the best at not having sex with just anybody."

The musicians also talked about classic man stuff – cars and guns, both of which are a feature of their homes. Matthew talked about his Corvette Z06 with enthusiasm: "It goes 200 miles an hour. I watch [the BBC car series] *Top Gear* all the time and they had my car on. [Presenter Jeremy] Clarkson said it was awesome but the ride was too rough. I'd love to be on *Top Gear*. Oh God, I would love to. I want to get in that reasonably priced car. I reckon I'd do pretty good. I'd have to have The Stig take me round first."

Jared referred to the Heckler & Koch handgun which he keeps at home with slight reluctance, saying: "The Notorious BIG used to rap about HK… It's kind of embarrassing. We thought someone broke in one night and it was a knee-jerk reaction. My mom talked me into it. It's so Tennessee of me." Of his own journey within the Kings, he explained: "When we first started I was just there for style purposes. Caleb and Nathan were doing something completely different, more country songs. I would make them mix-tapes of the Pixies, Joy Division, the White Stripes. I was the younger brother that knew all the cool stuff." When he was first introduced to cocaine, he refused to try it at first: "I was like, 'No thank you, I don't want to be a drug addict'. Somehow I got talked into it. It wasn't the most fun. Obviously it feels like maybe the best thing in the world for five or 10 minutes and then it's like, this fucking sucks. I can't go to sleep. By the time you've been doing it for a year or two it gets to the point of, I can't go to sleep and I kind of want to kill myself." Of LSD, he recalled: "An awful experience. It was in Chicago. We went to the U2 afterparty. A girl came up to me and said, 'Don't you just hate U2?' I thought she was wearing a wire and trying to incriminate me. I was like, 'No… I… love… them. Why… would… you… say… that?'"

After this many years in the public eye, the Followills were evidently aware that they had become a major target. In a revealing interview in *Spin* magazine, Caleb explained, perhaps with a slight lack of forethought: "We definitely got bigger than we wanted to be… You feel like you've done something wrong. That woman in mom jeans who'd never let me date her daughter? She likes my music. That's fucking not cool. You almost start doing damage control: when people ask you to do stuff, you're like, 'No, because I can already tell this record is going to get to a level where people will fucking hate us'."

The clear implication in Caleb's statement was that the Kings' level of success had meant that they had lost their critical credibility, and also that his fanbase was not what it had been. Jared seemed to share this sentiment, saying in the same intervew: "When our manager told us [that *Only By The Night*] had sold a million records, I was blown away. But it's also kind of bittersweet. Once you go platinum, you're automatically considered not cool… the first year I was in the band, I made $500. Now you start to feel like an asshole sometimes. You're on the plane, like, 'Dude, it's been 30 minutes – where's my sushi?'"

Caleb went on: "We used to play small clubs, go out to dive bars, drink with fans – it was a beautiful thing. Now you're backstage at a big arena with Wal-Mart lighting, and they're not letting anyone in. Our real fans, the ones who've been there for the last five years, are in the front row pissed off. They'll turn their backs on us during 'Sex On Fire' and 'Use Somebody', put their middle fingers up. I get it. We're definitely sellouts. But when you have success like we've had, you kind of have to feed the masses. As corny as it sounds."

However, Nathan was more sanguine about this issue, merely shrugging: "For every fan we lost by quote 'selling out', we've probably gained five… When we started this band, our goal was to sell 10,000 records and put on one concert a year for 10,000 people. We did that 179 times on this tour." Perhaps the band's unexpected success had telegraphed itself more clearly to him than to the others, helped along by a timely phone call from Pearl Jam frontman Eddie Vedder. As Caleb recalled, "[Eddie] said, 'You're about to ride a big wave'. I don't even think he liked the record. But he knew immediately we were about to go through something big."

'Big' was an understatement. 2009 had been a year like no other for the Kings. Walked through the events of the previous 12 months by the *Spin* interviewer, the Followills recalled the highlights of their fourth album's tour and press cycle. In January, evidence that the Kings' old partying ways hadn't quite deserted them came on Caleb's birthday when he combined booze and prescription sedatives for a high that caused him understandable anxiety. As he recalled, with a degree of candidness that would have other rock stars calling their lawyers on speed dial: "The night before my birthday, I really thought I was going to die. We were in LA, I was drunk, and someone handed me some devil pills – Vicodins or something. I remember lying in bed thinking, 'I'm gonna fuckin' die on my 27th birthday. I'm gonna be a rock cliché'. When I woke up the next morning, I looked at my girlfriend, and my first words were, 'I'm alive'…"

Later the same month, the Kings Of Leon had played a sold-out show at New York's prestigious Madison Square Garden – a venue which carried enough associations of greatness to fill even the most road-hardened musician with awe. "I don't get nervous hardly ever, but I was pretty nervous," recalled Matthew, adding: "The biggest and best play there." Caleb laughed: "When our manager first told us we were playing the Garden, I was like, 'Shut the fuck up!' When we got the tour schedule and it said Madison Square Garden, I was like, 'You actually booked it? Are you fuckin' crazy?'... I don't even remember how we played. I just remember after we hit that last note, I couldn't have a cold beer fast enough."

The small matter of the Grammys followed – another prominent milestone in the Kings' ascendance. "I can't lie," said Caleb. "I used to think the Grammys were a mockery of music. They made it this big, pop ball of bullshit. But I ate my words that night. You should have seen us before the show. We were like, 'We're up for not one, but multiple Grammys! That's fuckin' amazing!' We met some cool people. I remember [*The Nanny* actress] Fran Drescher was sitting right in front of us, and when we didn't win [the Rock Album of the Year award] she turned around and [made a sympathetic face]. We were like, 'The Nanny is disappointed for us!' As soon as we lost that one, though, we left. 'Cause you couldn't drink in there."

A full summer of festival slots, many of which were headliners, had stamped the Kings' presence on three continents. The London O2 shows had attracted high-level attention (Matt: "One of the princes of England came to the show – Harry. He was cool. We had a beer, played ping-pong. Maybe we'll be sirs someday...") and Stateside shows such as Austin City Limits had reassured the Followills that America was ready to embrace them at last. "If a band got to do just one of those [festivals]," said Nathan, "it would pretty much be the highlight of their year. *The Today Show* was awesome 'cause they said I was the first person ever to drink a beer on the air at 6:15 am. And Lollapalooza and Austin City Limits were phenomenal because that was kind of our American homecoming. The night before Austin City Limits was the drunkest I got all year – thanks to one Edward Vedder."

The sole bug in the Followill program – their unenthusiastically-received set at the Reading festival – was still a mystery. The festival organiser, Melvin Benn, was at a loss to explain it in an interview with the *NME*. "The performance was flawless," he said, "but the connectivity between the band and audience wasn't as good as it could have been.

The connectivity with the audience in Leeds was incredible… It's an incredibly strange one. They can't put their finger on it, we can't put our finger on it. Watching Kings Of Leon isn't hit or miss. It isn't likely that the band take the stage and you have no idea whether it's going to be the best performance in the world or the worst performance in the world. The truth is, musically, it was flawless."

Still, there were other things on the Followills' minds. Jared had been seen canoodling with yet another female celeb, this time country singer Julianne Hough. A source burbled to *People* magazine: "They were very affectionate, just hanging out at the table. They stayed for about an hour and enjoyed karaoke. None of them sang, but they just hung with their group. Only a few people noticed she was even there. They didn't make a spectacle of it."

Business was booming, too. Alongside their recently-launched clothing line, the Kings had lent their name to a record label. The Followills assumed the role of occasional A&R execs with a music publisher, Bug Music, and were on the lookout for new talent. The label's first signing was another Tennessee band, the Features, with whom the Kings had toured two years previously. In a stellar display of fawning, Bug Music CEO John Rudolph was quoted as saying: "Caleb, Jared, Matthew and Nathan are extraordinary tastemakers and constantly absorbing new sounds from all over the world. The honesty in their music is what draws them to genuine artists."

Clothing, a record label, relationships and marriage – it was a time of flux for the Kings, making their forthcoming vacation doubly welcome. Asked about the split of Oasis, who had announced what appeared to be a permanent schism in the summer of 2009, Nathan referenced his own band and the brotherly tensions that occasionally got out of hand. "I'm not sure what happened with those guys," he said. "All brothers fight, they just forgot to do the making-up bit. But then again, they seemed to be having the same family row for like, 10 or 15 years, so maybe it was time… But we have a special strength, because we had an upbringing where we didn't have outsiders in the social circle for the longest time. That makes a big difference. We bug the hell out of each other day to day, but the relationship is so deep it can be like we share a brain between us. We might kill each other, but I don't think we'd split."

So what might split the musicians up? Several interviews with the Followills had portrayed their existence in the more luxurious suburbs of Nashville as deeply intertwined with each other, with their mother and stepfather (the aforementioned Tom Murphy, who oversees their property portfolio) close at hand and the rest of the family never too far way. Surely only something deadly serious could come so far between the Kings as to force them to part ways forever?

Well, on occasions life hasn't been easy for the Followills. In their time as a band, the Kings had endured their fair share of conflict and ill-luck. As far back as 2004, Nathan had been stricken by a serious ailment that left him doubting whether he could perform. Caleb said at the time: "He's doing OK. It's a real bad kidney infection that he's had for the past week... he's been in real pain. But the minute he walked on stage, he felt a lot better. The adrenaline of the show got him through it. Our guitar tech has been on standby in case Nathan's too ill to finish the tour. Hopefully Nathan will be well enough to finish these British dates." He made it through, of course.

The band had also battled isolation. Caleb once explained, "You were in your hotel room all by yourself all day. You wake up and it's already dark out and you're so lonely. So at night, you go out with girls." That doesn't sound too galling, but then again the shallow rock-star life seemed only to indicate to Caleb just how far the band had to go to be taken seriously. He went on: "At the end of the day, you want to be doing something that will, hopefully, be remembered. You want that to be on the cover of the magazines, and the other stuff to be the blurb. As opposed to that on the magazine cover and the music as a blurb."

What was left to achieve, as 2009 became 2010, was that ethereal goal – critical as well as commercial success in a world of mediocre achievers. Jared stepped up to the plate when he said, with uncharacteristic bluntness, "We consider ourselves to be better than a lot of those bands that are big now, like Panic! At The Disco or Fall Out Boy. We would love to kick their asses out of there." However, it seems that total contentment won't be the Followills' due reward: they're too open about their insecurities for that. "I always felt that people would look at me as a guy who dropped out of high school, and point out everything I said that wasn't proper," said Caleb. "I was writing these melodies that I felt were so deserving to be heard, [and so] I just said, 'Sing the way you know how to sing. Just try it for one record, and, if it doesn't work, you can go back to your shelter'."

He went on: "It's an inner thing. I know this sounds a little dorky, but the Bible says, 'Pride comes before the fall'. It's one thing to be proud of the people you love, but to have a pride that comes off as arrogance, it's two different things. It's almost this thin line, but it's a tall thin line. It's a bit of a hurdle from pride to confidence. We have confidence, but none of us are cocky, or we try not to be. When you're on the road for two years and everyone's kissing your ass, after a while – if you don't watch yourself – you start to believe it. I think that's what's good about our success that we had in the UK and Europe first. Because we had to rise and become those people that we hate, then we came home and we're nothing, so we wrote a record about the people we hated that we're becoming. I think that's why we're humble. We're down to earth. We realise we're human and that we all fuck up, and no one's perfect."

Asked by *Risen* magazine if he'd ever experienced depression, Caleb replied: "We have our moments; we had a lot more in the beginning with always being away from home. Being in England where the sun never shines, that alone can get you really down. Like I said, I think we're getting better at what we do and I'm not talking about us playing, but better in the way we're taking it, taking all this shit in our stride. If it gets too bad we'll fly our mom into town. Honestly, we were in England and it had been raining well over a week. It was so gloomy and we were all in our rooms almost crying. We were feeling a depression we had never felt before. When our mom came to see us, there was the most beautiful sunshine for three days, and as soon as she left it went back to grey. Those kinds of things inspire us. That's what made us write [*Only By The Night*]. On our first album we were talking about the places we wish we could go and the girls we wish we had. Then we came home and wrote songs about people and not about celebrities. It's what really goes on. This album was all about emotions, even though it comes off as melancholy at times. But this is the shit that you go through."

Nathan had also given these matters some serious thought, it appeared. He explained: "Pride would be you have to tell yourself how good you are. Confidence is brought on by other people telling you how good you are… Everyone talks about being streetwise, but your idea of streetwise is way different than what streetwise really is. You come to find out that streetwise is understanding that the closest people around you, working with you, have an agenda. Everyone's got an agenda, everyone's got a purpose they've gotta fill. Everyone's gotta go up the ladder, it comes with the territory. I guess you gotta deal with it… When we come off the road, I would say we're all kind of down."

All this led to some confusion within the ranks, as is to be expected from a band which moves in as chaotic an environment as the Kings Of Leon. Witness two conflicting statements from Matthew, for example, in which he expresses both a liking and a revulsion for travel. Once he said, "I hope America wises up and starts to like us… I mean, it's fine in America. We play to 1500 kids, you know, and that's pretty good. It'll feel weird to come back and play for such a little crowd, and a crowd that might not care as much as a big crowd here, but as far as leaving here, I'm ready to get back to America, man." He also said: "[In the USA, rock is] not as big over here; they just don't really like good music over here at all. Over there they listen to decent stuff, but over here it's just really bad shit. Do I think we'll break through? I don't know – I mean, I hope so, that'd be great – but I don't think we really will, though… Everything is hip-hop over here and I hate it so much; I hate even being here, I wish I could move back to Europe or something."

Perhaps this is to be expected in a musician whose most devoted fanbase is thousands of miles from home. But there's a deeper thread of uncertainty inside all the Followills, it seems: one that they admit to on a regular basis. This stems from their itinerant childhood – a period in which stability was scarce. Caleb explained: "I think for us, the way we grew up, we've always been more accustomed to saying goodbye than hello, because we were always going somewhere else. It makes you a good person. In a way it makes you be able to communicate with people, but you don't put too much trust in relationships except the love that we have for one another. Not only as a family but as a band, we go through all the shit together.

He went on, with wince-making candour: "I would hate to ever be the band that thinks that they're the voice of their generation, but I do think that we are *part* of the voice of our generation. All these bands that had this great education, but didn't know what they wanted growing up. Being a band that's completely opposite of that, we're coming from a different place than most people. Where someone can take their education and make artsy music, we're gonna take what we know and make completely honest music. We know all these magazines are gonna say whatever they want to fucking say to sell their magazines, and they'll talk us up like were some model-fucking cocaine-using blah blah blah, this and that. But after this was all said and done, we came home and we were like 'If everyone wants to get so fucking personal, let's get more personal than they could ever imagine'. There's not many people writing songs about not being able to get it up. The funny thing is, if the people knew these women we couldn't get it up for, they would shit themselves."

This put an earlier comment by Matthew into context. Told that the UK press were depicting his band as sex gods, he laughed: "Sex gods? That's awesome! They're saying we're sex gods and hotties? That's weird… I mean, we do get more girls there than anywhere else. I don't know… we're certainly not sex gods, though… We don't try to dress any way, it's just that we don't cut our hair, and we just buy clothes that are too small for us. We don't have an image-consultant or anything like that."

The family ties that surrounded the Kings were thrown into sharp contrast by the celebrity culture in which the band moved. After all, which other group, brothers or not, would invite their parents to their aftershow parties? As Caleb explained, "We've always been really close with our family, like our uncles and aunts. You go through a time when you all love each other and you're proud of your family, and then you go through a time when your family embarrasses you. But I think the older we get and the more fucked up we get as people by relying on things that we used to frown upon… it makes your love totally change. I love having my mom and dad at a show with celebrities like Courtney Love and Juliette Lewis. You have celebrities walking around thinking they're big-time, and within 10 minutes our parents are the biggest stars of the party. Our big, jolly dad and our country mom that plays dumb half the time. These other people don't know what it's like…"

Then again, no-one knows what it's like to be the Kings Of Leon – at the time of writing, the band which can lay claim to the title of hottest new (or at least new-ish) rock band on the planet. No matter how much their music may change, people will never forget (or forgive) their country roots – as Matt once explained. "I had this interview earlier today," he said, "and I said 'Well, what do you think of the album?', and he said, 'It's really Southern rock'. And I was like, man, that's so bad… It seems like what everybody is doing is going, we're from the South, so we're automatically Southern rock. But we've never listened to all that Southern rock. I could tell you two songs [by] Lynyrd Skynyrd and I don't even know any Allman Brothers songs… here in America, we played to, like, 13 people – and the only reason they were there was because they were drunk – but in the UK, every show we've played there, whether it's been a little or a big one, they're pretty much always sold out… I don't really like [hype], because the *NME* will always have the chance to get people disappointed. They hear, like, 'This is the best band of the year', and then they listen to it and go 'That's not the best band!' – it just gets your hopes up. We try not to pay attention to that stuff too much, we don't want it to get to us."

It seems that as brothers the band have something most musicians don't have. Nathan insisted, "Oh, the whole family thing, it's definitely easier. Because when you're playing around on a new song or something, you don't have to be ashamed to do something that might sound bad; you don't really care… I've never been in a band with people that I didn't know, so I guess it would be harder. We get along, I don't think we really ever fight… we just do whatever. I mean, I hope we do good and people like us – in Europe it's going pretty good – but if we don't, we'll just quit and start a little church band."

This idea might not be too implausible, given Caleb's love of church music. Asked to name the songs which had been most influential to him as a kid, he said: "I would have to say gospel. It was a gospel song named 'On The Wings Of A Snow White Dove', sung by my uncle Buddy. Badass – it's a song I want to cover. The other song besides that was 'Crimson And Clover' by Tommy James & The Shondells. It blew my mind. My uncle went out and bought it the next day. The song freaked me out. I had never heard production before. Growing up with the broke-down church beats and clangy pianos that aren't even in tune, and so when I heard 'Crimson And Clover' in the back seat, I was like, 'What the fuck is that?'"

After a short period of recuperation, the Kings announced that recordings were taking place in New York City – once again with Petraglia and King – and that the new songs were taking a more relaxed, chilled-out form than their recent work. Of their decision to switch from their usual recording location of Nashville to the Big Apple, Caleb observed: "The hustle and the bustle of the city [made] us go somewhere differently, make us work harder. I just kept telling everyone, 'I'm going to go in there and try a dummy lyric', and everyone was like, 'You can't change it – what you said needs to be said'. And when I finally told what it is that I was saying, they were like, 'You can't say that, can you?' It was very raw and very natural, and it was very much the way I thought a New York artist would make a record."

The lyrics for the new album, which Caleb revealed would be titled *Come Around Sundown*, were improvised as he went along. "I didn't write lyrics," he explained. "I went in and ad-libbed, I free-floated everything. The closer it got to the end, I felt like, 'Man, you didn't do your job'… I kept thinking, 'When I go back and redo the lyrics, then I'll get it'. But when I went back in to try to do that, everyone was like, 'What are you doing? You can't change those lyrics. Those *are* the lyrics'."

Caleb being who he is, the recording of the new album was accompanied by a certain amount of angst and self-doubt. It emerged that he had been torturing himself with fears that the band had peaked, and that the stress of life on the road had got to him, explaining his guitar-smashing breakdown at Reading the previous year. "I wanted to do some interviews and just apologise for my attitude," he said. "Everything affected me and we took it out on a lot of people… I remember that we were on the road and I'd just found out that my house had gotten broken into, and the record was really doing good, and that was my kind of Kurt Cobain moment. I was hating the success and I was scared and I thought, you know, 'People are going to think that we did this on purpose and that we made this record so we could be big'."

Fortunately Lily Aldridge was on hand to supply reassurance, Caleb added: "I played her one song, and when I did, she looked at me and went, 'What the fuck? Why haven't you played me this? What are you scared of?' Before you know it, we had listened to every song, and she just loved it. That gave me the confidence to say, 'All right, well, maybe I'm in my head too much'."

Despite these feelings, by the time of the recording of *Come Around Sundown* Caleb seemed to be in control of his worries. Whereas in previous months he'd been concerned about the ongoing price of fame ("I didn't want the world to start to hate us because every time you'd turn on the radio, you'd hear one of our songs… I just got worried that the success was going to ruin what we'd been working hard for so long"), by this stage he'd found an inner peace, at least for a brief period. "I was no longer disgruntled about [fame] and, you know, the 'troubled artist' who thought that things had gotten too big," he mused. "I was really excited about where we were as a band and excited to take it to a different place, and see how many of the people who had just discovered the band on the last record, I wanted to take them on a little bit of a journey."

In June the Kings set off on a huge American and European tour, visiting more than 50 cities to deliver the message. While there were highlights such as the Bonnaroo festival – from whose stage Caleb declared, "There are very few times in my life when I've really felt like I was really, really proud of what we've done and what we've accomplished. And this is one of those times. I just want to say thank you to everybody who's been there with us since we were on the small stage" – the tour was completely overshadowed by an incident in St. Louis on July 24 that caused widespread hilarity among the band's many detractors. While playing a set at the city's Verizon Amphitheater, pigeon droppings began to rain onto the stage from the venue's rafters. Jared was the primary target, taking several hits on his face and clothing – and after three songs the band walked off-stage.

Reports immediately circulated worldwide of this humiliating event, and amusement levels among the band's critics spiralled. Where the Kings and their management erred was in responding to the incident over-seriously: had they issued an amused or otherwise relaxed statement about Pigeongate (as it was instantly dubbed) the fuss would have died down quickly. Instead, a representative from Vector Management stated, "Jared was hit several times during the first two songs. It's not only disgusting – it's a toxic health hazard. They really tried to hang in there." The bassist himself added, "I was hit by pigeons on each of the first three songs. We had 20 songs on the set list. By the end of the show, I would have been covered from head to toe... The last thing I was going to do was look up... but if that was only a couple [of birds], we must have caught them right after a big Thanksgiving dinner."

The opening bands The Postelles and The Stills had stayed the course, playing their allotted sets despite the storm of missiles. "We couldn't believe what [they] looked like after their sets," said Jared. "We didn't want to cancel the show, so we went for it. We tried to play. It was ridiculous." A serious sense-of-humour failure had occurred, it seems...

Fortunately, the incident was more or less forgotten by the time the lead single from *Come Around Sundown*, titled 'Radioactive', appeared on September 8. A departure from the Kings' usual style, the song was based on an almost Afrobeat chorus and rhythm and was a little hard to fathom on first spin. The rest of the album, which appeared on October 15, was both easier to assimilate and more recognisably derived from the band's previous work, notably the opening song 'The End', a stretched-out anthem with plenty of space for Jared's insistent, high-in-the-mix bass. Although no-one would be likely to accuse the band of more U2 plagiarism based on this song – and certainly not 'Radioactive', which followed it – there was a definite widescreen feel, with layers of reverbed guitar that gave it stadium-sized dimensions.

In 'Pyro', an excellent, somnolent song with acres of open space and an unhurried feel, Caleb sings the wistful line "Everything I cherish is slowly dying or it's gone" – a sentiment which caused several interviewers to ask if he'd become nostalgic as his thirties approached. "I might have been a little dramatic with that line," he admitted. "But sometimes I do reminisce about the days when we were on a bus. We'd play a gig, and then we'd go outside and drink in the parking lot with all our fans and just hang out. You feel different when you're in a big cold arena, and you walk offstage and fly to the next gig."

'Mary' is a full-production tune with overdriven guitars, a stamping beat and obvious pretensions towards the bigger stage. Caleb's vocals owe much to fifties rock'n'roll (listen to the chorus of 'Ah-ha-haaa' if you're sceptical) and Matthew's solos are similarly retro in feel. 'The Face' is the first example of the mellow, beach feel that the band had mentioned in the run-up to the album release, with a gentle organ figure filling the background between the bones of the song – which, like 'Pyro', were largely Caleb's emotive vocal and Jared's ever-present bass.

'The Immortals' is based on a mids-heavy Paul Simenon-style bass-line, around which Matthew and Caleb weave subtle guitar lines in the chorus and which then expands into a full, 'Sex On Fire'-alike chorus. Laden with religious images, the lyrics are – according to Caleb – "the way that I want to talk to my [future] children". He added that the song's opening line ("The open road, the path of greatness, is at your fingers / Go be the one that keeps on fighting, go be the stranger") speaks "definitely to myself".

A touch of downhome whimsy follows on the ethereal 'Back Down South' and 'Beach Side', two relaxed songs custom-made for summertime FM radio, while 'No Money' was, at least, the big 'Use Somebody'-type song that many of the Kings' fanbase had hoped for and which some had hoped would never reappear on a Kings Of Leon album. 'Pony Up' was yet another bass-driven song, and led some observers to muse that Jared was rapidly becoming the most prominent member of the band (and not just from a pigeon's point of view).

The album closes with a trio of disparate songs, 'Birthday', a rocker with a curiously busy feel; 'Mi Amigo', a ballad of surprising sweetness; and 'Pickup Truck', which builds slowly with peaks and troughs for a thoughtful conclusion to the record. The slick sound of the album drew much attention among reviewers, for good reason: while *Come Around Sundown* is hardly overproduced, it possesses a buffed-up polish that was lacking on the previous Kings albums. "We definitely don't sound as raw as we did early on," said Caleb. "But that's just because it's hard to teach yourself to be a bad guitar player again. [In the old days] we were playing as good as we could, and now our good is a little better than that."

The new album, Caleb explained to the *New York Times*, got its bigger sound from the band's expanded skills and ambition. "Something about the way that all of us come together, and the music that we've made here, at least in the last couple of years, it doesn't matter what we try to do," he said. "At the end of the day it has a bigger, richer quality to it than stuff that we used to do. I think for us to not write the songs that were on our minds and in our hearts, it would be a fraud. We don't want to go in there and do something that isn't real and something that doesn't really move us."

The fear that Caleb had felt before the album was recorded had receded, he said, when he realised that he had no reason to be apprehensive. "I would go home at night, and I would think, 'This music that we're making, is anyone going to be interested in it?'" he pondered "And I was scared at times because [it] sounded kind of big, and I didn't want it to have the big epic sound that people would expect from us. And the thing is, we were not at all trying to do that… Eventually I had a long look in the mirror and thought, 'What are you scared of?' When we first started making music, if you'd told me that we would have had a record that sold as many as [*Only By The Night*] did, I would have said, 'Absolutely, that's what we're here making music for'. Now, when we're playing concerts, I enjoy myself. Even if it's just people singing 'Use Somebody' or "Sex on Fire', I'm very appreciative of the fact that they're there."

Come Around Sundown performed as expected, debuting at the top of the album charts in many countries and doing especially well in the ever-loyal UK, where we merrie Englanders bought no fewer than 183,000 physical copies of it and almost 50,000 downloads in its first week on sale. Ultimately the album sold just under 700,000 copies in this country, a remarkable achievement in the YouTube and Spotify era.

As has been the vogue for some years since the rise of digital filming and laptop editing, a movie was made of the Followills in 2010 and shown in April the following year. Directed by Stephen C. Mitchell and titled *Talihina Sky* after the Kings Of Leon song of the same name, the film took the viewer into the band's private lives to an extent and was welcomed by fans, although it failed to make a serious impact outside a few American film festivals. No matter: in 2011 the band were focused on hitting the live circuit once again, outdoing their 02 Arena shows of 2010 with a set at Ireland's Slane Castle in front of 85,000 fans. Proof of their enormous popularity on this side of the Atlantic came when the Slane show sold out completely in less than half an hour.

The huge response to the band and their new album by audiences such as the Slane crowd gave the Followills cause to consider their rise, which has genuinely been meteoric – even given that phrase's clichéd qualities. "Everyone talks about indie this and indie that, but would you really want to be one of those indie bands that makes two albums and disappears? That's just sad," Caleb told *Rolling Stone* when asked about his band's shifting status over the years. "When we signed on with our manager, we all said we wanted to have a box-set career. We'll gladly be the next generation of bands that aren't going anywhere."

As to whether the Kings have retained any shreds of indie cool into their stadium years, he shrugged: "I think when we were considered 'hipsters,' if you will, we were never backing down from success; we were never doing that on purpose. When someone like U2 asked us to go on the road, we were immediately like, 'Yeah! Pearl Jam? Yeah! Bob Dylan? Yeah!' They were all different things, and we wanted to get ourselves out there and for people to hear our music. We weren't dumbing it down, and there was never a point in our career where we were like, 'Oh man, I think we should scale it back, otherwise we're going to be popular'. And anyone who acts like that, I think they're full of it."

He added: "No-one wants to not succeed in what they do, and I think in any walk of life, you wanna be the best at what it is you do, and that's always been our goal. And so, it's not even necessarily the hipsters I have a problem with, it's the critics that praise everything indie; everything indie is great… and it's like, 'Well, yeah, if that indie band is around in 10 years, you'll be talking bad about them, because they're no longer your little indie band'."

On May 12, 2011 Caleb joined his brother Nathan in the state of wedded bliss by marrying Aldridge in a family-only ceremony at San Ysidro Ranch in Montecito, California. Youth and young manhood? No longer…

The appeal of the Kings, over and above the success of their songs, lies in their contradictions as people, especially Caleb: this is what makes them so interesting to write about. The Followills are hard-drinking, ex-drug-taking party boys who swear by the Lord and the sanctity of family; they like nothing more than to go fishing and camping, but they own a clothing line and several fortunes' worth of designer clothes; they talk like yokels but they're savvy businessmen; they escort supermodels and raise cattle on their farm. Most of all, their ambitions exceed those of any artist that has ever come out of Tennesee, the small matter of Elvis

Presley aside. Asked how he hoped the band would be remembered, Nathan said: "As a band that rocked their asses off every night, and played for themselves. It's all about playing music... getting paid to play songs that you wrote, that you feel strongly about, and enjoy sharing with people. What else could you ask for?" Matthew added: "I don't really care if we're famous or anything, I just want people to listen to our records now, or years down the road, and think, 'Man, they're awesome'. I want to influence people later down the road."

This might well happen. After all, the Followills' confidence in their abilities was at a maximum after the global success of *Only By The Night* and *Come Around Sundown*. As Nathan put it, "You have your whole life to write your first record, so it better be amazing. Then you only have six months to write your second record, so it better be amazing. The third record is your make or break album, so it better be amazing. The fourth recording has no pressure associated with it, because you've just made it that far" – and the fifth, we assume given *Come Around Sundown*'s mellow nature, is easier still.

The band are too new to their success – on a world scale, anyway – to have found a predictable niche. Whether they're now part of the mainstream or still an alternative act is impossible to say, although their move from the latter to the former has been steady. Matthew certainly doesn't know. "I don't feel like we're in the mainstream really at all," he said. "I mean, I know we are now, because we'll hear our song on the radio and then the next song will be Kanye West or Britney Spears. But we're definitely still in the alternative vein. We just got lucky, I guess... I want people to think that our music is different, fresh, raw, not so polished. The new record was done mostly live. There was no vocal booth. Most bands will do the drums first, and we pretty much did the songs standing around looking at each other."

The band continue to stay in contact with their fans whenever this allows – a decreasing window of opportunity as their influence has widened. "After the show we definitely hang out and talk," Nathan once said. "They're the ones who buy the records and the tickets to the shows... It pisses me off when I see musicians who think they're much bigger than they really are. Anyone can have an attitude, but it takes a real rocker to hang out with normal folk, I guess."

Asked how the band had changed in recent years, their long-time collaborator Angelo Petraglia commented: "The changes you see in Kings Of Leon, as far as their image is concerned, are all coming from the band themselves, either collectively or individually. Probably what has changed most is their musicianship. They've come a long way when it comes to their abilities. When I first met Jared, he hadn't even started playing bass yet. As a matter of fact, I went with him to buy his first bass. Now he's one of my favourite players… There is no secret [to their success]. I just believe the Kings Of Leon are a killer band that are constantly evolving and not afraid to try new ideas."

Asked the same question, Nathan came at it from the angle of closeness between the band-members, saying: "We were all super close before the band started, and I'm sure we'll be super close once the band is gone… you know, our whole lives we have been forced to be each other's best friends… the only thing that's changed is the competition of who can have the nicest, fastest car. This is the first band any of us were ever in. Most bands play together for five or six years before they ever get a record deal. We formed because we got a record deal."

"Sure, we get in fist-fights every once in a while, just like all brothers," Jared added. "We argue a lot, but it's nothing we can't get over. We've been so close our whole life, physically close, in our car together. We've been our only friends at points. So, yeah, we're used to arguing. We learned to get over it and get on with it."

Probably the most clued-up Followill despite his junior status, Jared summed up the position that the Kings found themselves in at the start of 2010. Reminded how the UK press supported the band from the very beginning, he replied: "We never expected that. When people called and told us that they were saying that stuff, we were like, 'Really?' We didn't know what to say about it. It's cool. We're glad people like us, but we're not trying to be the top band or anything like that. We're just making music we want to hear… We always looked forward to going to the UK and Europe, because we were huge over there, but we also looked forward to coming home, because there was a certain level of anonymity. And it kept us hungry and humble. It's kind of hard to be cocky or get a big head when you come home and nobody knows who the hell you are. It definitely kept the fire under our butts. But everything happens for a reason, and we're really enjoying where we're at right now."

Where are they at right now, exactly? According to many end-of-decade polls, the Kings Of Leon were nothing less than the great white hopes of guitar music, after several years of 'landfill indie' from a succession of dishwater rock bands. In the UK at least, we have been plagued with so many pale, arrogant public-school bands with a line in sub-Franz Ferdinand/Kaiser Chiefs/Killers/Kasabian tunes that it's little wonder dance music is on the rise again. Faced with this turgid barrage of clowns, the Kings truly seem like something unique, with a very modern, post-Dubya, post-Strokes worldview that is equally at home in Nashville, London or Berlin.

The Followills have their critics, prominent among them being the many writers and music consumers who believe that the band are merely transposing the classic sixties and seventies rock tropes for an uninformed new generation – and perhaps they have a point. It could be argued that when you dissect the first two Kings albums you're left with The Strokes and Johnny Cash – and if you pick apart the threads that make up *Because Of The Times* and *Only By The Night*, it's basically all about U2. A whole lot of people with loud voices and a platform from which to exercise those voices have made this very point, and when you're listening to some of the Kings' less compelling songs, sometimes it feels as if they're right.

But there's something that these critics are forgetting, and that is the simple axiom that good songs shine through irrespective of the medium. A killer melody or a soaring hookline will grab you whether it is deployed in a reggae song, a blues song or a classical composition. In the case of stadium rock, which has to be unashamed about unsubtle mood changes and lighters-aloft euphoria, these devices can be very powerful indeed – and the Kings know this. You may like it, you may not, but the band have reaped enormous rewards on the back of it, so who's laughing?

How do we resolve the fact that the band executed a canny style-change halfway through their career to date? Until the very end of the band, the Kings will be accused of ripping off their elders and betters for a bigger, more lucrative sound that is a betrayal of their roots. They've protested on innumerable occasions that their new sound is nothing more than the natural result of a desire to explore new territory, but their reasoning seems to have largely landed on deaf ears, perhaps because of the endorsement of a more cynical view by contemporaries such as Liam Gallagher. As the Followills have noted many times, success in the UK is viewed with suspicion, while success in the USA is regarded as something to be proud of: it may simply be a symptom of our particularly British disease that many of us can't bring ourselves to congratulate the Kings' achievements and enjoy the ride.

Then again, there are plenty of American fans who dislike the recent, bigger 'Sex On Fire'-style sound, too – which brings us to another point, one that anchors the entire Kings story. Why was it that America just didn't get them for so long? Perhaps it was due to the physical size of the country, which takes years to penetrate, or maybe America is too obsessed with Disney pop and hip-hop to care about four country bums with guitars. Another possibility, which applies to other territories too, is that some observers noted the Kings' country look and sound and categorised them as roots musicians – only to be appalled further down the line when the band appeared dressed in designer labels and squiring trophy girlfriends in style magazines. This could offend a particularly American sense of its own heritage, it's reasonable to assume: after all, good ol' boys from Tennessee don't usually shop on Madison Avenue...

This sense that perhaps the Kings aren't true to themselves doesn't really hold water, though. The century is in its teens now: we're no longer in the fifties, when country and blues musicians confined themselves to the Grand Ol' Opry and package tours. This is the modern era (although that's going to look pretty funny if you're reading this 20 years from now) and Southern rock musicians aren't expected to be different to anyone else. Like I said, the Kings' worldview is one that is at home anywhere in the world.

Then there's the religion. In today's largely secular music scene, 'men of faith' (as Nathan described his band) are viewed as quaint at best and hypocrites at worst. Caleb in particular has described his family as 'sinners' for their rebellion against their upbringing, and all the Followills have noted that their bond with organised religion has weakened over the years. Some of this could be down to simple maturity, and some of could be due to the musicians having fornicated and used drugs – only to find that a bolt from above fails to appear. However this newfound freedom from the chains that bound them has emerged, more than a few people have taken the band less seriously as they've walked through life, professing their devout natures on one side and working their way through some of the world's most desirable females on the other. Most sensible people don't care about the ethics of the Followills' lifestyles, though, because we'd do exactly what they did in the same situation. Yes, you would.

Does the band have a long-term future? Assuredly, if the internal tensions between the four musicians don't lead to a breaking point. You will have noticed that Jared and Matthew have both expressed concerns about Caleb's alcohol intake, while Caleb himself has said openly that Nathan's alliance with Jessie Baylin troubled him at first. Then there's the royalties issue, about which the band spoke so openly in 2009: far too many great bands have been destroyed by arguments over money, and it's to be hoped that the Kings Of Leon don't join them.

The closest the band have yet come to jeopardising their future came in August 2011, when reports came in that the Followills had taken the dramatic step of cancelling their forthcoming American tour in its entirety. Perhaps this news wouldn't have pricked up as many ears as it did if the band hadn't issued an explanation that is as old as time, in rock'n'roll terms anyway - that of "exhaustion", long a euphemism for overindulgence. "The reason for the cancellation of the tour is [that] Caleb is under doctor's orders for vocal rest," insisted a spokesman for the band, adding: "They feel terrible about cancelling. They look forward to getting back on the road at the end of September." Watch this space, as they say.

Creatively speaking, the band could go more or less anywhere. Caleb mentioned a solo album further down the line, which might be a useful way for him to express himself without requiring the approval of his bandmates. The sixth Kings album and the ones that follow it could revert to the old *Youth And Young Manhood* style and still find a fanbase, or they could resume the arena-rock parameters first pursued on *Because Of The Times* and honed to perfection with *Only By The Night*. Either way, a fanbase will be there, and certainly the Kings will continue to be appreciated if their music falls somewhere in between those styles, as is the most likely scenario.

Then again, this is a band made up of four fairly volatile individuals, so predicting their future is an unwise endeavour. Caleb, who struggles with the contradictions of the rock'n'roll lifestyle the most, is a classic rock star: a man with a voice that draws people in and the looks to command any glossy photo shoot. He fights, he drinks, he sings, he worries – he possesses all the charm, and the right number of flaws, to make him one of today's quintessential rock icons. Nathan, the elder statesman of the band, is a businessman and now a settled-down husband – but even he flies into a rage when confronted with Caleb's worst excesses. If the band ever split, the impetus would be unlikely to come from him.

Jared, the junior member who has grown into the band's most interesting musician in many ways, is beginning to take up more space of his own in interviews and (it might reasonably be assumed) in the band's behind-the-scenes affairs. Whether he'll grow tired of his older brothers' dominance is a point for speculation. As for Matthew, the dark horse of the band who rarely speaks, who knows what he'll do next. In many ways he shaped the band's new, stadium-sized sound back when the Kings were recording *Only By The Night*: although he doesn't say much, what he says tends to be worth listening to.

There are bigger bands than the Kings Of Leon, but not many whose back story and interpersonal dynamic is as complex. One day they, and we, will look back in bemusement at exactly how the four Followills made it out of their background to become one of the world's most successful bands, which is why this book (hopefully) has some value – to help us make sense of it all when the time comes.

Whenever the Kings Of Leon story ends, it won't be the way you think it's going to be. The only certainties are that the Followills will stick to their own path, no matter what the critics say: asked if he thought people would always accuse him of sounding like U2's guitarist the Edge, he laughed and said: "Definitely, I'm sure they will be. Two more records down the road, they'll think we sound like someone else. Whatever, as long as they're listening, that's fine!"

The other thing that we can rely on, surprisingly, is the title of the last Kings album. Caleb surprised more than a few people when he promised: "I think we've all decided that maybe our final record will be called *The Altar Call*, which won't be five syllables, but until then I think we need to try to stick with five syllables. Who knows?"

The Altar Call? Hopefully the call will be to worship at the Kings' altar rather than to sacrifice them to the rock'n'roll cause. Only time will tell – but until then, the band and their fans are in for a ride like no other.

UK Discography

(all RCA; later SonyBMG)

Albums	Released
Youth And Young Manhood	2003
Aha Shake Heartbreak	2004
Because Of The Times	2007
Only By The Night	2008
Come Around Sundown	2010

Singles	Released
Holy Roller Novocaine	2003
What I Saw	2003
Molly's Chambers	2003
Wasted Time	2003
California Waiting	2004
The Bucket	2004
Four Kicks	2005
King Of The Rodeo	2005
On Call	2007
Fans	2007
Charmer	2007
Sex On Fire	2008

Use Somebody	2008
Revelry	2009
Notion	2009
Radioactive	2010
Pyro	2010
The Immortals	2011

Sources

Craig Ablitt, Adelaide Now, Andrew Almond, American Songwriter, Artistdirect, Billboard, Brisbane Times, Charleston City Paper, Chicago Innerview, Clash Music, James Clements, Contactmusic, CNN, Creative Loafing, Daily Mirror, Daily Record, Paul Elliott, Daily Telegraph, Jonathan Dekel, Drummers Republic, Entertainment Weekly, Esquire, EU Jacksonville, Fasterlouder, Flaunt, Gibson.com, Courtney Grimes, Guitar Center, Martin Halo, Incendiary Magazine, Independent, Khaleej Times, Molly Knight, Live On Rare, Gavin Martin, James McNair, Mojo, MTV, MTV News, Alex Murphy, Music OMH, NME, NY Mag, New York Times, People, Puremusic, Q, Rare FM, Reuters, Rhythm, Rip It Up, Risen, Rolling Stone, San Diego Union-Tribune, San Francisco Chronicle, Bud Scoppa, Scotland On Sunday, Seacoast, Shockhound, Spin, St. Louis Today, Stop Smiling, Sublime, Sydney Morning Herald, The Age, The Culture Shock, The Sun, Time Out, Total Guitar, Rob Townsend, Ultimate Guitar/Joe Matera, Uncut, Village Voice, Virtual Festivals. 2009 royalties argument: http://thealternateside.org/news/2009/oct/14/kings-leon-jared-followill-admits-brotherly-tensio/

Index